Prof. Dr. med. Walter van Laack

Nobody Ever Dies!

Author
Prof. Dr. med. Walter van Laack
Specialist for Orthopaedics, Orthopaedic Surgery
Physical Therapy, Sport Medicine, Chirotherapy, Chin. Acupuncture

Cover / pictures
The cover is designed by my son Martin
All pictures are designed by my sons Alexander and Martin

Translation
Translated by Anneliese Wolstenholme, Roetgen/Aachen/Germany
from the German original "Wer stirbt, ist nicht tot!", 1. Edition published on April 19, 2003.
Once more I thank her very much for her kind and patient cooperation.
Again I hope that she will continue translating my next books

For all my beloved ones

1. Edition, published in July, 2005

© 2005 by van Laack GmbH, Aachen/Germany
Book Publishers

All rights reserved. This book may not be translated, reproduced or transmitted in whole or in part in any form or by any means, electronic or mechanical, including photocopying and recording or by any information storage and retrieval system including the internet without the prior written permission of the author.

Printed by
BoD GmbH, Gutenbergring 53 , 22484 Norderstedt/Germany

Softcover/Paperback
ISBN 3 – 936624 – 03 – 8

Contents

Part 1:
A cross section of Science, faith and knowledge   5

1. Between hope and fear   6
2. The Hereafter in Religions and Myths   10
3. A Journey through Philosophy and Poetry   25
4. Our Cosmic View of the World in Doubt   44
5. Evolution's New Look: Body and Life, Brain and Spirit   63
6. There are two sides to everything   87
7. Progressive Spiritual Maturity   99
8. Sexuality reflected by Evolution and Spirit   109
9. Extraordinary: the Psychogenic Death   116
10. In the Shadow of Death   123
11. On the Threshold: Near-Death Experiences   132
12. Mysterious Phenomena   143
13. Reincarnation in Discussion   155
14. Where is Justice?   168
15. Coincidence or Predetermination   171
16. Are Contacts with the World Beyond conceivable?   175
17. Death is not the End of your life   187
18. Optimists have the advantage   190

Part 2:
Near-Death Experiences (NDE) under Discussion   193

Is this discussion at all necessary?   194
When are we dead?   196
Are NDEs only hallucinations?   197
Do NDEs show more cultural differences
                than previously thought?   201
Are there universal patterns for NDEs?   206
Are NDEs induced by a shortage of oxygen, or delirium?   208
Why is it that not all people experience NDEs?   211
Can out-of-body experiences provide proof of NDEs?   212
A grand concert with an amazing orchestra   214

The brain, the interface to the spirit 214
OBEs: Real excursions or visual hallucinations
                          of one's own double? 217
Are NDEs induced by psychogenic drugs? 220
Attempts at psychological explanations 222
Parapsychological explanations? 227
A comparative discussion of my perceptions 228

Part 3:
No Death is Final – Epilogue 231

Appendix 238

Glossary 249

References 264

Books from the author in English and German 272

Part 1:

A Cross Section of Science, Faith and Knowledge

"I went away and left you,
only for a moment and not very far.
When you follow me to where I went,
You will ask yourself why you wept."
Unknown author

Death is a horizon,
And the horizon is the limit of our vision.
If we mourn for someone,
Others beyond that horizon
Are delighted to see him again.
Unknown author

Nobody knows death. Nobody knows either,
Whether it is not the greatest gift to mankind.
Nevertheless it is dreaded as if it were in fact
The worst of all evils.
Socrates (469-399 AD)

1. Between Hope and Fear

Two outstanding events are the most important in any human life: birth and death.
While we do not experience our birth consciously, the knowledge of our own death influences us humans throughout our lives. Sickness and death of our loved ones remind us sooner or later that for each of us at some point in time our present life on earth will inevitably draw to an end.
We all have many different ways of handling this knowledge.
Many of us suffer greatly either consciously or at least subconsciously under the perception that we all have to die at some time or other. Some people, the older they get, experience panic fears and feel threatened by seemingly imminent death at the first sign of harmless ailments. Dying and death are a taboo for most people and thoughts about it are usually best suppressed.
Especially in our modern times people facing imminent death are often left alone with the process of their dying.
Others seek refuge with good or bad prophets who promise a "Hereafter" in innumerable variations which seem to provide people with the sense of security they lack. The influx of people to religions and religious sects or esoteric and occult groups is especially due to this promise.
Whether a prophet is good or bad seems to me to be not so much a question of his barely authentic perception or his promises concerning "death"; no human being can really know what happens after death. Whether there exists a "Hereafter", a "life after death", and if so the form it takes is completely beyond our knowledge and remains in the realm of faith and intuition.
No, I believe that the main difference between good and bad prophets lies in the fact that good prophets do not stand for dogmatic fundamentalism, they do not speak ill of people who do not agree with them and they do not see differently minded people condemned to suffer torments in hell after death. Although they do have the legitimate desire to convince people of their own ideas and to discuss their theories they always do this without grim missionary determination and with great tolerance. In this respect most doctrines and especially the great

world religions have failed sadly time and again. Nevertheless it is gratifying to notice that some of them have actually changed and developed more tolerance.

However, others still have to go through their time of change and develop the necessary maturity.

For many critics, especially for die-hard modern scientists, any perception of a "Hereafter", possibly even of a personal survival of a merely physical death, appears to be the result of an understandable human hope not just to disappear without trace – simply the result of wishful thinking. Since the human being does not exist before he is born and there is not the slightest idea or trace of him enriching this world it would be only consequential to believe that he will disappear without trace when he dies.

At best he might live on in the memory of his relatives and friends – at least until they follow the inevitable way of all mortals.

Such putative consolation is expressed in many obituaries today. This theory corresponds with the spirit of our age and is simultaneously, accordingly the theory I already expressed in my earlier books, at the root of so much evil in our society. For me this perception is an accessory to the presently almost overwhelmingly dominant egoistic lifestyle, the increasing "me-first" mentality, uncaring alienations between humans and not least the growing number of criminal excesses.

Even if hope and wishful thinking should play an important role when practically all myths and religious traditions in the world from time immemorial suggest a "Hereafter" – even a personal survival after death – there is no reason at all why this "Hereafter" should not exist.

Without doubt, natural science plays a key role in our present time in explaining the world, matter, life and hence human beings and their spirits; and without doubt it has every right to occupy this important position. Only a few hundred years ago religions took this position, which in our western cultural area was mainly Christianity. And they established their apparently irrefutable religious dogmas in the same way as natural scientists establish theirs today.

Time and again philosophers had to take corrective action and relativize religious views. Over hundreds of years philosophers also paved the way for natural scientists enabling them to gain their victory over long-cemented but nevertheless untenable religious dogmas.

Today, I believe, such corrective actions by philosophers are needed again whereby modern natural scientific dogmas should be relativized, since it seems to me that many of those dogmas are leading mankind into dead ends again.

The pendulum of knowledge swings today into the other, the purely materialistic, direction. However, this direction seems to be just as wrong as the religious fundamentalist one. Every day we can see that both entail the most tragic consequences for humans either due to the abuse of technology and biology, or due to political-ideological and religious terrorism.

In some of my previous books – e.g. "An Argument for Life after Death and a slightly different View of the World", "Key to Eternity" as well as the trilogy "A Better History of Our World" – I attempted to grab the pendulum in the middle between the poles and to stop it. The aim and objective of my books is to establish a comprehensive perception which goes beyond the limits of single fields of science and knowledge combining them with one another.

The trilogy especially is an attempt to explain this alternative perspective of our world in a clear, logical and easily understandable way which is also mostly concurrent with the actual knowledge of our time and age.

I have always made it perfectly clear that a theory which combines the sciences only makes sense if it does not simply ignore the many spiritual experiences countless people have had repeatedly throughout history and all over the world.

I myself have been fortunate in having gone through a number of such experiences in the course of my life, even though the circumstances leading to them were rarely nice or pleasant. All this tells me that spirit must exist just like matter. Spirit is not merely a product of matter. On the contrary spirit rather uses matter as a medium.

Life and death can only be really understood in their complete significance if the spiritual part is not simply eradicated.

Therefore it only makes sense to talk about death and a "Hereafter" if we have previously thought about the spirituality in our world and the spirit in every living individual in this world. Confirmed knowledge of natural science was not to be impugned but a number of mere interpretations had to be questioned critically.

I consider my books to be the long sought-after but missing philosophical corrective of natural science which dominates everything in our world today. They should also be a still necessary corrective for religious doctrines and above all for the growing number of dubious pseudo-religious and esoteric or occult movements.

As a result, death as the irrevocable end of us all is finally losing its mystery. I wish to convey to every reader the well-founded hope that he will survive his physical death – and that in full possession of his individual personality!
Finally some remarks to the form of this book:
Similar to the trilogy published between 2000 and 2001, I will discuss those points which seem most important to me in the first part of the book. In the second part I discuss the subject "Death" in a virtual *Dialogue* with my two sons *Alexander* and *Martin*. Basically the elements of a near death experience (NDE) are critically examined here, especially with regard to possible proof of a survival after our physical death. The third part concludes this book with an epilogue. Since you will repeatedly find references to my earlier books, especially to their natural scientific and logical models, I collected the most important basic principles of those books and added them as a separate *Appendix*. This appendix is followed by a comprehensive *Glossary* and a *List of References*.
There you will find all the important persons, references and terms to which I refer in this book, especially those printed in Italics.
This book corresponds in the main with the last volume of the trilogy subtitled "Death", the English translation of which was first published in August 2003. However, I not only added 2 chapters but I also replenished this book with many new examples and, wherever necessary, with the latest scientific observations. In other instances I rephrased some sentences which were not clear enough in an attempt to make them easier to understand. So I hope to have made this very complex and alternative view of the world more easily and clearly understandable.
Even before the third volume of the trilogy was published I had decided to publish this present book under the title of the lectures I have given on this subject over the last years as a completely separate and independent work with some additions and amendments.

Aachen, 5th February 2003 (German Original)
in remembrance of my deceased father's birthday,
Aachen, 11th May 2005, (Last changes in the English Version)

Prof. Dr. med. Walter van Laack

2. The Hereafter in Religions and Myths

From time immemorial death seems to affect, to fascinate and to frighten us more than anything else. Humans are the only creatures on earth who know for sure that they will die one day. The consciousness of our own death extends without any doubt far beyond the purely instinctive fascination and aversion felt by anthropoids which are our nearest animal relatives.

At the same time, this makes the history of mankind unlike that of any other living creature on earth for it tells the story of how humans view their own death. Interestingly, this always seemed to pose the question of whether death is the terminal end; to be sure, this finality has always been doubted or even denied. Death and the question of the creation of the universe and life occupies the most important focal point in all religions and myths. According to the Latin meaning of the word, religions are something that should find *considerate and conscientious observance* and something that *leads us to the true core of the matter.*

Their reason and purpose are mainly to be found in their endeavour to save the human soul. It is this idea, the notion of an immaterial natural basis, a soul, which includes and requires something *transcendental* which must be especially honoured, thoroughly protected and always cherished! The evidence of any kind of faith which our human ancestors or their nearest human relatives (e.g. Neanderthal Man) had in a post mortal existence is merely a few ten thousand years old and is documented by loving funeral rites and artful cave-paintings.

We do not possess such clear and well-preserved evidence from earlier generations. But we should not jump to the conclusion that humans at the earliest times of their appearance on earth did not have similar perceptions. The so-called Peking Man, for example, lived about half a million years ago. From the meagre evidence we have of his existence we can, for example, gather that people decapitated their dead in a very special systematic way. Why they did this we do not really know. But we may at least assume that they disposed of their dead with much care, indeed, later civilizations went to a lot of trouble in burying the severed heads separately. This kind of burial, as well as the perforating of the skulls which appeared later, suggests that the people believed in an

immaterial soul which could leave the head more easily if the skull was opened or if the head was severed and buried separately.
In the *Shanidar-Cave* in *Iraq*, which is about 60,000 years old, evidence was found that the dead were buried lovingly on flowering herbs.
The American religious scholar *Carol Zaleski*[1] talks in this context of a real "funeral industry" which was already widespread many thousands of years ago.
In one of my earlier books I already established the theory that the development of mankind was primarily a spiritual act which was only secondarily expressed in the development of the typical human physique such as the upright posture.
Life itself is something spiritual. It only functions if organic structures of sufficient complexity are developed. This is so because, as I already plausibly explained in several of my previous books, spirit and matter are two symmetrical and simultaneously polar sides of the same coin, the "World". They are interdependent after having developed the necessary preconditions piece by piece from their side. Just as *life* is rather underdeveloped, undifferentiated and unspecified at the beginning, so is the *spirit*. Living matter has developed a nervous system which has been striving consistently to an ever higher and strictly hierarchically structured order and has developed and matured without making any detours. This becomes, I believe, the central constant of evolution.
With this nervous system it has been possible to reach an ever greater spiritual perfection, i.e. an ever more refined and pronounced differentiation of the really existing (world-) spirit. This spirit can be considered as an immaterial global information field which in turn makes the development of ever more complex and perfect bodies and body organs possible. At the end of this development on earth stands – provisionally – the human being (anthropical principle).
The human hand as a tool and the human ability to walk upright and to interact are, therefore, characteristic *consequences* of human development and not its cause. One important aspect of the spiritual background inherent in humans which is already well developed is their "intuitive conviction" that this "spirituality" will survive their physical death. Such primeval human intuition leaves no doubt as to the lasting existence of a spirituality which is in fact born of itself. It is only independent, conscious and controlled thinking that has gradually led us to question

---

[1] Carol Zaleski, "Otherworld Journeys. Accounts of near-Death Experience in Medieval and Modern Times", Oxford Univ. Press (1987), see List of References

this intuitive knowledge, since in the course of time humans wanted to rely increasingly on their purely sensory perception as being the basis of all existence.

Those of us who are on principle non-believers and who deny any intuitive knowledge are, in my opinion, descending rather than climbing up the ladder of spiritual evolution because they misunderstood the meaning of "emancipation" of thought.

Prehistoric shamans many thousands of years ago used to "travel" in a trance and experienced other spiritual or dreamlike worlds. Their ability to fall into ecstasy enabled them, so it is reported, to leave their bodies by pure will power and to go on mystical travels through the cosmos. Shamans are said to have been able to accompany the souls of deceased persons or to visit them and to connect heaven and earth, thereby helping incarnated humans in the case of sickness, for example. The experiences of such travels in dream worlds and to the next world has certainly resulted in an unbelievably diverse mixture of facts and tales, legends and fairytales due to their having been passed down from generation to generation. Together with perceptions which were sometimes deliberately influenced by peoples and powers, cultural convictions, myths and also religions have developed over thousands of years. All religions, however, have always been based on three major doctrines on which everything else stood:

First and foremost, the question was always as to whether there is a creative power, a creative dimension, one creating God or several Gods or deities structured in hierarchies or in dynasties. *Secondly,* all religions identify a spiritual dimension which must be strictly differentiated from the physical level and which can be perceived by senses. Humans are, of course, part of this spiritual sphere.

Thirdly, there has always been a precise perception of some kind of continued existence after physical death.

Even where immense differences exist between various civilizations, their perceptions of an existence after death, the principle of a survival after death, is the same in all religions. *Jakob Ozols,* professor for prehistory and ancient history, summarizes: *"After death the soul leaves the body and continues to live its own life separated from the body.... It [the soul] can easily cover great distances .... It is no longer dependent on any particular time scale and can experience the past as well as the future."*

And, in the concordant view of early civilizations, not only the soul of a deceased, but also the soul of a living person can in principle do something similar. *Jakob Ozols* continues: *"The soul of a living person leaves the body only at night or in unusual situations, such as a sudden fright or a serious disease or in extraordinary circumstances such as trance or ecstasy. However, the soul may not leave the body for too long a period of time. If it does not return soon enough, the person is taken ill, he is exposed to many dangers, and if the soul is absent for too long he must even die …. The soul may meet the souls of other humans who are long deceased, it may meet spirits and experience unusual adventures."*

In the ancient Orient the dead led a kind of mute shadow-life. In the Old Testament *Job* lamented that his short life had not been a better one as he had to leave soon for the Kingdom of Darkness and Shadow.[2]
The ancient Greeks had a similar perception. According to *Homer* the *psyche* leaves the *body* after death. However, what he called psyche does not mean the same as the phenomenon we call *soul* today.
It is nothing but a *delicate waft*, a more or less meaningless memory or a shadow, which moves around the underworld, the *Hades*, but is still able to show itself to the living.
In this way the dead which *Odysseus* met on his travels, were extraordinarily hopeless figures, and the shadow of *Achilles* mourns that he would prefer an existence as a slave on earth to being the ruler of the entire kingdom of the dead.
However, the dead souls could regain their consciousness for a certain time if they drank sacrificial blood. This perception changes during the fifth century before Christ, probably under the influence of the ancient Egyptians who had a completely different picture of the other world. The luxurious burial chambers in the huge pyramids are a classical indication for this change. They symbolize the cosmic hierarchy and the ascent into other dimensions. In their burial chambers the deceased Pharaohs had everything they needed for their life in the next world. By means of incantations and prayers which were engraved in the walls it was made easier for the deceased to rise into the presence of the god(s) and finally to merge with *Osiris*, the God of Death. A judgement on the life of the deceased was made in the other world: he was judged by the morality of his actions and also by the seriousness of his ritual preparation for his own death. The judgement was followed by a reward

---

[2] The Bible, Old Testament, Job 10.20-22: "Are not my days few? Cease then and let me alone that I may take comfort a little, before I go whence I shall not return, even to the land of darkness and the shadow of death; and the land of darkness as darkness itself; and of the shadow of death without any order and where the light is as darkness."

or a punishment. For those who were accepted into the other world, life was not much different from their earthly life.

On the contrary, in the realm of death the deceased had access not only to all kinds of pleasures and beautiful things but also to all the knowledge in the world and to the mystery of time! Later on, this perception became the basis for the Christian belief in the existence of a *heaven*.

Parallel to this, there also existed a realm of terror for the dead where the bad people had to go and from where they tried with all their means to escape again. If they did not succeed they died a second death which was then final. Much later, this ancient Egyptian perception shaped the Christian belief in the existence of a *hell*. It also influenced significantly the Greek imagination of death and the beyond. The formerly shadow-like psyche was enhanced. It became an independent medium of the personal human identity. During that time there appeared for the first time the belief in a *reincarnation* in flesh, the transmigration of souls or the *rebirth* of the flesh.

For the Greeks the life in the other world was mainly determined by their actions during their life on earth. They differentiated between the spirit, which merged with the collective spirit of the world, and the individual soul which – after the physical death – joined the hopeless realm of shadows in the underworld, *Hades*.

It was only during the late classical antiquity that a differentiation was finally drawn between the descent of the souls of the dead into Hades and the ascent into higher spiritual dimensions. And so it came about that for the late classical Greek Gnostic birth itself was considered as the descent into the underworld from where, depending on a satisfactorily good behaviour, only the ascent was possible.

The Romans had no specific perception of the world beyond. They orientated themselves on the perceptions of their neighbours, especially those of the Greeks and the Etruscans. The dead were honoured and it was assumed that somehow they were able to keep up the connection with their descendants.

In intellectual circles especially, perceptions of the world beyond did not play a major role and in general people did not believe that after their own death they could be either rewarded or punished for their actions. However, it was considered to be a politically welcome means of influencing other people in accordance with ones own requirements.

Going back to the roots of Christianity and Judaism we find that initially neither had a detailed concept of the world beyond.
There was a *Scheol*, a realm of the shadows of the dead which was the exact opposite of the earthly life. Much later the doctrine of the "resurrection of the flesh" gained more and more in importance. This is supposed to have taken place in a "Messianic era" and the time spent in the grave was somehow a "time of waiting" for this event. There is also talk of a soul later on. If this had behaved well enough during its lifetime on earth it was allowed to go to the heavenly paradise to wait for the "final decision" and its later resurrection.
A wicked soul on the other hand had to go to hell *(Deshehenna)*. This change in Judaism was primarily due to the Jewish mystics, e.g. the supporters of maccabean mysticism, an esoteric movement which developed in Palestine and Babylon within rabbinical Judaism.[3] *Carol Zaleski* writes that this rabbinical kind of literature was obviously very popular and it also caused the legends of biblical prophets and rulers to be embellished. For example, Moses' vision of the "Promised Land" in the so-called *midrash scripts* of the Middle Ages became a complete journey through heaven and hell.
Journeys to the "world beyond" were always the basic starting point of detailed perceptions of the other world. Some chosen people experienced them in perfect health, i.e. without being close to death. Therefore, it would probably be more accurate to use the term "wandering consciousness".
Their experiences, however, are very much like the "real" near death experiences which are reported by many people who very nearly died and which will of course be discussed in detail later in this book. Therefore, I will just use the term "travel to the beyond" here which is admittedly ambiguous.
Passed down through many generations these tales became legends and over long periods of time they even became, interwoven with other legends, complex religious doctrines.
Such legends are to be found in all civilizations. Celtic legends about journeys to other countries "beneath the waves" or "above the fog" tell these tales as well as the Germanic mythology which tells about *Hel* and

---

[3] Scholem, G.G., "Major Trends in Jewish Mysticism" Schocken Books (1995), see List of References.

Valhalla[4]. An Irish-Celtic legend tells about the soul of a deceased which looks back to its lifeless former body and addresses and kisses it for the last time with the words: "Thank you for having given me shelter and being good to me for such a long time" before it passes on to the "other world".

And in a Persian-zarathustrian book *Arda Viraz* tells the story of a priest who voluntarily took a narcotic enabling him to travel to the other world[5].

From the Old Testament of the Bible we learn very little about travels to the beyond which does not mean, however, that the Jewish religion did not engender such legends. They are just not part of the "legitimate", i.e. the canonic scripts. All the more may be found in the secret records, the so-called *Apocrypha*. *Henoch,* a descendant of *Adam,* gave a detailed account of a journey to the other world which became especially well known.

The (apocryphal) Ethiopian book of Henoch describes his journey to the other world: *"...They took me away and put me in another place where all things were like flaming fire and if they wished they appeared like humans. ... I saw places of lights, the stockpiles of lightning and thunder and in the deepest depths I saw an arc of fire. ... They put me near the living water and the fire of the West which receives each time the setting sun. I came to a stream of fire whose fire was flowing like water and which was gushing forth into a huge ocean in the West. (...) ... three rooms were prepared to separate the spirits of the dead; and there was a special room prepared for the spirits of the righteous, where there was a bright source of water ... ."*

One of the uncanonical scripts also relates the tale of the "Ascension of Isaiah" in which, according to Stefan Hoegl, it says at the end: *"And the angel who was leading me could sense what I was thinking and he said: If you are already delighted with this light how much happier you will be when you see the light in the seventh heaven where God and his beloved one are, whence I was sent, and who will be named Son in the world. (...) For the light there is great and wonderful."*

Some religions were possibly initiated due to their respective founder having undergone a profound spiritual transformation after an experience which, according to the reports, had the typical characteristics of travels to the world beyond. Examples for this are probably Islam and Buddhism.

Islam goes back to *Mohammed,* an Arabian businessman, born in Mecca, who in 610 AD claimed that he had received messages directly from

---
[4] H.R. Patch, "The Other World", see List of References.
[5] Martin Haug et al., "The book of Arda Viraf", see List of References.

God *(Allah,)* probably by means of travels to the other world, and who originally developed his doctrines in Medina. According to *Muslim* belief the revelations he received are the ultimate and absolute expression of God's divine command. The Islamic doctrines are written down in the Koran and were to be disseminated to all humans. From this missionary perception is derived the idea of the "holy war", the *"Jihat"*, which originally did not have a bellicose meaning at all.

The Islamic concept of the other world is similar to that of Christianity. Death is no longer the real end of life, but merely a time of transition from a transient physical life to a lasting eternal life. Soon after his death the deceased is interrogated by the angels *Mungkar* and *Nakir* to whom he has to prove his faith in Allah. Therefore, Muslims are traditionally buried covered by only a shroud and with no coffin; otherwise it would be impossible for the angels to wake them up for their interrogation.

After the interrogation – and here the Jewish-Christian element brings its influence to bear – they are allowed to rest until "Doomsday".

According to Islamic doctrines this is also the day on which the good are separated from the evil. The righteous go to paradise and the bad go to hell, a place of eternal damnation. The difference between a Muslim and a non-Muslim, an unbeliever, is that at some time or other Allah will have mercy on the faithful Muslim and will in the end release him from the torments of hell.

Siddhartha Gautama, named *Buddha* or "the Enlightened One", was originally a rich prince in what is Nepal today. In about 500 years BC, when he was a young adult, he had a crucial experience in which he was confronted with poverty, sickness and death – conditions completely unknown to him previously – and he became a Hindu mendicant monk. After extensive meditation during which he was probably also able to travel to the other world he experienced a profound religious change. Based on his perceptions he founded a new religious movement, known as Buddhism, which was derived from Hinduism. In the Hindu tradition of India and the Far East as well as in Buddhism an impressive number of travels to the other world are reported.[6] In his famous fire sermon Buddha compares life to a flame which keeps on burning because it is always kindled anew by the three misdemeanours "greed", "hate" and "delusion". Humans should abstain from these bad habits in order to

---

[6] e.g. Edward Conze, "Buddhist Scriptures", see List of References.

reach *Nirvana* and thus break the ever repeating circle of birth, death and rebirth.

For Buddha this circle was the logical consequence of his observation that all physical matter in the universe is created and perishes only to emerge again in a different form. He based his doctrines on Hindu perceptions which were already known at that time. But in contrast to the general western opinion Nirvana is by no means a mere "nothing" but rather a condition of eternal and unchangeable calmness of the soul, a state of blessed salvation or enduring, calm and simultaneously content stillness of the (self-) aware soul. In his *Suttapitaka* Buddha himself vehemently rejects the idea that in Nirvana the being comes to an end.

Buddhism also knows a great number of heavenly paradises. One example is the "Pure Land of Amitabha", which is abundant in trees decorated with valuable jewels and sweetly fragrant rivers; but there are also fiery hells where sinners are chained to anvils and are roasted by smirking devils.[7]

In the *Upanishads*, holy scripts of Hindu tradition in India, we also find a number of stories of descents into the realm of death. Such excursions also help to purge the living so that they can break the circle of their continuous return.[8]

A unique and also very detailed version of the other world is described in the "Bardo Thodoel" or "Bar do thos grol", better known as the *Tibetan Book of the Dead* of Tibetan Buddhism, known as *Lamaism*.

Although this is only one of many records of an existence after death, I think it is the best known one. It is very similar to the ancient Egyptian book of death and describes in great detail the path consciousness takes from the moment of death through various phases of actually being dead in a kind of "twilight world" up to the subsequent reincarnation, i.e. being physically reborn into a new life on earth.

As in almost all other myths and religions as well, the deceased, after slowly becoming aware of the fact that his physical body is dead, is confronted with the deeds and misdeeds he performed during his former life. One of the fundamental principles of this sphere, the "Bardo of experiencing reality", is the perception that thoughts can create reality and experience. Every thought becomes a complete and total experience. From this point of view, heaven and hell become after death images of

---

[7] Edward Conze, "Buddhist Scriptures", see List of References.
[8] e.g. Radhakrishnan, "The Principal Upanishads", see List of References.

themselves. According to the adage "birds of a feather flock together", related souls go through this phase together.

In Christianity the basic concept of "doomsday", the day of God's mighty judgement, with a carnal resurrection, which can actually be experienced in the flesh, is still taken literally by the Churches today. There are surely several reasons for this. On the one hand it is based on the same perceptions as the religion of Zoroastrianism which the Persian prophet Zoroastra had already established in approximately 600 BC. Its Holy Scriptures, the Avesta, already describes the resurrection of the soul as well as that of the physical body. Later on it tells us that the resurrection will take place when the world is completed. *"The glory of fame is inherent in the Lord so that the Lord may create the creatures, the many and beautiful, the many and splendid, the many and wonderful, the many and marvellous; so that they will make life wonderful, not ageing, not putrefying, not rotting, eternally living, eternally thriving, so that there is a free choice. When the dead will be resurrected again and for the living there is life without destruction then he will renew existence according to his own will."* The religious scholar *Hans-Joachim Klimkeit* summarizes the final phase of resurrection: *"... in the end the joyful mutual welcome of all righteous human souls which can reunify with their bodies. They go forth into the realm of light of our Lord to immortal and eternal life."*
On the other hand the belief in a carnal resurrection is probably based on contemporary Jewish perceptions. It was virtually proven in retrospect by the story of Jesus Christ's resurrection on the third day after his crucifixion.
This gives the Catholic dogmatists the problem of explaining Christ's empty grave which was supposedly confirmed by several witnesses.
The theology professor *Otmar Meuffels* of Wuerzburg, Germany, pointed out, however, in his presentation at the occasion of the meeting at the Academy of the Cathedral at Wuerzburg[9] in October 2001, that the biblical story of the "empty grave of Jesus" is not mentioned in the oldest testimonies of the resurrection[10]. It seems to be a generally synoptic *Easter story, which presupposed that there was a resurrection and served to illustrate its central message ... [11]. The preaching of experiences of the living God is evident in the faith and the stories of the empty grave serve as a secondary illustration*

---

[9] I also had the privilege of giving a presentation at this meeting on October 03. 2001 entitled: "He who dies is not dead ".
[10] The Bible, I. Corinthians 15, 03-05
[11] The Bible, Mark 16, 06

to support this. They are a mere testimony of faith ingeniously explaining experienced blessings and resurrections; they are not to be taken as reports of a historical fact which may – or may not – be corroborated.

There has always been a tripartite structure of levels in the world beyond within the popular, "illustrated" doctrines of Christianity. There is heaven, hell and purgatory, where souls apparently were obliged or were allowed to stay, depending on their demeanour on earth, until doomsday. And heaven had long since been a place for angels and saints and, of course, God himself.
Another typical example of after-death perspectives of faith being obtained by wandering consciousness or by journeys to the other world is, for me, the Apostle *Paul*. At first, as *Saul*, he persecuted the Christians[12]. Later, however, he became the most ardent worshipper of Jesus Christ and Christianity[13]. There are some indications that Paul himself had a near death experience which caused his "travel to the beyond" due to which he started to consider things from a different point of view.
In his Second Letter to the Corinthians he told of his experiences of the other world although he was apparently advised not to boast too much about it, for he talks in the third person (12.01-04):
I know a Christian man who fourteen years ago (whether in the body or out of the body, I do not know – God knows) was caught up as far as the third heaven. And I know that this same man (whether in the body or out of the body, I do not know – God knows) was caught up into paradise, and heard words so secret that human lips may not repeat them."
Especially interesting here is the twice repeated clause "*whether in the body or out of the body, I do not know – God knows*". I think that this could be caused by the understandable uncertainty of all travellers to the beyond: without exception they all have the impression that they are "physically intact". At the same time, however they seem to feel that they are not so, at least not in the common, i.e. in the known mortal-carnal sense!
According to early Christian perception it seems that life does not end with death at all and that it does not even "take a break" until "doomsday". This is supported by Jesus Christ himself when, after the

---

[12] e.g. in the Bible, I. Corinthians, 15, 09: "For I am the least of the apostles, indeed not fit to be called an apostle because I had persecuted the church of God."
[13] The Bible, I. Corinthians, 15, 10: "However, by God's grace I am what I am, and his grace to me has not proved vain ...."

crucifixion on Golgotha, he addresses one of his two fellow-sufferers with the words[14]: *"Truly I tell you: today you will be with me in Paradise."*
With regard to his resurrection, Apostle Paul helps us again even more. And thus the Christian perception fits harmoniously into an apparent *globally identical, basic human* perception. The physical death of a human being is followed immediately by another form of existence, the actual real and spiritual life. Apostle Paul's answer to the "how" of the resurrection[15] we find in the First Letter of Paul to the Corinthians (15.42-47):
"...So it is with the resurrection of the dead: what is sown as a perishable thing is raised imperishable. ... sown a physical body, it is raised a spiritual body. If there is such a thing as a physical body, there is also a spiritual body .... Observe, the spiritual does not come first; the physical body comes first and then the spiritual. The first man is from earth, made of dust: the second man is from heaven."
This for me seems to be one of the many testimonies which shows that with the term "resurrection of the dead" the early Christian faith rather meant some kind of "change" –by which was meant a change from a physical identity to a spiritual one which was, however, already inherent in the human being before his death because it was given to him by God as his (true) "character".
This interpretation is also supported by the following passage which is also taken from the First Letter of Paul to the Corinthians (15.35-37):
"... In what kind of body? What stupid questions! The seed you sow does not come to life unless it has first died; and what you sow is not the body that shall be, but a bare grain, ... God gives it the body of his choice, each seed its own particular body."
According to Paul, the mortal body is replaced by a heavenly body, the spiritual body, at the moment of death.
In this passage there is an additional testimony for the spiritual element in each life. Matter does not *live* on its own accord.
Thus death becomes also in the Christian tradition a divide between two adjacent and merging dimensions of life, the one before and the one after death. Again it is Paul who, this time in his letter to the Philippians, submits an unambiguous testimony (01.21-24):
"For to me life is Christ, and death is gain. If I am to go on living in the body there is fruitful work for me to do which then am I to choose? I cannot tell. I am pulled two ways: my own desire is to depart and be with Christ – that is better by far; but for your sake the greater need is for me to remain in the body."

---

[14] The Bible, Luke, 23.43
[15] The Bible, I. Corinthians 15.35: "But, you may ask, how are the dead raised?"

In practically all myths and religions the survival of ones own death is a fundamental cognition. Death is always merely the end of the physical body. At all times religious perceptions have all supported the belief in at least an early phase of a purely spiritual existence which was nevertheless perceived physically. The more people have tried to obtain further knowledge of developments taking place after their physical death the more the information, which was passed on, differed.

For various reasons these more or less fundamental experiences were embellished by exuberant accessories and in the end whole doctrines were established. Some of these probably go back to observations in nature with its many periodical courses, philosophising about ethical-moral matters, such as justice, and, connected with that, some efforts to explain or to interpret the very different courses life takes for different people. Certainly some rather base motives have very often played a role too, such as the desire to manipulate people and whole countries by opportunistic interpretations.

Many of these doctrines are no longer congruent with modern scientific knowledge about nature.

This is certainly an important reason for the dwindling trust some people have in religious traditions today. Others unfortunately adopt an almost exotic and very often tragically unrestrained fundamentalism which is unacceptable and inexcusable, especially in view of the effect it has on the people concerned.

In my opinion, both these extreme developments are quite simply wrong. Furthermore, neither of them does justice to the real core of all religions.

The countless number of reports in religions and myths of people having survived their own physical death should be taken seriously because such reports are basically identical in all civilizations – although in some cases those civilizations were geographically and temporally so far apart that their making contact with one another was practically impossible.

After all, such reports have been forthcoming in astonishing continuity since the birth of mankind or, at least, we have good reason to believe so.

This should be reason enough for us not to ignore or reject them. On the contrary, we should consider them as being serious and respectable hypotheses and we should integrate them into our interpretations and discuss them. Furthermore: I believe that perceptions which ignore these reports and consciously exclude them cannot claim to being nearer to the truth than anybody else.

And this is exactly the current most significant problem of modern science. Scientists often admit to their efforts towards explaining away any immaterial spirituality in the world. They have not actually succeeded in this yet and, of course, they *cannot* succeed. Unfortunately, this does not restrain them in their efforts by formulating their explanatory models as "flexibly" as possible if need be. So much so that, contrary to all previous experience, they render laws of nature and other regularities pliable so that they may adhere to the purely materialistic idea which they favour.

The fundamental conviction of ancient myths and of all religions is based on intuitive experience. For a long time it was regarded as quite natural to accept them as possible sources of cognition. When, in spite of all criticism, natural science made its rightfully triumphant progress and with it the growing significance of sensory experiences, it was philosophers like *Immanuel Kant* who started to appreciate less and less the value of an intuitive search for cognition.

A form of life after death, whatever it may be like, is ultimately an intuitive fundamental conviction of mankind and, as already mentioned, probably has been since the beginning of human existence.

Sociology and psychology like to explain this today with the stark human fear of death as being the unavoidable and utter end.

Life after death is thus reduced to a simple illusion, to a kind of wishful thinking due to the permanent human longing for it.

Superficially these arguments cannot be dismissed. But the question must be allowed as to whether the idea of a life after death must remain an illusion simply because there are good reasons that it might be so?

I do not believe that!

Even if the doctrines of significant myths and religions may appear so very complex and it may seem impossible for some to accept them in our modern times, ultimately they all contain the same three central ideas with varying degrees of embellishment:

1) Creator – Creation – superior "divine" dimension – God – deities – "almighty love" – "sense", etc..
2 Spiritual dimension – spiritual level – "realm of souls", etc..
3) Survival after physical death.

These central ideas seem to be a kind of "collective inner knowledge" of man who recognizes himself as a living being.

It is the synopsis of our intuitive cognition. Even if it is caused by wandering consciousness or journeys to the other world, of waking dreams or other visions, representing themselves in an abundant colourful mix of pictures – it is of no consequence.

All these pictures reflect a truth which will probably remain unfathomable for us humans even far into the future. We do not understand them today nor did our forbears in earlier times. Depending on time, culture, education, progress and state of human development, therefore, they *must* be objectively indescribable and hence utterly subjective. They can only be of a symbolic character. And exactly that is the crucial point because it actually increases significantly the value of myths and religions in being the most important cultural treasures of human history. After all, they are really all quite correct!

And it follows that any kind of fundamentalism, any religious fanaticism or any one-sided dogmatic missionary work is sacrilegious. "To each his own" is truly wise advice which illustrates the required degree of tolerance which we must at long last show towards other religions. We can do this because we are sure that in the end the universal core of intuitive cognition will be magnificent. Irrespective of what each of us believes in, any faith can basically assist humans to orientate themselves in this world in which they would otherwise have to live with little guidance. As the ideological chaos in the world has proven only too clearly over the last century, humans are unable to provide this guidance for themselves.

Myths and religions are mainly based on intuitive experiences. In my opinion, and in this I agree with *Plato,* intuitive experience should be considered as being one of several possibilities for obtaining higher cognition, since the essential theses and basic beliefs are more or less identical in all myths and religions of all known cultures and their traditions. For me, they even represent an important characteristic of human evolution. And thus the survival of our physical death becomes an intuitively recognized reality.

In the next chapter I will take a closer look at philosophical contributions on the subject of death and perceptions of the "beyond".

3. A Journey through Philosophy and Poetry

Nearly two and half thousand years ago the very wise and famous Greek scholar *Plato* once said that philosophy was a preparation for death. Nobody else, I think, has ever made such a direct and succinct statement with regard to the key issue of philosophical contemplations. Let me take up Plato's theory and expand on it: philosophy is the path of the individual thinker leading him to the most important questions of his existence. Religion, on the other hand, is the path of the broad mass of the population.

And the most important issues are still those concerning creation, the creator, the spirit and survival after physical death, even if many people like to repress this, especially in our modern times.

Or, in other words: Who or what am I? Where do I come from and where am I going? Religions and myths offer a plethora of theories, obtained mainly by intuition, which are not strictly and exclusively perceived by the senses. Natural science, on the other hand, is based on sensory experiences.

Philosophy now means that – by taking into careful, logical consideration the entire circumstantial evidence – knowledge is optimised by individual thinking. Intuitive experience should not be discredited as being inferior. The wise Chinese philosopher *Lao Tzu* wrote very appositely during the 7th century BC: *"Without going outdoors, one knows the world. Without looking out of the window one sees the DAO (the way, the sense) of heaven. – The further out one goes the lesser one's knowledge becomes."* As far as I understand it, philosophy is meant to be a kind of mediator between completely different sources, especially in cases in which they seem to be utterly irreconcilable.

From my point of view it should in addition be a corrective for both sides, for religions and myths as well as for scientific dogmas which unfortunately very often seem to be chaotically exaggerated today. For a long period of time philosophy had great difficulty defending itself from religious dogmas.

Christianity especially, and its institution "Church", have impeded and prevented scientific development over long periods of time. That the Earth is a sphere and not the centre of a geocentric world was simply suppressed, although already proven, for more than one and a half thousand years: the Greek astronomer *Aristarchus of Samos* discovered a good 250 years before the birth of Christ that the Earth moves around the Sun and could not, therefore, be the centre of the world. Between the 17th and 19th century natural sciences started their overwhelming, triumphant progress – they positively swept aside the predominant Christian view of the world and led to a new, materialistic perception of all things. It almost seems as if natural sciences made the attempt (and are still doing today) at eradicating all the foundations of religion by research. Creation and creator seem to have become increasingly outdated concepts. Life, the spirit, the soul, consciousness and personal identity became so-called epiphenomena and products of complex matter which organized itself over immeasurably long periods of time.

And what has become of the belief in a life after death? – It is the mere illusion of hope and wishful thinking of dim-witted humans. It is not just that propagating such perceptions is not fashionable but that one places one's reputation as a serious scientist at risk.

How fragile this "enlightened materialistic world" really is, however, even within the contemporary emotional fundamental structure of mankind, is demonstrated by the unbelievable success of a few books which, since the 70's of the last century, have swept a world that seemed to have said farewell forever to metaphysical perceptions. The first one was the book *"On Death and Dying"* (1969) by the Swiss-American physician *Elisabeth Kübler-Ross*, followed by *Raymond Moody's*, *"Life after Death"* (1975) which had already sold several million copies shortly after it was published. Here people who nearly died in accidents or during illnesses report on unusual out-of-body experiences they had, for example, during short periods while their heart had stopped beating. I will discuss this in detail later, especially in the second part of this book, the "Discussion".

Of course, the reports in these books are by no means anything new. As I already defined in the previous chapter with the term "travels to the beyond", such stories are abundant and have probably existed since time immemorial. They are possibly just one of the decisive issues on which myths and religions are based. But here they are placed on a new, an especially respectable (since scientific) level.

And that is why this kind of book has been catapulted to the top of the bestseller lists all over the world for a long period of time.

In spite of the highly scientific basis of our modern life mankind still seems to be especially receptive to metaphysics. Pure reason with a seemingly rational rejection of metaphysics and a simultaneous

acceptance of purely sensory experiences in natural science – as vehemently called for by *Immanuel Kant* – seems not to be persistent in this form.
Unfortunately, an effective philosophical corrective with the ability to monitor modern scientific views as critically as the tenets of the old religions has been missing for the last two hundred years during which materialism gained a predominant position which it was able to extend so rigorously. It seems to me that the new dogmas also stand on shaky foundations in more cases than one might expect.
In all my books I have always endeavoured not just to criticize the mainly materialistic interpretations of contemporary scientific conclusions. On the contrary, I try to respond with a possible better perspective. At the same time I will continue giving any kind of religious fundamentalism a clear rebuff – irrespective of the direction from which it comes, and most certainly the same applies to political ideologies be they from the left or the right: I do not appreciate either!

The oldest literary work which still exists was probably written about three and a half thousand years ago in cuneiform script on clay tablets. It was written by one of the first advanced civilizations of mankind which we know of, the *Sumerians,* who ruled the country between the Euphrates and the Tigris, the two rivers in today's Iraq in Asia Minor. *Gilgamesh* was the name of a very powerful king, ruler of Uruk, an important town at the time. King Gilgamesh was the subject of a number of heroic legends originating from this time. Much later these legends were collected by the poet S*in-leqe-unnini*, probably during the 12th century BC, who then composed the famous epic poem *Gilgamesh* from them.
The theme of the poem is the recognition of the inevitability of human death. Gilgamesh has to suffer the painful experience in the example of his friend Enkidu who was killed in revenge by the gods. In his sorrow the hero sets out upon a rather adventurous quest for his friend and searches for possibilities to obtain immortality by means of magic. In the end he finds Enkidu "living" in a rather dreary realm of death which probably became a model for the Greek Hades.
The journey to Hades is described by the famous poet *Homer* in several of his works of which the eleventh book of the "Odyssey" should receive special attention. In the "Realm of the Greek Dead" the hero also meets miserable, hopeless figures (see Chapter 2). Homer conceived the perception that the soul was some "trace of matter" just like air. Much

later it became "psyche" and was thus equipped with a personal quality. About 500 years BC the great Greek philosopher and mathematician *Pythagoras* adopted the idea of transmigration of souls or *reincarnation* which had meanwhile developed in Hinduism and was spread to the western civilizations by merchants. It is believed that every single still rather abstract soul reincarnates in a new animal or human body depending on its *Karma,* i.e. the degree of guilt it has burdened upon itself in the course of life. As a side remark only, I would like to point out here that it was Pythagoras who was probably the first to ascribe a real existence to numbers and who realized that there was an inner connection between numbers and the cosmos. His famous theorem[16] has been taught in schools all over the world ever since. I explained in detail why I believe this theorem to be of fundamental significance for understanding the entire cosmic existence in one of my earlier books entitled "Key to Eternity". A number of people in Pythagoras's time and day also reported of travels to the beyond and their stories are still recorded.

Heraclitus was a contemporary of Pythagoras. In my opinion some of his views are still relevant today.

Heraclitus believed in a world soul and compared it to a fire in which the souls of the dead are the flames. Thereby he creates a connection between the whole and the individual as an inseparable part of the whole. We come across this idea regularly especially in latter-day religions and philosophical perceptions. In my previous books I discussed in detail my model of a spiritual field which is the basis of everything in this world. If we look upon it as a kind of "cosmic internet" it is something continuous just like, metaphorically speaking, fire. At the very beginning of all matter it was still rather undifferentiated. It might be seen as a field of spiritual possibilities lying nearly fallow but becoming increasingly differentiated with time thereby undergoing consistent development in the course of a gigantic cosmic development.

Theoretically, it is also possible to add new information to the internet, continuously and without limit, thereby differentiating and structuring it further and further. Such structures are, for example, independent intranets. And the equivalent would be, for example, the human spirit.

---

[16] $a^2 + b^2 = c^2$ (In a right-angled triangle the area of the square on the hypotenuse is equal to the sum of the areas of the squares drawn on the other two sides) is *"Pythagoras's theorem".*

Sooner or later there comes a point in the evolution of all life when a sufficiently differentiated spirit recognizes itself for the very first time. Humans were the first to develop self-consciousness and self-awareness. Thus every individual gets the chance consistently to develop his very own spiritual intranet, i.e. his very own personal area within a really existing spiritual dimensionality, and to recognize himself as an individual personality with all his personal attributes. Each single spirit, each personal intranet could be compared to the flames of Heraclitus's world-fire. The individual flames of human beings, however, are enabled to recognize themselves and will not lose the thread of self-recognition again, since by means of their consciousness they have reached a significantly higher level of development.

The flames of a fire are not static. They rather give evidence of progression, a dynamic process. Since the outlines of the flames seem to retreat into the fire, however, and to reappear out of the fire, this comparison could depict the eternal return of souls in the form of reincarnations. Here, however, I cannot agree with Heraclitus, since I do not believe in carnal reincarnation. I will discuss this in further detail in Chapter 13.

I do agree, however, with Heraclitus's perception that the entire cosmos, life and all existence is an everlasting process of transformation. Heraclitus uttered the famous words "Panta Rhei" (everything flows). And behind the process of transformation is the great objective principle of order in the world, the "Logos". Thus the connection to a (spiritual) creator, a creating dimension, a "God" is made.

Another interesting theory was proclaimed by the Greek physician Hippocrates in about 450 BC:

He saw the brain as some kind of messenger to the consciousness *(synesis)* or as an interpreter *(hermeneus)* of conscious thoughts and desires. Here we notice the concept of a *dualism* which differentiates between an immaterial spirit and a physical brain and which runs like a thread through the entire history of philosophy. Today such perceptions are rejected by the majority of neuro-physiologists and brain researchers who consider the spirit to be a mere product of the physical brain *(monism)*. The existence of dualism is disclaimed since, according to general physical notions, there is no explanation for such forms of communication.

As I have already pointed out in my book "Life" and also in earlier publications I believe this view to be wrong, the social-political consequences of which could be downright fatal.
The fundamental problem is to be found in the natural sciences and their non-acceptance of a spiritual dimension which, although not physical, still possesses some interfaces with the physical world which was ultimately produced by it.
It seems to me that numbers play an important role here, e.g. the sequence of ordinal numbers – which Pythagoras believed to be of significant importance: if we succeeded in presenting the *real existence* of a purely spiritual world as being "extremely probable" – and I hope to have some good arguments for suggesting this myself – then the communication between the two worlds, the spiritual and the physical, would be completely redefined. Then it could no longer be considered as being a purely physical communication taking place exclusively between two physical things. It is also possible that physics needs only to be defined more widely and the extremely complex flow of data, which up to now has been considered to be of purely virtual nature, must be considered as a reality. The seemingly implausible dualism between spirit and brain would thus be given a completely new quality. And it would become possible to imagine that a spirit, which uses the brain as an exceedingly well-developed tool, could also exist without it. This would open the way for the perception that, after their physical death (brain death), all human beings, who are (also) spiritual beings, and who are aware of their own spiritual individuality, will go on to an individual spiritual further existence. That is exactly the intention I have in writing my books. I will discuss some of these connections between brain and spirit in further detail in special chapters of this volume. Here I see many correlations with the wise old Greek masters such as *Heraclitus, Phythagoras* or *Hippocrates*, with *Socrates* and, of course, with *Plato*, as well as, with certain restrictions, with *Aristotle*.
Socrates and his student Plato also maintained that the spirit, or the soul, and the physical body are two qualitatively completely different things. For Socrates the soul is the prisoner of the human body as long as the person lives and it is only after death that the soul is released from the *"chains of the body"*. Especially interesting is his reasoning with regard to survival after death: among other things he simply points out that everything in this world emerges from its opposite (polarity!): the large from the small and vice versa, the powerful from the weak and vice

versa, the fast from the slow and vice versa and so on, always and everywhere. And life is in opposition to death in the same way as being awake is to being asleep. And as there are always transitional phases between opposite conditions, such as the phase of falling asleep and of waking up, there must also be transitional phases between life and death, those of dying and coming back to life. If there were only the phase of going to sleep and not of waking up, then we would all be asleep in the end. If there were no coming back to life after death then everything would be dead in the end. Socrates reasons that the souls of the dead really exist. They *do*!

In his student *Plato's* work about the doctrines of souls, the *Phaedo*, we find the ideas of Socrates, who never wrote anything himself.

I started this chapter with Plato's statement: *"Philosophy is the preparation for death"*. He gave as a reason for this opinion that *"... striving for wisdom demands a severing from the body and a teaching of the spirit"*[17]. Plato adopted Pythagoras's notion, and he believed that Pythagoras was the first Greek philosopher to express the idea that *"in the face of death the soul notices a forked road"* which leads either to blissful happiness or to an arduous and again agonizing rebirth.

Leucippus of Milet and his pupil *Democritus*[18] were, in contrast to the above-mentioned philosophers, early materialists. For them the entire world is made of a substance consisting of the most minute of indivisible particles which Democritus called *atoms*. But these minute particles had, according to Democritus, two sides, the purely physical one and the non-physical, the side of thought *(logicus)*.

Therefore, Democritus was not a genuine materialist, although he believed that the end of a physical life, the death of a human, most certainly also meant the end of everything that was attached to it, such as thought, and hence the personal soul would perish.

Please allow me a short digression to East Asia, China to be exact, to Lao Tzu. While little is known of detailed perceptions Chinese wise men might have had of the beyond, we can find some very clear statements about their fundamental philosophical attitudes. And it seems they were strongly convinced that a self-recognizing immaterial soul was immortal. The following quotations from two of Lao Tzu's poems illustrate this:

"... I have heard that whosoever knows how to live life well wanders through the land and meets neither rhinoceros nor tiger. He walks through an army and avoids neither

---

[17] from Plato *Phaedo*.
[18] They both also lived during the 6th and 5th century BC, see Glossary.

armour nor weapons. The rhinoceros finds nothing to sink its horn into. The tiger finds nothing to sink its claws into. The weapon finds nothing to receive its sharpness. Why is this so? Because he has no mortal spot." And another example: *"... To see the smallest means to be clear. To guard wisdom means to be strong. If one uses one's light in order to return to this clarity one does not endanger one's person. This is called the hull of eternity."*[19]

But let us go back to orient and occident:

Aristotle, one of Plato's pupils and later the teacher of *Alexander the Great*, thought he could prove the existence of a self-aware human soul: *"If someone does not notice that a finger is pressed beneath his eye, he will not only see two objects instead of one, but he will even believe that there are two objects, but if he does know* (that a finger is pressed beneath his eye) *he will still notice two objects but he will* (no longer) *think that there are two."*

Later he dismissed the belief in an immortal human soul, and said that only God's soul was immortal.

Many of his contemporaries criticized him for this and said that the human soul must be immortal if a connection did indeed exist between God the creator and humans as his creatures. Therefore, Aristotle differentiated between the human soul and the spirit. While the soul remained mortal, the spirit, which enabled humans to think and to recognize, was immortal. This spirit, however, was neither tangible nor individually independent, but was merely a non-self-aware part of some kind of worldly spirit or divine information. Therefore, he did not draw up any detailed perceptions of a lasting existence after death.

Plato had mentioned a forked path on which the human soul wandered after death to ascend or to descend, depending on the kind of life it had led.

The Platonic, Stoic and neo-Pythagorean scholars that followed concentrated only on the ascent into higher spheres. The Roman Consul and gifted orator *Cicero*, who lived during the first century BC and who was killed a year after Caesar by the Roman Emperor *Marcus Antonius*, ended his work "On the State" *(De re publica)* with a tribute to Plato in which he describes the philosophical life as an astral journey.

The Greek philosopher *Plotinus*, founder of the neo-Platonic philosophical school in Rome during the 3rd century AD, took the view that all material things are the shadow of the real One, namely God, from whom all matter derives *(the concept of emanations)*. Besides

---

[19] Translation by Richard Wilhelm/H.G. Ostwald, published by the Penguin Group: "Lao Tzu – Tao Te Ching", The Richard William Edition, Arkana Penguin Books (1989)

maintaining rather modern ideas even for us today about the nature of the universe, of the beginning and the end of the world and the nature of time *(time is "relative")*, Plotinus and the neo-Platonic philosophers held the view that human life was by no means terminated by death. Most interesting is Plotinus' indication that he developed his theories by means of meditation (extra-sensual) and he even described special techniques.

For *Augustine*, one of the early fathers of the church and a teacher, who lived in the Roman Empire during the early Middle Ages, the immaterial human soul is defined by three characteristics: reason, will and memory. For him the human soul is a direct image of the triune God and survives physical death.

Pope *Gregory the Great,* an admirer of Augustine, was very much interested in spiritual scripts and he obviously influenced medieval discussion significantly with regard to miracles and visions. In the fourth and last book of his dialogues he claimed that on the strength of visions experienced by dying people, travels to the beyond and spiritual apparitions, he could offer *proof* of the immortality of the soul. Important and reoccurring components of his concepts of the beyond are hell, meadows full of flowers in paradise, heavenly hosts clothed in white gowns and the "Judgement" of human actions. It is important to note that Christians in those days believed in the *direct* survival of death through the immortal soul. However, due to the famous biblical perception of an apocalyptic end to the world at the end of all days, the "Day of Final Judgement", it became an "intermediate phase" which starts with death and ends with the "Day of Final Judgement". On that day the bodies of those saved by God are supposed to be resurrected while the condemned ones go to hell for ever.

The late medieval 13th century AD is known as the "Century of the Occident" because people then tried to reconcile the antipodes religion and secularism as well as the ancient world and the Middle Ages. The naturalist, theologian and philosopher *Albertus Magnus* who was born in Bavaria and later lived and worked in Cologne, my home-town, is the only scholar described as "the Great". His real name was Count Albrecht von Bollstädt. He considered the world as being filled with God. He strongly believed in the immortality of the soul and fought fiercely against the Arab belief that humans possess merely a kind of general soul which is only individualized by them during their physical lives. Each soul, Albertus Magnus tells us, is created directly by God and, since there is a significant difference between body and soul, it is not affected by the death of the body. The soul has the same (external) shape as the body and its intrinsic principle is movement.

His most famous student was *Thomas Aquinas* who accompanied him to Cologne and helped to found Cologne University. For Thomas Aquinas every human possesses a body *and* a bodiless soul. An interaction takes place between these two which must, of course, be of non-mechanical nature. The soul gives life to the body and thus the ability to work.

Whereas the human body has reached the highest hierarchical level of all life on earth, the soul is on the lowest level of the "absolute forms", i.e. the divine.

Eternal life is the final aim of every human. His blissful happiness is derived from the knowledge of God. It is necessary solely due to the hierarchy of being and must thus be considered as proven. The third member of the Cologne "epistemological trio" – whom I mention not merely for reasons of local patriotism but because their ideas were significant contributions – was *Meister (=Master) Eckhart*, a member of the Dominican order. Although he taught in many places all over Germany it was in Cologne of all places where he was indicted for religious controversy because the Church condemned some of his theses. In contrast to Thomas of Aquinas and Albertus Magnus, whose philosophical grandson he was, his ideas were governed less by logic and systematic but rather, as *Ernst Sandvoss* wrote, by religious experience, ecstasy, experience of God and visions. For him the soul did not go to any special place after death. "Where should the soul go?" he asked. "Where else should it go, where else does eternity exist? The soul stays here."

Living almost 200 years after the visionary Benedictine abbess *Hildegard von Bingen*, who probably experienced travels to the beyond[20], Meister Eckhart is another important German mystic. He wrote that God needs us as we need God, and that the only virtue consists of three parts: love, beauty and harmony.

Medieval perceptions of the beyond are also shaped by a number of visions documented in literature. Among others there are the tales of *Drythelm*, a pious English family father who, after serious illness, died at nightfall and came back to life in the first light of the following day. When he arose from his deathbed the gathered mourners were shocked.

---

[20] Very famous are her visions of the "living light".

In Drythelm's tale, as was always the case in those days, a more or less drawn out journey through hell played a major role before the wandering soul was allowed to take a glimpse into the heavenly worlds of paradise before returning to its body. During this journey the soul is accompanied by a higher being of the beyond.
Following the example of the "Aeneid", written by the Roman writer Virgil who lived during the 1st century BC, the Italian poet *Alighieri Dante* wrote the greatest poem of the Christian world *"La Divina Commedia"* *("The Commedia")* at the beginning of the 14th century. This epic poem describes the poet's travels to the beyond in 100 songs with more than 14,000 verses. However, it probably does not really describe Dante's own vision but is rather to be considered as a document of the generally existing belief in the beyond at that time. Therefore, Dante's journey takes him through hell before he reaches paradise via purgatory and he finally catches sight of God.
Such travels to the beyond always effected a lasting *inner change* of the travellers. This extremely remarkable fact differentiates the earlier "travels to the beyond" or modern "near-death experiences" from practically all similar but "artificial" phenomena either induced by medicine or provoked by any kind of experiment. I will come back to this in detail later.

Our present time is characterized by extremely fast progress in natural science. Sensory perceptions become ever more important. At the same time this leads people to turn away from their religious beliefs. For a long time the dominant Christian church in the occident fought against this trend in a completely unchristian way. Although the slow but triumphant progress of scientific research has been severely hampered by this attitude it never completely prevented it. The most important period of spiritual change was most certainly between the 17th and 18th century. Most of the great masters of natural philosophy, I believe, lived and worked and philosophised about problems of existential theories at that time. I would like to name just a few of the most important ones: *Descartes, Pascal, Leibniz, de Spinoza, Newton, Locke, Hume, Berkeley, Laplace* and *Kant*.
With the three most famous words *"Cogito, ergo sum"* *(I think, therefore, I am)* René Descartes became one of the acknowledged architects of the modern age. Everything could and should be doubted except that we *exist* because we are *thinking*.

That, approximately, is the gist of the statement. The philosopher Descartes believed that the entire world is a huge cosmic machine, a gigantic clockwork in which only humans possess an immaterial spirit which influences their bodies *(dualism)*. The natural scientist Descartes discovered the laws of impact and considered the action of thought to be the result of smallest impacts taking place. And here lies the root of the problem we have today with understanding the whole matter. Adequate indications for dualistic interactions of quasi mechanical nature between spirit and brain are presently still missing. Many among us unfortunately lack the fantasy to imagine that there must be a qualitatively polar form of existence to all matter; and most also lack the realization of its logical necessity. They prefer to ignore and suppress the phenomena which, were they accepted at face value, may only be explained in this way.

Descartes located the immaterial spirit, which is only inherent in humans, in the pineal gland and he described it as being indestructible. After death the human spirit is separated from the body and remains in existence without its brain. A spirit which can survive without a body cannot be explained in our world by means of matter.

It was probably a typical example for a journey to the beyond in the context of a near-death experience which occurred to the French philosopher and mathematician *Blaise Pascal* on the 23rd November 1646. On exactly that day he had a "divine vision" in connection with an OBE[21]. For Pascal, too, this experience was a turning-point in his life. Previously he had been a busy epicurean and a brilliant scientist who had made many extremely important discoveries and had written treatises on mathematical and physical problems. After that day he retreated into a monastery and he pursued exclusively religious and philosophical studies until his early death in 1662. Pascal maintained at that time that there is a higher immaterial cosmic order whose highest quality is love. For him intuition, defined as *"inner feeling and sensing"*, gained a new and important status which had not been recognized before. The final questions of this world, he maintained, lie beyond the scope of sensible and rational answers. The devout experience of God could alone give a *subjectively* satisfying answer. Pascal talks of an immaterial immortal soul which characterizes each individual. The human spirit is part of that soul, but not the most important one. Its real core is emotionality and, above all, love. I myself can follow this line of thought without reservations.

---

[21] Generally used term for an **Out-of-Body Experience**.

The English scientist *Isaac Newton* was certainly one of the greatest scientists of all time. Among many other things he explained space, time and gravitation and established the laws of motion. He recognized that light consists of smallest "particles", and as a brilliant mathematician he developed the infinitesimal calculus independently of the German natural scientist *Gottfried Wilhelm Leibniz*. Hardly anybody knows, however, that he studied the Bible at least with as much fervour as he did the cosmos. After his death his theological manuscripts were found which in pure volume exceeded all his scientific works. And the English philosopher *John Locke* said about Newton's biblical knowledge that he *"knew only few people who were a match for him in this respect"*. It is said that Newton was a strict believer in the word of the Bible. One of the greatest natural scientists was simultaneously a mystic.

Newton's perceptions of the world beyond probably corresponded to a large extent with the contemporary Christian concepts.

Among the greatest natural scientists at that period were also, of course, *Gottfried Wilhelm Leibniz* and *Baruch de Spinoza*, a Dutchman.

Leibniz, the Englishman *George Berkeley* and *Baruch de Spinoza* maintained a kind of panpsychism according to which a certain mental element is present in everything that exists. Leibniz developed the Monads Theory. Monads being the smallest, indivisible and complete power points present in any form of matter. Furthermore, for him matter in the authentic substantial sense did not exist. Everything material is only an illusion, a manifestation of purely spiritual monads due to the *"effective power"* inherent in them.

All monads possess a soul in so far as they are able to sense and to react; but not every soul possesses a consciousness. Humans are colonies of monads regulated by a constant order which also defines the soul. *"When this soul is raised to the level of reason then it will recognize itself as a spirit."* If it recognizes the eternal order and the soul of the world, then it will become God's mirror. God is the prime monad and, therefore, a pure and fully conscious spirit, completely separated from body and mechanisms. Between spirit and body there is no interaction in a mechanical sense!

Physical and spiritual processes take place simultaneously due to *"(pre-stabilized) harmony* which was established in advance by God in the same way as *"two clocks identically designed, wound up and set so that they tick the seconds and chime the hours simultaneously without any interaction or mutual influence taking place."*

Basically, Leibniz maintained that matter and spirit are two sides of one and the same "proto-spiritual" coin. The seemingly separate, simultaneous processes of mechanics and life, of motion and of thought are one and the same. It depends on the standpoint from which we look upon these processes – if from outside, then they are physical; if from inside, then they are spiritual. I think that *Leibniz* was basically right here, but I do not believe that Leibniz really meant that everything was "imperatively predetermined by God", since a *harmony* of matter and spirit is the inevitable result if they are considered as being two sides of the same coin – they must be synchronized without influencing each other in the mechanical sense. However, quality, quantity and complexity of such "synchronized things" are not necessarily (pre-) determined. This would only be the case if all spirituality in the world were an extension of God's spirit – but not if the spirit were a mere seed sown by God which still has to grow and mature. In this case any kind of *emergence*, i.e. free development, is imaginable and only a certain frame is determined.

De Spinoza goes a step further. For him God alone is the unique and absolute substance from which everything else emerges. Therefore, everything in this world exists as a *"mode of God" (pantheism)*. It follows that all deeds done by the things developed by God must be divine deeds and all his "living developments" must be divine beings. It also means that everything is basically God's will, predetermined and non-influenceable.

This is called radical determinism. The human being has no free will. He must try to recognize, acknowledge and accept unconditionally every event in this world as being the necessity of God. *Pierre-Simon de Laplace* rightly contradicted this concept. Laplace held the view that the total course of, if anyone were to have knowledge of all conditions and effective mechanisms of a certain state of the world at any arbitrary point in time, then he could predict the course of all future events. Then everything without exception would be predetermined and even God himself would have no freedom of will.

For Leibniz the human soul, unlike God's soul, is immortal and is always connected to a body. However, I cannot agree with that. And in this Leibniz contradicts his own logic, probably due to his fear of the inquisition. Prepared to make concessions he continues: the immortality of the soul will become apparent in the reincarnation of the dead on the "Day of the Last Judgement". It followed that the bodies of the dead must also be resurrected, thereby towing the Church's line. De Spinoza, on the other hand, saw the soul under the predominance of the laws of the (physical) universe, which made it impersonal and mortal. The English philosopher *John Locke* and the Scottish philosopher *David Hume* thought likewise. They both adhered to *empiricism* and thought that it was only a question of time before natural science would finally be able to eliminate any kind of metaphysics such as God and creation in Christian religion. Real knowledge could only be obtained by sensory experience, in his opinion, but not by pure reason and even less by the intuitive basis of religions.

During the 18th century *Immanuel Kant* opposed this idea and, at first, he even believed that *reason (rationalism)* alone could lead to knowledge. However, later on, influenced by his contemporary *David Hume*, he changes his opinion and maintains that this must be a misconception.

But he did not concede that *Hume* might have been right when he says that everything can be perceived by our senses. Kant looked for the happy medium and came to realise that both, sensory experience as well as reason, must work together. However, he rejected intuitive cognition completely, unlike the medieval Jewish physician, theologian and philosopher *Moses Maimonides,* who advocated in the 12th century the interpretation of religious scripts as being allegories or symbols, if contradictions between religion and science were found. In my opinion, that recommendation seems very sensible. In his time Maimonides was held in equally high esteem among Jews, Christians and Arabs for his attempts at interpreting religious scripts in a rational way. I believe that even today, this could be an acceptable way towards the elimination of the utterly senseless and superfluous dissension between religions.

Kant sought a third option between *rationalism* and *empirical scepticism* (sensory experience) and he found it when he combined these two to form two sides of the same coin but this left no space for a third party, such as religion and thus intuitive cognition.

For Kant, God and immortality were unfortunately the subject of mere speculation: they could neither be experienced with our senses nor could they be evaluated or categorized by reason. A metaphysical proof of the existence of God would be outside of any sensory experience and would thus only be subject to pure rational thinking. But that would not be sufficient for gaining real cognition. Yet, the notion of God and immortality still makes sense, as he states in his *"Critique of Practical Reason",* because we must believe in them for *"reasons of morality"* alone. Whether they really exist or not is actually of secondary importance.

It becomes apparent how dramatically philosophical perceptions with regard to God, spirit, soul or a survival after death have changed in the course of modern times. This is mainly due to the growing influence of natural science – but it can also be understood as the real reaction to the remorseless indoctrination practiced by the Christian Church over a long period of time.

All religions suffered from increasing criticism over the following centuries. Describing religion as being *"opium for the masses"* was a bold and simple expression coined by *Karl Marx* and harnessed for the initiation of a number of dramatic social-political reorientations especially during the 20th century, influenced mainly by the Germans *Ludwig Feuerbach, Karl Marx* and *Friedrich Engels.*

These new structures, detached from any faith in God or metaphysical matters, with which people attempted to stand on their own (spiritual) feet like a youth in puberty, were basically in their oppressiveness in no way different from the churches and their rigorous religious dogmas. Yet, their consequences, which were in part also due to the tremendous technical progress unfurling at the same time, represented an even bigger catastrophe for the affected people and countries in the end.

A gradual spiritual change finally took place during the last century, mostly a period of sadness and oppression. The Austrian philosopher and psychologist *Karl Popper* was one of the instigators of that change. He stressed that in principle phenomena based on experience, i.e. *empirically*[22] verifiable phenomena, could none the less also be true. Only an error could refute a hypothesis. Verifiability, however, has never been a proof that a theses is correct because at some time before the end of time we have to expect that it may yet be proven wrong. However, the fact that we will never really be sure of the truth should not encourage complacency. The search for truth should always be accompanied by a plethora of different hypotheses, by discussion and comparison as well as logical checks. In free adaptation to the theory of the evolution researcher *Charles Darwin,* Popper stated that this was the only way in which a "viable contest" of theories could develop, leading to higher knowledge in the end. *Popper* who, as a young man, was fascinated by Marxism but became soon utterly disillusioned by it, recognized that the human spirit obviously possessed a completely new quality which went far beyond its equivalent in the physical world. The human ability to

---

[22] Not to be confused with "empiristic", i.e. based on perception by senses which is practically identical with "natural science".

think has become independent and has created its *own world*. There exist, said Popper, mental conditions which have a completely different quality than physical ones and which interact. From this theory Popper developed the idea of an emergent world, i.e. a world that creates itself, in which new things are created without being predestined *(indeterminism)*. Human thoughts possess their own status of reality.

They *are*!

Here Popper sees a chance to solve the problem as to *why* it is that humans, with their rather limited life-span, can participate in timeless ideas: everything has already been thought of at some time or other by someone. Therefore, all thoughts are reality now and gain their own dynamic. This enables any individual spirit to retrieve them at will.

Popper introduced the theses of a globally existing spiritual, i.e. immaterial, network of ideas, thoughts and perceptions since for him this perspective seemed to be conclusive. Popper thus forced the rejection of a purely materialistic view of the world.

In my opinion, as I already explained in my previous books, both exist: emergence as postulated by Popper, as well as a number of already existing pre-conditions within which this emergence is made possible and where it can, may, must and should work. This frame-work, I believe, is of purely spiritual nature. As well as being a kind of spiritual blue-print it also contains a mathematical plan which is primarily a geometrical plan for structuring physical matters.

In spite of these perceptions which were rather revolutionary for his time, Popper did not succeed in leaping over his own shadow and accepting also that a lasting individual spiritual personality indeed exists.

The famous Australian brain researcher *John Eccles*, however, who died in 1997 when he was 94 years old, did so. In his *"dualistic interactive hypotheses"*, which I consider to be quite plausible and conclusive and which he had to defend vehemently against much criticism from his own ranks, he talks of interactions between a body-independent spirit which exists and acts outside the brain and *his* brain as the physical instrument for communication in this world.

While *Popper* does not yet believe in a survival after death, due to his restricted viewpoint, Eccles is convinced of this theory.

During a conversation with Karl Popper on 29.04.1974 which he mentioned in a book, Eccles said the following: *Karl, I think that you are nauseated by all these rather clumsy attempts at 'describing' life after death. I too am sickened by them. However, I do believe that a great mystery lies behind all this.*

What does this life mean? First we start to exist and then we stop existing? We find ourselves going through this wonderful, rich and vivid experience which lasts all our life, but then, is that the end? Our very own self-conscious spirit possesses a mysterious relationship with our brain and is thus enabled to experience human love and friendship, the wonderful beauty of nature and intellectual excitement and pleasure by enjoying and understanding our cultural inheritance. Should this current life end completely when we die or may we hope that some further sense will be discovered? (...) I believe that we live in complete ignorance of our future, but then we came from the unknown. Is it really so that our life is only an episode of consciousness, between two phases of unconsciousness or is there a 'transcendental experience' of which we 'know' nothing? Our start of existence is just as mysterious as our end in death. (the inverted commas '...' are mine).

Finally, at the end of this chapter, I would like to mention some aspects discussed by the great philosopher and anthropologist *Pierre Teilhard de Chardin*. In his book *"The Phenomenon of Humanity"* [23] he maintains, using strictly logical arguments, that there is a non-physical "omnipotent power" which regulates everything in the universe with precision. In the course of cosmic evolution certain phenomena have kept occurring which at first appeared to be special cases, but later proved to be something universal.

According to *Teilhard de Chardin* this also applies to the spirit and human consciousness. Spirit and consciousness must also have their smallest origin in the far distant past, in the same way as all physical matter. He also maintains that there is an immaterial energy of things which is expressed in life and which in a continuing evolutionary process has led to individualization and finally to a personal consciousness. Only love can set in motion the increasing integration of all matter in this universe and simultaneously act as a tireless engine and keep everything running at all times. Although love is a universal principle humans put up a strong resistance to it. Humans are presently representing the highest level of evolution, but they are by no means the final result of a convergent development of the universe which is inexorably progressing further.

A central problem for humans on their path to cognition and to themselves is their *"paralysing anti-personality complex"*: humans show neither respect for the value of their individuality nor for their immense personal responsibility. For me this is the result of severe social

---

[23] First published under the title "Le Phénomène humain" (1948)

deficiencies which I already criticized earlier. In my opinion, the prevalent aversions people had over the last two centuries against all things metaphysical are responsible for this development. As long as the collective group absorbs or seems to absorb the individual person, it kills love before it is born, so Teilhard. Viewed thus, the collective group appears "rather undesirable". Individualization is, therefore, a necessary pre-condition for the "continuing development" towards more harmony based on a binding love between brethren in the community. This development requires that the *spirit* be able to grow *(noogenese)*.

The emergence of an individual spirit and its steady increase in size are, therefore, a general, i.e. a universal, principle with a purposefully directed development towards God, the convergence of *"all conscious centres of the world"* which then become *"one with God"*, not, however, by being *"identified with God (so that God becomes everything), but by the differentiating and unifying effect of 'love' (God is in everything)"*.

Evolution still has far to go. In a sense, we are *all God,* said Teilhard de Chardin --- God in emergence. And in this point I wholeheartedly agree with him.

It is obvious that the acceptance of an individual spirit, existing as a basically body-independent and evolutionary principle, inevitably includes the survival of physical death.

Expanding on this it follows that the physical death no longer plays a role when the development of an individual human being is contemplated. It is reduced to a sort of turning-point which becomes necessary for several reasons in the course of our individual development which has practically only just started and which remains completely inexplicable to us.

The Czech poet *Rainer Maria Rilke* once said very aptly: *"There is no escape from eternity."*

4. Our Cosmic View of the World in Doubt

Modern natural sciences currently provide a rather complicated view of the world, which for most of us is barely understandable. Nevertheless it is accepted almost everywhere without criticism. Certainly, some people just respond with a shrug, since hardly anyone feels himself to be in a position to contradict this obviously overwhelming scientific evidence.

Everything seems to be so complicated: This applies to the generation of the cosmos as well as to the evolution of life on Earth. The certainly most remarkable, even most important, aspect of all modern perceptions is without doubt the fact that they are of purely materialistic nature. For things such as spirit, soul, God, creator, immaterial reality, etc. there seems no longer to be any place in the eyes of natural scientists.

We have to state this fact so clearly and unambiguously since for all imaginable non-physical things there remains, if at all, only a small enclave where science has not declared it out of existence. And with time this enclave should, according to most scientists, become even smaller and disappear completely sooner rather than later.

The so-called quantum mechanics deals with the smallest physical components in the world, the smallest particle or quanta. Some aspects of quantum phenomena are still so baffling for modern scientists that they admit to the limits of their comprehension. However, this "inexplicable fuzziness" should not obscure the fact that there is in effect no room left for immaterial and spiritual things.

In order to describe the subject of my book clearly and to explain the problem I will simplify the matter and bring it to a point: according to the present generally accepted scientific view of the world, any vague notion of a survival of our physical death, especially the survival even of an integer, human personality, is, in short, utter nonsense.

In the very best case it is disqualified as an understandable relict of pious wishful thinking and as a consequence of the conscious or unconscious fear of having to face our final and irrevocable end. Briefly, I consider this in "respected" scientific circles almost uncontested view on death as being entirely wrong and, for social-political reasons, even contraproductive and also dangerous.

Therefore, discussion about death and an assumed or even possible personal survival of death only makes sense for me if we express our legitimate doubts about the current scientifically accepted view of the world, and if we can simultaneously offer a more plausible, alternative intellectual model of the world. This is exactly what I already attempted to do in my previous books. This chapter and the next ones will provide a short comparative summary of my previous books, so that readers who have not had the chance to read them are better prepared to understand this book.

According to the currently accepted cosmic view of the world our universe emerged after an incredibly small point of inconceivably high density exploded with a big bang about 15 billion years ago. Within an extremely short period of time a ball of fire of unimaginably high temperature was generated. Soon after it started to cool down, a kind of thick soup developed containing minute particles of matter and electromagnetic radiation (light). Over long periods of time the continuous collisions of radiation particles and their mutual bombardments caused clusters of matter to be created, and much later gigantic piles of matter. Finally all celestial bodies and galaxies were formed from these piles of matter, among others also our solar system.
Since then the galaxies have all been moving away from one another. The universe is expanding – and indeed the expansion is accelerating. Scientists are convinced that a certain observation, a phenomenon known as red-shift, indicates that their assumption is correct. A physical phenomenon know as "Doppler effect", named after the 19th century Austrian physicist *Christian Doppler,* states the following: when an ambulance passes by sounding its siren, the tone of the siren seems higher (higher frequency) while the ambulance is approaching and lower (lower frequency) when it is moving away. Accordingly it is assumed that the colour emitted by distant galaxies which is admittedly shifted to the red spectrum and indicates a lower frequency, must mean that the galaxies are moving away.
Furthermore, a very low, evenly distributed microwave radiation is detectable everywhere and fills the universe. It is supposed to have developed a few hundred thousand years after the Big Bang while the universe constantly cooled down and scientists assume that they might thus gain information of the earliest days of the universe. Its temperature

of exactly 2.73° Kelvin[24] is only slightly higher than that of "absolute zero" (= 0 degree Kelvin or minus 273 degree Celsius).
Due to these observations, the currently accepted Big Bang theory sounds plausible, but leads to a number of explanatory deficiencies:
First of all we have to ask ourselves inevitably what was there before the Big Bang happened or what caused the Big Bang. Scientists usually do not permit the first part of this question; they reason that also time as we know it was generated by the Big Bang. Before that, they say, time did not exist. Therefore, that part of the question is inadmissible. The answer to the second part is that the Big Bang emerged from a "void", because it could not have been caused by "something".
Otherwise, we would inevitably be bound to ask of what quality and origin this "something" was. Some quantum physicists of our time believe, however, that even in the "void of quantum physics", i.e. on the level of unimaginably small particles, virtual particles could suddenly emerge. The Big Bang could have been caused by an incidental accumulation of an unimaginably huge number of such so-called quanta fluctuations. However, had the universe been generated in this way it would inevitably be finite and, therefore, would come to an end one day, since none of these quanta fluctuations could provide the infinite amount of energy required for an infinite eternal cosmos.
The void could also be a real *"singularity"* which is something like an infinitesimally small version of infinity[25].
At this point one feels obliged to remark critically that even firmly established "serious" physics touches on the usually discarded "metaphysics", since infinity exists neither for "real", i.e. physical, things nor for their infinite quantities – even when applied to galaxies. Everything which is divisible, and that includes any kind of matter, is finite.
Today's most famous cosmologist, the English physicist *Stephen Hawking*, who has been confined to a wheelchair by a terrible disease, once said: *"in the transition between the void and being, the key to 'God's plan' is hidden.*[26].
Hawking's words can be almost described as cutting irony.
In my opinion, none of the solutions put forward leaves much room for the "divine", that which we should really approach (and I make the daily attempt to realize this) with the greatest humility, since this whiff of

---

[24] ± further figures after the third decimal position
[25] Physically a singularity is an infinite point for which physical laws are no longer valid.
[26] Interview of Stephen Hawking by the German magazine "Focus" 36 (2001).

nothingness, this singularity, must already contain complete information on every single thing ever conceived in this cosmos including life itself and the human spirit and immeasurably more beyond it.

The mere fact that every existence in this world with its so highly complex structure must adhere to extremely narrowly defined and restricted cosmic laws (laws of nature) and constants, renders the popular Big Bang theory more than unlikely. Cosmologists are desperately searching for methods of selection by means of which they could effectively narrow down the huge improbability of the accidental emergence of all irrefutable yet existing laws of nature. To venture a bold and simple comparison: it would be much more probable that every inhabitant of the world since the beginning of mankind had won one million Euro in a "World Lottery" every day of his life than that we could really have come into existence in the way which is currently assumed. The head of the research centre of the Max-Planck-Institute of Astrophysics in Munich-Garchinger, Gerhard Börger, said in this context that "the age-old questions: "where do we come from?" and "where are we going?" are of even more pressing importance today than ever before."[27]

In addition to other unexplained or at least not unequivocally answered questions such as the asymmetry of matter and anti-matter[28], doubt seems to be cast on the "key proofs" for the Big Bang theory. Above all, we have to record the fact that the temperature of **2.73 ...** degrees Kelvin of the background radiation is subject to fluctuations which are, however, almost negligible in the entire universe. [29] The number sequence **2-7-3** alone is of great interest here and I will come back to this again later.

As regards the red shift of light arriving here from distant galaxies, we must recognize today, now that our vision penetrates vast distances into the cosmos that the assumed escape velocity must soon travel at the speed of light, or even faster than that.

---

[27] Professor Dr. Gerhard Börger in conversation with Thomas Bührke. In: Spektrum der Wissenschaft-Spezial: Forschung im 21. Jahrhundert (Research in the 21st century)
[28] Even if some new explanatory models exist today the problem still remains unsolved and is not supported by observations.
[29] The COBE space telescope could only detect fluctuations of a mere one thirty millionth of a degree. The latest experiments with balloons (Boomerang and Maxima) showed significantly smaller fluctuations. The background temperature is completely isotropic, i.e. absolutely even in all directions of the entire cosmos!

That, however, is impossible since matter travelling at such speed would become infinitely inert and would, therefore, possess infinite mass.[30] Again we would be confronted with infinities which cannot be applied to finite bodies. Cosmologists managed to eliminate this problem by simply altering the calculation basis for increasing velocities of expansion.[31] I certainly do not exaggerate when I say that, in my opinion, in doing so they try to save the currently accepted world model from disrepute. However, this seems to be the only sufficiently plausible explanation to them, which may even be correct from a purely materialistic point of view.

After all, we know that the distribution of cosmic matter in galaxies is by no means as even as it would be if it were due to a Big Bang. The astronomer *Vera Rubin* discovered this fact back in 1954. However, the Big Bang was the "in" thing – and Rubin's discoveries were, therefore, not accepted. In 1986, however, the American astronomer *Margaret Geller* was able to prove that our universe is rather like a big sponge: almost completely empty bubbles of different sizes are surrounded by galaxies. They form the structure of the sponge. Viewed from afar it all looks rather homogenous, but not precisely like a typical Big Bang induced pattern!

The genius *Albert Einstein*, the German physicist who became so very famous all over the world, discovered a four-dimensionality with his *relativity theories*. He interpreted it as a four-dimensional space-time continuum.

Included are the three dimensions of space which we already know and an additional fourth dimension as a single-dimensioned, directed axis of time. Time, however, is relative, i.e. depending on the velocity of object from which it is experienced – the same applies to objects which are attracted by gravitational forces. Of course, it is correct that we all experience time as something that is one-dimensional and directed. We cannot relive the past. The question now arising is whether this single-dimension of time is objectively not just as relative as time itself as an objective quantity. Should that be so, then conditions must exist in which time is a multi-dimension.

In earlier books I have already pointed out – and I will come back to this later – that this is probably the case and furthermore, that time and space are symmetrical and polar to each other, i.e. they are exact opposites in

---

[30] According to Albert Einstein and Hendrik Lorentz, see Glossary and previous books.
[31] By altering the Hubble constant with growing distance.

the same way as is every number to its reciprocal value – or as is a horizontal line to a vertical. From this perspective time would also be three-dimensional, but space would only appear as a single dimension.
Keeping these thoughts in mind, we can see the possibility that Einstein's four-dimensionality is in fact a real spatial four-dimensionality! This would mean that the space of our universe is not three-dimensional, as previously assumed, but (genuinely) four-dimensional.
As far as I know, *Peter Plichta* was the first to explain the theory of 4-D space, although his explanations were based on a completely different chain of arguments. I thankfully took up his chain of thoughts and later on I was able to show[32] for the first time that this kind of space inevitably results when we apply the laws of elementary logic – in the same way as many prevailing conditions all over the world catch the eye. This, however, requires that we explain the generation of our universe on the bases of a *completely new model* which, of course, must not omit any really confirmed knowledge.
Einstein's assumption that a four-dimensional space-time continuum existed caused scientists to predict the curvature of cosmic space.
In this context we must remember that, according to previous perceptions, space was limited by the expansion of light, since nothing can move faster than light. In other words: if we assume that a Big Bang did indeed occur about 15 billion years ago, then our cosmos should have the size of a "three-dimensional balloon" with a radius of 15 billion light-years. Einstein assumes correctly that forces of attraction must also bend the light on its path. By the same reasoning this must mean that space itself is curved.
In the meantime science has progressed and we can see much further into space. Yet, cosmologists have not been able to detect the slightest curvature of space up till now.
The universe appears to be absolutely flat and plane (Euclidean). Yet, scientists observed decades ago that the path of a ray of light passing a large mass, e.g. the Sun, is indeed curved.
Therefore, it is accepted today that at least local curvatures must happen. If we assume, however, that light and space are not absolutely congruent then the deviation of light – without doubt a proven fact – does not necessarily mean that space itself must also be curved. This perception is usually not taken seriously; what else should determine the limits of

---

[32] Volume 1, "The Universe", Monologue, Chapter, "Straight to the Point", see also Appendix.

space? And what else should be the nature of space itself if not a "cone of light" generated by an unbelievable Big Bang?

An absolutely plane space would contradict all laws of gravitation, if indeed, as Einstein postulated, gravitation could curve space, a fact which was confirmed only last year.

However, in my opinion gravitation does not do this. Cosmologists are again busy trying to find new explanations without questioning their basic model. Anti-gravitational forces are already "invented" or huge masses, so-called dark matter. Nobody has found anything yet, however – and I claim that there is nothing to be found.

Gravitation also is something "mystical". Newton explained *how* it works: he established the "inverse distance square law" according to which the attraction between two physical quantities decreases with the square of the distance between the sources of gravitation. This is pure mathematical law found in abundance in our world. Unfortunately, most scientists today believe it most unlikely that these laws themselves could be anything real or even be the underlying reason for many observations and for the properties of our world. More than two thousand years ago it was quite different as we can see in the works of *Pythagoras* and *Plato*.

For a long time, scientists were convinced that the universe was filled with some kind of ether. It was over a hundred years ago, however, that the American scientists *Edward Morley* and *Albert Michelson* could rule this out. In spite of huge celestial bodies with their gigantic masses, the universe is absolutely empty, a near vacuum, apart from some drifting atoms which are very few and far between[33]. – This knowledge finally led to our present perception of light:

It was *Isaac Newton* who established that light must be composed of the tiniest of particles, and *Albert Einstein* as well as *Max Planck* and many others confirmed this perception. Today, we experiment and work with light particles, *photons*, for example in communication electronics. All types of radiation consist of particles or, in general, of *quanta*.

It is also true to say that, in a vacuum like the cosmos, light cannot move freely as a pure succession of such particles. If no (physical) medium exists in the universe, therefore, light must be something more than just particles. This cognition led to the presently accepted perception that light must possess a wave-particle duality. Light, i.e. any kind of electro-

---

[33] It is assumed today that there is approx. 1 atom per cubic metre in the cosmos.

magnetic radiation, is assumed to consist of particles and *independent* waves.
All observations and indeed our daily life indicate that this perception must be correct, although it is difficult even for some physicists to understand. And I am almost ashamed to admit that nevertheless, in my opinion, this perception is wrong. The following comparison may support the reason for my doubts:
If we throw a stone into water we create waves. These waves, however, are not the waves of the stone but those of the water. If we shout we will cause waves. They are, however, not the waves of our vocal cords but those of the surrounding air. In both cases waves are generated in the surrounding medium. In the universe, however, there is no medium. This fact caused headaches for generations of scientists who came up with the presently accepted theory that light consists of waves and particles simultaneously.
Difficulties also exist when modern scientists attempt to envision the end of the cosmos: the latest results of cosmology research[34] indicate that the universe is flat and extends into infinity, a perception which was absolutely rejected for a very long time. Finally, at some unfathomably distant point in time, it will thin itself out and will practically disappear into a hopeless void.
The quanta fluctuations which supposedly brought about the Big Bang would thus be relegated, however, since the infinite amount of energy needed at the beginning could not have been available even if the universe were to become infinitely thin in eternity. In spite of this old new idea, we still seem to be naturally unable to imagine infinity in a plausible way, since in our imagination the limits of space must be marked by some kind of matter, light in this case. Although a "flat universe" already denotes two-dimensional planes, limits induced by light would mean that there are also "frameworks" which would contradict any theory of infinite expansion.
It seems to me that it is entirely due to their own unbelievably fantastic hypotheses that cosmologists indeed find themselves entangled in a self-induced web of contradictions from which they are hardly able to escape.

---

[34] These perceptions were established in 2001.

Nevertheless, some of them, among others *Stephen Hawking*[35], whom many regard as a genius, possess the impertinence to believe that they are "at last" very close to describing an all-explaining world model.

In my previous books I already defended the theory always supported by famous scientists that only simplicity can hold the truth. Simplex sigillum veri est.[36] Again, I claim that the universe, too, with all its complexity, adheres to a very simple, i.e. divine plan.

To illustrate this I developed a small intellectual experiment (see Appendix)[37]: just think of a tiny finite dot, which, be it as small as we can possibly imagine, is still a minute circle[38] since it is still finite. Then I only assume two important pre-requisites:

1) strict orientation to the "biblical call" to "be fruitful and multiply" and
– 2) observation of the purely logical laws of symmetry and polarity which prevail throughout the world. By mirroring and enlarging the first small basic circle by observing these clear specifications and the defined points, we obtain after only a few steps an area of four basic circles arranged in a square. This first expansion of a finite point into an area (two dimensions, mathematically: *xy-plane*) automatically creates a number of ideal basic geometrical patterns and certain number constellations. In addition to the circle (start: smallest finite point) and the square (formed by four finite points, i.e. circles) we also find the rectangular triangle and the equilateral triangle when we connect the circle centres.

If we juggled about with numbers we would start with "**1**" which stands for the circle and via "**2**" and "**3**" we would soon arrive at "**4**" which stands for the square made up of four standard circles.

If we add up the numbers **1, 2, 3** and **4**, by means of which the square can be obtained by creating a mirror-image, we arrive at the number **10**.

If we multiply these numbers by each other we arrive at the number **24**.

And by a rational combination of multiplication and exponentiation (see Appendix) we arrive at the number **81**[39].

---

[35] However, I do not consider it as being impertinent or arrogant that in a reader's letter to the German magazine FOCUS (38, 2001) I described him as the greatest fairy-tale teller since the Grimm brothers.
[36] Latin: Simplicity carries the stamp of truth.
[37] See the detailed explanations in Volume 1, "The Universe" of my trilogy "A Better History of the World", Monologue, Chapter 8: "Straight to the Point"
[38] In every "rational" circle is hidden the "irrational" number π, one of the most remarkable construction components of our world.
[39] See my book "The Universe", Monologue, Chapter 5, "The Three Musketeers"

Furthermore, the number sequences **618,** which denotes the "Golden Section" and is simultaneously the measure of beauty and optimal conditions in our world, and **273,** which is, as I postulate it, the measure of maximum rational expansion and physical manifestation of matter, are also generated automatically (see Appendix and my previous books).

If we wish to expand this two-dimensional plane into a three-dimensional space, we must again mirror the plane if we intend to remain within the strict logic of this successive and continuously controlled development. Hence we obtain two planes at right angles to each other and whose geometries ("xy") must, therefore, be multiplied. Hence we obtain the x^2y^2-geometry of two intersecting planes or areas perpendicular to each other.

It only takes one small step further: my entire intellectual experiment is based solely on the first four ordinal numbers. All we do is simply imagine that numbers are just as real as we are ourselves. Numbers really do exist as forms of information like data in the "ether". Now we assume that, in the beginning, really existing numbers as a kind of information are behind the development of my finite points, the smallest circles. Then we can imagine that these numbers keep running once the sequence has been set in motion. In contrast to finite i.e. physical matter, numbers can be considered as being infinite. If we accept that the finite circle is the smallest (physical) expansion, then we must expect that a circular expansion of (spiritual or informative) numbers also exists. It would thus expand over two planes into infinity. Since these two planes are perpendicular to each other (symmetrical and polar) and intersect each other we arrive at a "genuine four-dimensional", infinite, pure number space!

This perception enables us to find answers to all cosmic problems in the simplest possible way: the universe, imagined as a pure number space is pure information and would be infinite, which agrees with the latest assumption of cosmologists. In addition space would no longer be congruent with the expansion of light. The observed curvature of light due to its gravitational attraction no longer means that space is also curved.

Space would be absolutely flat, *plane*, i.e. Euclidean, a description which all the latest observations seem to verify, very much to the amazement of cosmologists. There would no longer be a necessity for anti-gravitational forces, and cosmologists could stop looking for dark matter.

Space would (at long last) possess a "medium" – that of really existing numbers which means: structural information. And waves of light would no longer be considered as "real" light waves, but rather as the transport of light *particles* (photons), which are also just information, over spherically arranged, concentric number shells into infinity. The wave length of the so-called light curve of a photon would thus be the result of the distance between the number shells which are responsible for the transport of light. I will come back to this later when we discuss whether or not the redshift of light proves that the universe is expanding.

As you see, in this model all confirmed laws of physics remain unimpaired since the accepted wave-pattern remains intact. It is no longer just the wave of light itself. Only the interpretation of the pattern and its derivation has changed.

Gravitation, too, would thus be a force with finite speed as Einstein, in contrast to Newton, predicted. The speeds of light and gravitation would by the nature of things be identical and predetermined solely by the "spiritual", i.e. number-controlled, expansion of space.

Since the number 4 stands for infinity and since we label finite bodies as "three-dimensional" this would certainly orientate the finite speeds of light and gravitation to the number 3. This idea is, of course, only to be understood as a concept and not as scientific proof. In fact, it has been known for a long time that the measured speed of light is practically **$3:10^n$**. /[40]

It is not so long ago that American astronomers measured the speed of gravitation at the German radio telescope Effelsberg in the Eifel and confirmed this result exactly.

All this sounds rather crazy at first – I know – but let us go on "spinning this yarn": the space of our universe would now be something spiritual since in reality it consists exclusively of really existing numbers. In other words, our cosmos would be an unbelievably gigantic field of information.

The spirit as an expression of organized immaterial information would return to our world – long overdue in my opinion.

To crown it all, and very much to the chagrin of all disciples of materialism, there would even be an especially important role allocated to it!

---

[40] The exact speed of light measured in a vacuum is $2.9979 \cdot 10^8$ m/s

Having arrived at this point, it is only a very small step to the notion that really existing numbers do not represent everything, not the entire spirit but rather only a (small) part of the entire really existing, spiritual information field. Exactly the same applies, of course, to certain geometrical basic forms since they are the raw material of any number development: after all, with the help of ideal basic patterns, they provide the number material for the world without the assistance of a calculating system!

We may now claim quite rightly that we have (re-)discovered a plan – an absolutely "divine plan" – derived from an "abundance of spirit".

One last small intellectual step:

My smallest point was conceived to be a finite point, i.e. a circle. As such it is the smallest and *ideal* representative of physical matter. Any circle can be exactly defined by exactly **three** bits of information on its outline. This information is, of course, something purely immaterial. The logical deduction can only be that something spiritual directly generates – or, expressed in a more religious way – creates physical matter.

The first verses in St. John's Gospel tell us: *In the beginning was the Word – and the Word was with God and the Word was God"*. "Word" is, in my opinion, a beautiful symbol for immaterial information.

The biblical account of the creation takes on a completely new meaning and importance provided we are prepared not to take it literally, but rather as being of symbolic value as with other biblical tenets or in the same way as in other religions.

Information is spiritual material in the same way as atoms are physical material. Something physical –depicted in my example as the tiniest point imaginable, the (standard) circle – is created by information and thus by spirit. And such information is also a component of each new circle. Everything in this world is like a coin with two symmetrical and simultaneously polar sides: one physical side with a finite expansion and finite existence and an immaterial spiritual side with infinite expansion and infinite existence.

If numbers, being part of this really existing spirit, really exist themselves, then they form a kind of eternal spiritual or informative trelliswork around any kind of physical existence in our world. The information concerning the "BEING" of any "physical matter", however small, will use this trelliswork to grow forever into the vast space of the increasingly physical world which stretches into infinity.

In other words, an infinite sequence of really existing whole numbers is set into motion around every finite, i.e. physical, point. In fact, there are two number sequences around every finite existence, one over each of the two perpendicularly intersecting circle areas $(x^2 y^2$-geometry$)$.
Therefore, we must consider the expansion of numbers proceeding in squares – or in other words: square number spaces are created which are infinite in their expansion and are, therefore, eternal.
It forms a "spiritual corset" of each and every physical point in our universe.
As far as I know, *Plichta* was the first to envisage such a number space. I was intuitively attracted to the notion.
However, I believe that this model is given a conclusive logical meaning only by my simplified intellectual experiment based on the growth and procreation of smallest finite points while taking account of the rules of symmetry and polarity. Unfortunately *Plichta* broke off all former relations to me in January 2000 since, it seems to me, he considered my own perceptions and my own publications as unwelcome competition. I believe my line of thought is very plausible, and I very much regret that he was, therefore, unable to become acquainted with it by first-hand knowledge or to discuss it with me.
The development of all ordinal numbers around any finite point, i.e. around any physical component, progresses in circles.
An ancient adage of Native Americans says: *"Everything comes in circles."* Any number space consists of an infinite number of concentric circles arranged like onion skins.
My intellectual experiment plausibly suggests that each one of these shells contains exactly 24 (= 1·2·3·4) numbers. This is in accordance with *Plichta's* perceptions, who assumed the same, based on his earlier and different intellectual approach.
Light[41] itself consists of small particles known as photons possessing, as we now know, no physical mass.
Viewed from this perspective, light is not really something physical. Nevertheless, it belongs without doubt to our physical world. It takes effect in our physical world. In my opinion, light possesses a form of dualism which is completely different to the one currently claimed by physicists:

---

[41] Light stands here for any kind of electromagnetic radiation.

We can now consider light to be a kind of *interface* between the physical, i.e. truly corpuscular part of the universe, and its spiritual basis and eternal background: without possessing any mass and expansion of its own, each photon is in fact a pure point of *information* (spiritual, informative effect) which seems to shine when it collides with perceptive matter such as the retina of our eyes (physical effect).

Light as an *interface* between spirit and matter, is subject to the known physical laws of nature in the cosmos, such as the laws of spatial expansion and gravitation. Each influences the other.

As already indicated, light is one of the many effects *within* space (and not the producer *of* space) is mainly limited by the maximum expansion of the (spiritual) number space.

Based on its assumed number rhythm of **24** this suggests an expansion speed of $3 \cdot 10^n$./[42] This provides another more scientific derivation for the speed of light and gravitation. In fact, light is assumed to possess a velocity of 300.000 km/s, i.e. $3 \cdot 10^8$ m/s. The latest measured value is 299.792,458 km/s and is very close to the assumed speed.

The intensity or luminosity of mass-less light *particles* which expand into infinite space reduces in proportion to the square of the distance: Light becomes weaker. The intensity of light can be strengthened by the gravitation of massive objects in the same proportion[43]: it becomes brighter again. When observed from a great distance this effect can be interpreted as the curvature of light. However, since the limits of light and space are no longer congruent, this increase in the intensity of light (= attraction of light particles) no longer represents the curvature of space. If we assume, as I do, that there exists an immaterial spiritual number space then the curvature of space is simply impossible.

According to this model, gravitation can also be explained in a very simple way: it is the *effect* of masses and the space between them which has the same characteristics but an opposed effect to light. This follows from the eternal laws of symmetry and polarity:

In my opinion light must be considered primarily as "spiritual information" with a certain portion of physical matter:

By this I mean the quantization of light, i.e. the (discontinuous or interrupted) division into mass-less smallest particles.

---

[42] For detailed information see Volume 1, "The Universe", or my other books "Plädoyer für ein Leben nach dem Tod und eine etwas andere Sicht der Welt", or "The Key to Eternity ". The calculation of the expansion of space is based on *Plichta's* theories.
[43] Reversing Newton's "inverse distance square law".

Therefore, there must be a symmetrical and polar "physical counter-effect": i.e. there must be an effect of mass with an informative (spiritual) and thus continuous component. Gravitation fulfils these requirements. It is exerted by every mass. And Newton's discovery that gravitation seems to function according to a simple basic mathematical principle, the "inverse distance square law", can now be explained in a plausible way by the squared construction of number space consisting of two planes and governed by ordinal numbers.

Therefore, the search for all kinds of a particle, which, for example, exert or mediate gravitation (so-called gravitons), becomes utterly obsolete. Such particles do not exist. And also, the latest idea that gravitation is in fact the result of the pressure exerted by the smallest invisible particles, which are whirring at random around the universe, belongs to the realm of science fiction. In this case the apparent attraction was actually pressure. This new idea goes back to the Swiss physicists and mathematicians *Nicola Fatio de Duillier* and *Feorges Louis Le Sage* (beginning to middle of the 18th century).

But what about the Big Bang at the beginning of our universe? The background radiation of **2,73** degrees Kelvin above the absolute zero of **−273°C** is, as you will remember, important evidence for scientists that there must have been a Big Bang: they consider it as being a kind of aftermath of a cooling down period. That the background radiation is distributed in such a homogeneous way *(isotropic)* and that it displays only very slight fluctuations surprisingly does not induce any scientist seriously to doubt the evidence. On the contrary, it seems even to confirm the conventional view of the world.

Does anything strike you about this? The number sequence **273** is also an early result of my intellectual experiment on the growth and procreation of smallest finite points as being the ratio of the area of the square to that of the starting circle (see Appendix).

And in fact − wherever we look in this world − at important key positions, we are continually confronted with exactly this number sequence. It has no significance at all if the numbers after the decimal point vary or if the number is not quite exact. In the same way, as the circle constant π cannot be expressed as an exact value, although it is still completely and perfectly represented in the geometry of every circle, this also applies to all other arithmetically measurable values: they merely correspond with the "physical implementation" of geometrically perfect patterns of a spiritual world which stands behind all this.

And we will find the number sequence **618** of the "Golden Section" in everything that seems perfect to us.

In my previous books I have already discussed this notion in detail and supported it by many examples (see Appendix).

This often-quoted small intellectual experiment which starts with the smallest unit, the circle, and leads to the next higher unit the multitude[44], the square formed by four circles, also points to further important conclusions: we can assume that the calculation based on the decimal system, i.e. based on the number **10**, may be an important discovery made by humans, but it is by no means a human invention **(1+2+3+4 = 10)**.

Dividing a day into **24** hours **(1 · 2 · 3 · 4 = 24)** may have been very sensible for the same reasons – in many cultures it was already introduced thousands of years ago and is still fully accepted today.

Finally, some remarks concerning the number **81** which can be derived from the "sensible combination" of the first four ordinal numbers[45]: on the one hand, it represents the maximum number of all naturally existing and stable chemical elements[46] in the entire cosmos. On the other hand, there are exactly 81 *possible positions* for the so-called nucleotides which carry amino acids[47] in the genetic code of the genotype and in the entire universe that applies to all known living beings and, probably, also to all possible forms of life. You will remember: amino acids are the building components of proteins. And all living beings consist of "proteins". With no more than exactly 81 possible positions nature is able to provide exact and definite details about related forms of life and their differences – one of the reasons is probably that frequent errors due to copying are thereby compensated: one incorrect character within the code of the genotype (by mutation) does not render the entire code unreadable (see Appendix).

I was the first to postulate and to prove that all especially important natural constants can be deduced in a simple and plausible way from a few decisive numbers (see Appendix).[48]

The second very important proof for scientists on which they base the Big Bang theory is the redshift of light.

---

[44] After only a few steps the smallest unit, the circle, becomes a multitude consisting of four circles with the next higher unit, the square.
[45] It follows: $1^2 \cdot 3^4 = 81$ (see Appendix)
[46] Peter Plichta was the first to discover and describe this.
[47] I was the first in 1999 to discover and describe this, (see Appendix)
[48] See my book "Life", Monologue, Chapter 3

In previous books I already explained in detail two counter-arguments which allow alternative explanations:
First, the very age of the stars alone will cause a redshift. Another reason, in my opinion, is to be found in the special conditions of the real number space, which from the outset define the speed and the intensity of light. Therefore, we may fairly safely assume that the redshift, which only indicates a decrease of various light frequencies, can also be attributed to the prevailing special space conditions of this alternative world model.
For this I have already suggested *Plichta's* prime number ray as being the conductor giving the rhythm, as he describes it himself. It contains nothing but real prime numbers and prime number squares. The higher the numbers grow and the more number shells that stretch into infinity, the less frequent prime number squares on the prime number ray become. If we now imagine that light frequency is encoded by prime numbers, then we might assume that the reduction of prime number squares in our square number space could lead to a decreased light frequency. We can practically conclude that light itself is "growing old" as well. However, this would only be really significant over very great distances.
Furthermore, the following is true: If with the increasing distance of the number space from its origin, e.g. a source of light, the prime number squares become less frequent, this simply imitates the steady expansion of space since the distances increase between single prime number squares. The result could be compared to the famous balloon which is blown up after a certain distance is marked on it: the distance between two marked points increases. In this way the expansion of the so-called light curve, which has actually been observed, may also be explained. However, it is now caused by a really existing square number code which is the true space structure.
Therefore, the reason for the observed redshift of light may simply be found in the huge distances over which these objects are observed. This would also explain some other very paradoxical phenomena in the sky.
There are, for example, things called *quasars*. These are presumably dead galaxies which often seem to be very close to or even connected with one another.

The redshift of the emitted light, however, varies tremendously.[49] According to all conventional perceptions it must be assumed that they are moving so unbelievably fast that all known basic physical laws are contradicted and, furthermore, the speed of their escape must differ although they are obviously interconnected. And this seems more than dubious and is still a big mystery.

If the redshift were to be explained differently than hitherto by means other than the *Doppler-effect* and the expansion of the light curve as being the result of the expansion of space, then the most important argument for the assumed steady expansion of the cosmos would fall away. This would blow the theory of the Big Bang sky-high.

I do not doubt at all, however, that celestial bodies do indeed move with great speed through the cosmos – but my theory does not permit them to move away from each other at an ever increasing speed which then should very soon reach trans-light velocity.

With my theory we do not need the Big Bang either and I believe that this would give us a much better starting position for explaining our universe and avoiding contradictions. For example, only a short time ago a star was discovered at a distance of only 36,000 light years away from us, which, according to scientists, must have been some kind of "premature birth" about 15 billion years ago, i.e. very soon after the presumed Big Bang.[50] However, the whole theory has one flaw: the star contains very little iron and, therefore, its mass is so low that it could not possibly have come into existence at such an early point in time.

Without the Big Bang theory there would be not just one beginning in which every later existence is already inherent, but many small beginnings, which would again and again create "space within space" in various places.

We could rather imagine a continuous "creation" which is still going on today and which is by no means all over and done with.

Matter is still being created today; it condenses to form stars and galaxies, it moves restlessly through space and perishes again at some time or other. You may have seen the very impressive pictures of the huge star factories which the *space telescope COBE* transmitted back to us only a few years ago.

---

[49] e.g. Galaxy NGC4319, which is connected to the Quasar Markarian 205 by a bright band of light.
[50] It is labelled HE0107-5240

But what is the substance of which this matter is made in these breeding places?
It is radiation or, in one simple word, light. The real origin of light is spirit: light has two sides and is, like spirit, pure information.
Hence light is the interface between spirit and physical matter.
Later on in the course of the creation and evolution of life certain pieces of information combined to become complicated, complex and interconnected information structures.
With the aid of its manifestation in complex physical structures a spirit, rather undifferentiated at the beginning, slowly becomes more and more differentiated in this way. The next chapter will give you an even more detailed explanation on this matter.

The recognition and deep conviction that only a completely new view of the universe can give us a balanced picture of our world and really explain it to us is the most important point at the end of this chapter. Such a model or our entire cosmos not only includes something spiritual but is actually based on something spiritual.
First and foremost, this spirit offers the decisive framework and the background for an eternal cosmic existence.
And besides all that, it seems to me that, at the beginning of all matter, this "primeval spirit" itself seems to have been rather "spiritless". This would mean that we have to imagine it more as a mechanical tool in a similar way as genes which determine the structure and function of a living being.
This notion makes the creation and the creator not only possible, but also essential.
The Old Testament of the Bible starts with the words:" In the beginning God created the heavens and the earth." In a sense we could say: God created spirit and matter. In the Bible it seems to have happened quietly, smoothly and unspectacularly. Why should there ever have been such a dramatic event as the Big Bang?
Creation and the creator are an essential part of our infinite and eternal world and make it simultaneously transcendent. If now a creation and a creating being exist which make the universal spirit transcendent then the world can only be understood as the awakening of the spirit finding the way to itself via the universe.
The spirit, originally undifferentiated, not only seeks manifestation in and with this world, it actually needs it in order to materialize, to grow and to

prosper away from this physical environment. In fact the spirit creates all these things and makes use of them thereby enabling it to be passed on and developed further with the greatest possible diversity in its own spiritual world: it creates life. Life is a purely spiritual quality which makes the difference between a complex heap of matter, which we may call an animal or human body, and something we may call a rock.

As purely spiritual qualities, a number sequence, or an information, spirit or life could never come to an end in this infinite and eternal cosmos. For all these death does not exist.

5. Evolution's New Look: Body and Life, Brain and Spirit

In the previous chapter, I demonstrated that our current perceptions of the creation, evolution and structure of the universe present many contradictions and leave us with a plethora of unanswered questions.

Therefore, I believed it necessary to look out for a more plausible and possibly more comprehensive alternative world model to solve the dilemma. In my previous books I already presented my own, different thoughts on this subject.

Among the complex issues which obviously leave more questions open than answered is the question of how life was created and how evolution has functioned and everything to do with our "spirit". I concentrated on these topics especially in Volume 2 of my trilogy.

Science regards "life" as being a purely biochemical property of organic complexes. It is assumed that life happens spontaneously and automatically after a certain level of organization has been reached. In my opinion this is basically correct, but biologists usually assume in this case that spirit must inevitably be the *product* of this complex matter. However, I see the complex matter as being only the suitable "equipment" which enables us to "receive" spirit.

The perception of suddenly changing system characteristics goes back mainly to the theory of the Belgian biochemist Ilya Prigogine on *"dissipative structures"* for which he was awarded the Nobel Prize for Chemistry in 1977. He established that a constant supply of energy enables organic components to be transformed from a previously disorderly state to a higher level of order. When the energy supply is cut off, however, they fall back to their previous state.

At the beginning of the 1950s the American *Stanley Miller* caused quite a stir when he succeeded in producing some basic components of life after having treated a mixture of water, oxygen, methane and ammoniac with electric lightening under high temperature for about a week. Similar to the creation of Frankenstein's monster in the movie, Miller found in his mixture carbon monoxide and dioxide in addition to some organic compounds such as amino acids which are so important for the creation of life. Miller's experiments were successfully repeated later. But that is not all – in other experiments even components of the genotype were found, such as nucleic acids.

Presently a number of research teams, for example in Switzerland and in America, are trying to produce membranes, the shells of cellular bodies. The idea is still the following: produce all the necessary components of cells, mix them together and, there you are, new life is created.

To create life artificially is no longer a utopian dream as we all know. Just think of the cloned sheep "Dolly" and its many "brothers and sisters in a test tube", it has meanwhile become a very controversially discussed reality. In this context I would also like to mention the births of allegedly cloned human babies acclaimed by the world media – in my opinion the rather perverse action by an unbelievably obscure sect in the USA.

However, in all these cases without exception it is a creation of life from already existing life – but never from inanimate, organic matter. Scientists believe they will soon be able to overcome this hurdle.

It seems to me that this is just wishful thinking and will remain so.

And to this I can only say: thank God! Life is much more than just the sum of its single components.

Several theories of evolution deal with the continuous development of life and of all living beings on Earth – beginning with the organic preliminary stages through to the appearance of man. The whole complex is known as "evolution". In all evolution theories coincidence is one of the main aspects. Coincidence alone is responsible for changes in the genotype, known as *mutations*. Coincidence is also made responsible

for the emergence of life itself. And it is also assumed that it has always provided the necessary ignition for the evolution of such an unbelievable variety and number of species in the course of the Earth's history.
The general perception today is that the huge time span between the beginning of life and today is proof enough for this assumption.
It is due to the fact that we humans cannot conceive of such immense periods of time that we are completely unable to follow this argument.
Every living being consists of countless single cells which are interconnected. Of course, there are also unicellular organisms existing as independent forms of life such as bacteria. There does seem to be a number of reasons, however, as to why it is that unicellular organisms do not, or at least, do not exclusively, characterize the beginning of all life. Presumably there were just as many multi-cellular organisms around in those early times. It is quite likely that many unicellular organisms developed later from multi-cellular organisms by regression.
It does not really matter how it happened, since every unicellular organism is already a complete system of "irreducible complexity" on a micro-biological level as some scientists rightly and critically claim against the general perceptions of today.[51]
For the micro-biologist *Michael Behe* this means that within such a unicellular system all components must work together to a set order and no single one of them may be removed. Otherwise a collapse of the entire system would be unavoidable.
Outside of their "irreducible complex system", however, the single components make no sense at all.
That the single components of life have developed at all is, in spite of some of the more daring arithmetical acrobatics aimed at increasing its probability, so incredible that we may justifiably describe it as a miracle. Even the most favourable yet honestly calculated degree of probability ought to frustrate any materialist who is still dead set on sticking to the commonly accepted theories.
But it is not only the correct measurement and the correct composition of all the single components necessary which decide whether life is created or not; it is that all these components must then unanimously follow the predetermined rhythm of one and the same baton and must work together in utmost harmony in accordance with an inner order

---

[51] e.g. Carlos Bustamante, Jed Macosko and Michael Behe, microbiologists at the Berkeley University San Francisco, California (SF weekly, 2001)

whose origin is as yet unknown. But, what is the baton, and who is the conductor?

Should you, dear reader, be a faithful follower of any religious community and believe in a *direct* act of creation – do not rejoice too soon:

All forms of life, and here I am in complete accord with common evolutionary theories, developed from their organic preliminary forms without *direct* creation. This certainly *also* happened *with the aid* of those mechanisms which have been known for over a hundred years as "coincidence", i.e. mutation, "selection", and, according to the latest concepts, "cooperation".

However, and here I go beyond currently accepted models, although these mechanisms may play a very important role they were in all probability *not the only means* of evolution.

Maybe we could compare it to the dodgem-cars so popular on fairgrounds: if the power supply of the wire netting under the roof is switched off the cars stop moving. Any heap of organic matter, however complex, lacks what is most needed for life, the "power supply". The spirit is missing!

Life seems to be something spiritual, as I already explained in detail in the volume "Life" of my trilogy. It is only the ability of suitable biochemical compounds to receive information from their "spiritual environment" which slowly leads to the necessary order and complexity which is essential for the development of life.

As already explained, numbers seem to be a truly existing part of this spirit or, if you like, of the all enveloping and permeating world of information.

They represent, so to speak, the body of laws, operate discretely in the background and maintain the order which is so amazingly omnipresent and inherent in our universe.

Even the slightest divergence from this order renders the existence of our universe impossible. This is an incontestable fact which fills even the most materialistic cosmologists with awe. The same also applies to all kinds of life. Numbers seem to play an equally important role here if only we were prepared to open our eyes to it.

The "Golden Section", for example, not only determines the arrangement and positions of leaves and fir-needles but also lays down the standard proportions of all animals and humans: e.g. the distances from the human feet to the navel and from the navel to the top of the head usually have the same ratio as the golden section. The same applies to the ratio of the length of the human humerus to the length of the bones in the forearm or the length of the leg bones and the ratio of the length of the bones in fingers or toes.

Furthermore, psychological tests which scientists still use to try to find criteria which determine whether a face or a body is "beautiful", establish clearly that proportions which correspond to the golden section are usually considered beautiful. In the face of a beautiful woman, for example, the width of the mouth and the width of the nose have the ratio of the golden section, and the same applies to a number of other facial proportions. Also, if the ratio of waist to hips approximates the golden section a female body is considered as being beautiful.

And something else: adjacent spirals of a snail-shell have the same proportional distances as the arms of galaxies: and, of course, the ratio of the distances is that of the golden section. Such examples are endless; to cite more here would, however, go beyond the scope of this book, but some more are listed in the Appendix.

The living being most investigated by evolutionary biologists is currently a small worm, known as *C. elegans*. An interesting and hardly known fact is the number of its cells. Female worms possess exactly 1031 and male worms 959 cells.

These are both prime numbers which seem to have a kind of leading function in the universe. The difference between these two numbers is 72 or 3·24 cells.

These numbers seem to be of great importance for the development and the structure of our physical world, as my intellectual experiment, revolving around the growth and propagation of a smallest finite point, indicated and which I quoted in the previous chapter.[52]

Meanwhile, we know with certainty that some animals and plants are even able to count. Even insects, such as certain cicadas, *count* the number of vegetation cycles and base their calculation on prime numbers so that they do not mix their various species when mating.[53]

By the way, it seems that toddlers are also capable of counting long before they learn arithmetic! They use their fingers for counting right from the start. The renowned mathematician and neuroscientist *Stanislas Dehaene*[54] supports this opinion. Without going into too much detail here

---

[52] see my book "The Universe", Monologue, Chapter 8 and this book, last chapter
[53] see my book, "Life", Monologue, Chapter 10.
[54] from: Deutsches Wirtschaftsmagazin 1 (2002)

about the various, currently accepted and mostly materialistic attempts at interpretation, it suffices to say that this is an amazing fact which should make us think.

Something else: renowned evolutionary biologists talk about positional information which determines the correct time and place at which various parts of the body are developed. In the example of the cockroach the British biologist *Lewis Wolpert* was even able to demonstrate that such positional determinations must be arranged around an extremity as are the figures on the face of a clock with 2 times 12 (= 24) positions – again the same numbers which we can constantly discover everywhere in our world.[55] We can find such information about positions in abundance. *Olaf Breidbach*, professor of evolutionary biology in Jena, changed such positions while experimenting with meal-worms. He twisted the relevant areas of tissue in opposite directions and left the dislocated cells to grow back on in the new position. The results were amazing and, I believe, indicated that they kept growing with the aid of ordinal numbers. Professor Breidbach himself said in an interview with the German magazine "Geo" (01/2003): *"The processes which bring such results are much more than a reflex of the genome sequences of single cells.... Whatever is predetermined in the genome is read by the organism in a constantly new manner. Exactly this process is a phenomenon which has remained incomprehensible up to now and which demands completely new explanations.*

If we consider the numerical arrangement of bones in the arms and legs of animals or humans, we are confronted again with the first five ordinal numbers: the human arm has **1** humerus, followed by **2** bones of the forearm, then there are **3** bones in the first row of the carpus[56] and **4** bones in the second row of the carpus and finally **5** bones in the metacarpus. The same applies, of course, to the bones in the feet. This arrangement seems to be a law of universal validity and can be found in every animal with the exception of spiders and insects which, being in principal a completely different form of life, follow other numerical laws.[57] Due to regression or specialization, some animal species have lost some of these extremities although they are still genetically planned and in some cases appear as stumps (e.g. hoofed animals).

---

[55] see my book, "Life", Monologue, Chapter 7.
[56] Scaphoid bone, lunate bone and triquetral bone. The pisiform bone is not one of them since it is a so-called sesamoid bone which serves as a roll or trochlea for a muscle.
[57] For them the numerical laws for an enclosed space are applicable as 2^n, since they are limited to the outside. See. "Arguments for a Life after Death and a slightly different View of the World "

Remarkable also is the fact that, although there are some more phalanxes following the rows of the metacarpus and the metatarsus, their number does not increase. Since the extremities and their components always come in pairs we have 2·5 and we arrive again at the number **10**, i.e. the sum of the first four ordinal numbers.

Numbers also control the performance of our central nervous system (CNS): for example, the processing of sounds of varying frequencies alternates constantly between the left and the right ear and the left and the right hemisphere of the brain.

The alternation of hemispheres occurs each time the frequency of tones reaches an exact multiple of 40 or 60 Hz, i.e. 1·40Hz, 2·40Hz, 3·40Hz, or 1·60Hz, 2·60Hz, 3·60Hz, etc.! Ordinal numbers are taking over again.

The latest results of brain research tell us something about the way the human memory works. Scientists at the *Bonn Clinic for Epilepsy* found out that information reaching the brain is classified as important or unimportant by certain structures in the so-called *limbic system*. Unimportant items are forgotten immediately, i.e. they are not admitted to higher brain centres if the "doorman", the limbic system, and the relevant higher processing centre of the cerebrum vibrate in harmony at a frequency of exactly (**4·10** Hz) = 40Hz each (and possibly a multiple of that?).

The processing or, more precisely, the admission of visual stimulations to the cerebrum shows the same pattern of "phase synchronized" 40 Hz-vibrations and has been known for a long time. I expect that further control functions will be discovered in future which are encoded by the first four ordinal numbers.

I am also convinced that, no matter where we might find life in the universe, at some time or other (and I am certain life is endemic throughout the universe!) we will find that such creatures also adhere to the same basic principles as those of terrestrial life.

I believe that universal numerical laws are at work here and everywhere. They play an important role in the determination and construction of all our lives.

There is another aspect which we should take into consideration in this context: the specialization of species which is almost universal, combined with the greatest possible perfection in shape, appearance, function, socialization and behaviour.

In my book "Life" I mentioned a deep sea mussel which adorns itself with the perfect imitation of a fish, although simple *mimicry* would have been quite sufficient to irritate other fishes which then help the mussel to propagate. The phantom squid is also an excellent mimic: one moment it pretends to be a sea-serpent and the next it imitates a fire-fish. Both are highly poisonous creatures. By imitating them in such a perfect way the squid is reliably protected against predators.

Many species of fish like to imitate others: the well-known weedy sea-dragons, for example, can look like a torn off piece of bladder-wrack seaweed. They are perfectly camouflaged against any kind of background since they are able to imitate exactly any live or inanimate object.

There are countless examples of mimicry or, more generally, specialization involving a high degree of perfection. We only have to look at the trunk of an elephant. It is not solely a respiratory organ, but also the best equipped olfactory organ of all terrestrial mammals. In addition, it is a very sensitive tactile organ and a finely tuned prehensile organ comparable to the human hand. An elephant's trunk is a highly specialized multi-functional device. The obvious striving for highest perfection clearly exceeds the evolutionary pressure to develop advantages which would merely guarantee the survival of a certain species for a longer period of time. In Mexico scientists are researching the behavioural pattern of special meat-flies which purposefully fly to the centre of a spider's web. They seem to "know" that there it is not sticky. Alarmed by the vibrations of the web the spider approaches the assumed victim which quickly flies off to the spider's eggs which are now unprotected. The meat-fly lays a few larvae which quickly find their way into the eggs and eat them. Here we find a reversal of roles between the predator and the victim. This form of parasitism is not even necessary for the fly's survival since it usually feeds off carrion. Nevertheless, this most complex and perfect pattern of behaviour has developed. In my opinion, this phenomenon cannot be explained by hitherto accepted evolutionary factors.

Let me mention another example: a normal domesticated cat. As we know all cats possess extremely well-developed eye sight which is the result of their eyes making optimal use of weak light which is reflected on to the retina. In addition they possess extremely sensitive whiskers which respond to the slightest stir in the air caused by stationary objects. This enables them to move safely even in the dark. But what is the benefit of all this?

After all, cats (and not only our domesticated cats) spend two thirds of their lives asleep and the remaining third mainly with personal hygiene.

So what is the reason for all this perfection? As in the above-mentioned examples, there is no really plausible reason for all this. It is often said in such cases that it was all at one time an advantage necessary for survival. However, this cannot always have been true.

There are many kinds of deep sea fish which are of outstanding beauty, but nobody can see them. They must have developed this beauty on the spur of an "internal motivation" but without having achieved any advantage in the struggle for survival. The Berlin historian *Leopold von Ranke*, who was an adviser to emperors and kings during the 19th century, once said: *"All life carries its own ideal within itself."* I find this very apt: for every species, it seems, there is an ideal and a kind of aim towards which it seems to strive; for many things which characterize e.g. its appearance, functions or behaviour seem to be unimportant for the survival of the species. Sometimes certain features are quite bizarre, and this statement is supported by many impressive examples of *convergence* in the animal world. I will come back to this shortly. I dedicated a whole chapter to the phenomenon of convergence in my book "Life". Convergence means that plants or animals although not related to one another and not living in the same geographical environment or at the same time – their life-time could even be many million years apart – show identical or very similar features. Obviously there are certain patterns which keep reappearing and which adjust themselves to changing environmental conditions.

Take the kangaroo: it is an Australian marsupial. Nowhere else in the world can you find this species. Compare its appearance with that of a typical dinosaur, e.g. Tyrannosaurus rex: both go upright, have short stumps of forelegs (arms), big hind legs and a huge tail with which they control their balance. Both seem to follow a basic model. There was also a species of dinosaur called Gallimimus. It possessed the same kind of sieve for its feed which can be found today in ducks. These two species are not related to one another. The common explanation today is that evolution must have invented such a sieve twice. Considering the most gigantic improbability of possibly "inventing" the same gadget twice independently from one another by chance and to develop the same complex attributes by selection alone in the course of time, such an explanation may not be taken seriously, in my opinion.

Another convergent behaviour is shown by tadpoles of a certain species of frog which are only a few millimetres long[58]: with the aid of a rather sophisticated and complex mouth opening they create, as American biologists discovered, a strong suction and swallow the tiniest animals of prey within a few milliseconds – a fraction of the time it takes for the human eye to blink. The important point is that this method of feeding is absolutely unique among frogs and can only be found in fish with which they are not related.

Another example: Up to now it has been the general belief that something as complicated as an eye, for example, could only have been invented once. Any evolutionary biologist would support this view; even the immensely long periods of time available would hardly suffice to create the eye twice by coincidence (mutations) or by selection. Until a short time ago scientists still believed that they could confirm the conventional assumption of a common origin. They had discovered the so-called Pax-6 gene which stands at the top of the hierarchy and controls more than one hundred other genes which are involved in the development of the eye. This gene seems to be nearly the same in all animals. If a Pax-6 gene of a mouse is implanted into a fly it still develops the normal compound eye.

However, recent research shows completely different results: gene analyses carried out by the American scientists *Todd Oakley* and *Clifford Cunningham* at the *Duke University* in *North Carolina* established that even in closely related animals such as the Crustaceans the eyes must have been developed several times and independently. The same seems to apply for other animals, and especially for those of different species.[59] These results seem to contradict one another. However, I believe that first impressions are deceptive and view the matter in a different light.

I believe quite the opposite to be the case, namely that these two results together would even support my theory of constantly recurring (spiritual, immaterial information-) patterns – if only scientists would stop describing coincidence as being the sole instigator of all evolutionary development. My model, adjusted to this example, renders the following conceivable: there is an information pattern called "Two Eyes". Its biochemical correlate is the "leading-gene" Pax-6 inherent in all living beings. To make the comparison easier, imagine now that you are working with normal index cards like those I still use in my surgery in

---

[58] Hymenochirus boettgeri, see "Nature", Vol. 420
[59] Proc. Nat. Acad. Sci. 99 (2001)

spite of the computer. Each one of them is a file and bears only the name of the relevant patient on the outside. Within these files all the examination results for this patient have been collected over the years.
The gene Pax-6 is just the unspecific file named "Two Eyes". This tells us nothing about its contents; Pax-6 gives no further details about certain versions and features of the "two eyes" – just as little as the outside of each file tells us about its patient. Both, file and Pax-6 gene, only determine the framework within which we are working. And in the same way as the once preferred system of index cards for collecting information was used for all patients, the gene can be considered as the collector of information for all kinds of eyes. All information relevant for the development of eyes is *bound* in the file "Pax-6" and can, therefore, be translated into a biochemical language, i.e. into genes. Therefore, eyes have not been incidentally invented several times, but neither are they the result of one single database for genes which was generated at some time by coincidence and adjusted to different conditions by further coincidence.
Often there seems to be no reason for the recurrence of similar patterns which sometimes seem quite absurd.
Why is it, for example, that among mammals it is only elephants, monkeys and humans which have developed two breasts with which to feed their young? Somewhere in the "rag-bag" of evolution this pattern still exists and for reasons unknown to us it is wheeled out again "if needed". Another example for this theory is the Australian duck-billed platypus. On the one hand it lays eggs, on the other hand, however, it suckles its offspring.
Why is it, as I already asked earlier, that the unrelated Arctic musk-ox and the takin from the Himalayas, a mixture of sheep and goat, display an almost identical defensive behaviour: both form a kind of „body fortress". Takins, however, inhabit dense vegetation and this kind of defence is ineffective for them. In the face of looming danger they would do better by running away.
Obviously there are pre-existent patterns at work. In combination with changing environmental conditions they turn every living being, in the course of time and in harmonious creativity, into a perfect creature in the end. In the course of this development it can happen that features are brought to perfection which exceed by far those necessary or which are even counterproductive for their specific purpose.

However, they do not always provide special advantages for the survival of the species and it is this which contradicts the arguments of evolutionary biologists.

Up until the appearance of humans, perfection was always directed at physical features only; be it the development of wings, long beaks, long necks or an outstanding visual or tactile sense.

The Australian thorny devil, for example, has perfected its outer skin to becoming a very sensitive sponge over which even the finest droplets of water are absorbed thus protecting the animal from dehydration.

A large brain is also at first a potential physical advantage – a sign that every brain is, of course, *also* a computer and that the larger the brain the more potential capacity it possesses. Later on, however, the size alone is no longer decisive. Over the last 500,000 years at least all humans have had a large brain. Or think of the elephants, which, in comparison to humans, possess a much larger brain. However, there is a world of difference between the spiritual capabilities of an elephant and those of a human being. In saying this I do not at all intend to belittle the amazing spiritual capabilities of elephants. And yes, the brain of Neanderthal man, a close relative of the Homo sapiens, was indeed larger than ours.

And although today's humans seem to have mixed well with Neanderthal man about 40,000 years ago, as the latest research in the USA indicates, their larger brain clearly did not prevail.

On the contrary, the average brain-volume of Europeans has diminished by more than 10% since the Neolithic period. However, modern mankind shows a much greater *spiritual* variety although there have been only 1,600 generations between the end of the Neanderthal man and modern times. The famous archaeologist, *Richard Klein*, of Stanford University California, points out that mankind underwent an abrupt *cultural* leap, which may have been very abrupt, about 50,000 years ago and which cannot be explained anatomically. Klein assumes, however, in line with contemporary thinking, that this was caused by a genetic mutation; this is no reasonable explanation to my mind.[60]

In any case, the hypothesis that more complex behaviour requires a relatively larger brain is simply wrong.

Evolution shows that, in addition to constantly recurring typical basic patterns in similar creatures on new levels, it still bears something special: not only the quantity but, especially, the quality of newly acquired

---

[60] Interview with Richard Klein in "Der Spiegel", 5/2003

characteristics within the system is substantially increased from one level to the next in ever shorter periods of time. Green plants appeared approx. 400 million years ago, but it took another 40 million years before leaves began to grow on their stems.

Take another example: the horse needed about 60 million years to develop proper hooves. Yet, the development of the human cerebrum, which, compared to leaves and hooves, is far more complicated, was completed within a fraction of that time. From the purely anatomical point of view, there had already been a quantum leap from the brain of primates and an even greater one from the brain of other mammals to the human brain with its complexity of circuits.

Ever since, the brain has remained by and large at this level of development although, amazingly enough, it seems to have diminished again slightly. However, this brain, which has remained almost unchanged, achieved a *spiritual* development in the course of only a few thousand years which can only be described as phenomenal. It seems that evolution itself is characterized by the ability to constantly create something new with ever improving quality in ever shorter periods.

Our common sense should stop us here for a moment and ask whether all this could be made possible by the previously known mechanisms of evolution alone, i.e. "mutation", "selection" and "cooperation".

This question bears special relevance today since it is mutation alone which induces new developments by coincidence and is a process which may exert direct influence on our biochemical genotype thereby instigate changes which are passed on to further generations. If we search for other, additional possibilities of how to influence development, as I do, we have to start thinking about other methods than the presently known hereditary mechanisms. To claim that the evolution of life is merely based on coincidence could be compared to the attempt to construct a jumbo jet or an ocean liner with the aid of a hurricane tearing at high speed across a scrap metal yard.

Therefore, on the strength of a number of arguments, I have been convinced for a long time that the history of evolution must be bound together with the development of evolutionary mechanisms. I assume that the further the development of life progresses the more often and more consistently new and more advanced mechanisms exert their influence in order to control and accelerate the unique process called "evolution" significantly. At the beginning of this gigantic process there was only mutation available to set the ball rolling and to determine everything new, and selection to discriminate between all things useful and useless. Of course, both these mechanisms still accompany the evolutionary process today. But in the course of time others complemented them and slowly pushed mutation especially as the decisive igniting spark into the background.

Communication, between individuals of the same species as well as different species, became another important influence.

This is basic knowledge today since it is the pre-requisite for a successful cooperation. Communication, however, is, at least in its advanced form, of spiritual quality.

Instincts are soon developed which induce and support certain patterns of behaviour in creatures thereby helping them to survive. How and why they really developed is still a mystery. In my opinion instincts are clearly new, spiritual evolutionary factors. They developed from previous experiences made by a particular group of species and are, therefore, based on a kind of collective memory of the species. It might be that "copies" thereof and countless automatic reaction patterns are indeed stored *within* the brains of organisms – but I believe that in animals their origin is the result of an impersonal species-specific influence from "outside". There are indeed anatomical indications which lend credence to this as the famous brain scientist and Nobel Prize winner *John Eccles* explained in his books shortly before he died a few years ago: the micro-anatomy of the furrowed grey surface of a mammal's brain and, of course, that of a human brain especially, indicates that it is by no means merely a kind of super computer, although this might be the dominating function in most animals.

In addition the brain, especially the human brain, seems to be an outstanding multi-functional receiver and transmitter, functions which could enable it to keep a constant interactive contact with its spiritual environment which is, in my opinion, exactly what it does do constantly.

This constant "online-connection" between the "physical hardware" and the "spiritual internet" may be the crucial factor in the introduction of a certain feature which becomes apparent much later in the history of evolution and which gradually grows into an "evolutionary torpedo" discriminating between animals and humans: consciousness.

For this to occur, however, the brain must have reached a sufficiently high level of development. I would compare this perhaps with the do-it-yourself construction of a radio: not before all necessary parts are available and assembled, can the radio receive programs. If the last screw is still missing it will not work. As already indicated consciousness is by no means a purely human characteristic. We will detect some kind of consciousness in most mammals at least, in various degrees perhaps and on a much smaller scale. The better the brain of an organism is developed the more its interactive connection to the omnipresent and all-permeating spiritual field becomes the actual fundament of its existence.

Its consciousness will probably cause the organism to repeatedly do things in the purposeful and controlled manner which it has learned in the course of its life by "trial and error", and which it *recognized* as being useful. Man, however, is the first species which has really become aware of this fact and of his consciousness. We call this our self-awareness which, to a certain rudimentary degree, seems to exist already in mammals and to a more mature degree in some primates, especially in chimpanzees. I am of the opinion that consciousness is purely spiritual and possesses *primarily* no corresponding correlate *in* the brain. Of course, this does not exclude the possibility that constant learning and repetition of conscious actions could then *secondarily* also leave traces *in* the brain, in the same way as *"cookies"* are stored on the fixed-disk of your computer when you surf the internet, so that the same page can be found more easily next time, and some information will certainly also be stored completely as a copy, or – as we know from the computer – as a cache memory.

Since babies show no consciousness, although most brain researchers today believe that consciousness is located *in* the front lobe of the brain, the so-called prefrontal cortex, it was assumed that this region lies dormant and inactive in very small children. In the meantime, however, French neuro-scientists have detected considerable activity patterns in the brains of babies also. There is no plausible materialistic explanation for this.

The core of all spiritual matter is its immaterial information content which is not necessarily tied to any kind of physical matter.

I believe that information is being constantly exchanged by interactions between a living organism and its spiritual world. This process is beneficial to both and together they can progress in their development. It is the neuronal system especially which benefits from this: throughout the history of evolution this communication system has been characterized by its consistent and continual striving for a higher level.

With regard to other physical matters, however, life itself has repeatedly made detours which have sometimes ended in dead ends.

Here lies the real mystery of evolution of all life in this world. From a physical point of view every organism in itself is completely independent and is separate from its brethren. Yet no animal ever possesses a personal biography. Each one is firmly integrated in the collective of their species. Due to their very own, unique individuality (not appointed to them or invented for them) only humans go beyond the collective. From the spiritual point of view, however, all spiritual matter in humans also seems to be only part of a uniform and homogeneous unity. Regarded superficially, it seems as if a differentiation is not possible. In fact, however, this spiritual unity of the human species comes up with the greatest variety of individuals we can imagine.

Instincts and consciousness are, in my opinion, new and purely spiritual factors which contribute greatly to evolution. They are the result of the constant interaction between the growing (physical) nervous system and an omnipresent spiritual field which, due to the interactive spiritual exchange, is increasingly differentiated. Every new generation of animals of the same species is more able to perform such interaction. Every new individual animal thereby learns automatically the collective instructions relevant for the species. With the aid of the nervous system they then facilitate appropriate, peripheral body reactions.

Humans thus developed their perfect human hand and their ability to speak. Generations of scientists used to believe that the ability to speak was an acquired property. But, as French scientists have recently been able to establish, long before babies are able to speak, the same left lobe brain regions as in adults are activated when they listen to their parents. This means that the processing of language is congenital. A new neuronal structure is developed and used. The externally noticeable phenomenon, in this case our language, is the secondary expression of this new acquisition.

The question that remains to be discussed is how it is possible that changes in the biochemical genotype can possibly be caused by transfer of information alone. If immaterial information causes the development of new evolutionary mechanisms of higher quality, which not only control certain behavioural patterns but also possibly produce genetically transferable physical adjustments, then the question as to how heredity works must be clarified. How shall we imagine immaterial information to influence, for example, genes?

The very latest results of research could literally bring "light" to the dark. In my previous books I repeatedly explained that a number of scientists, the first of which was the Russian *Alexander Gurwitsch* and, more recently, the German physicist *Fritz Albert Popp* among others, were able to prove that live tissue emits radiation. They emit mainly weak laser light which is especially suited for transmitting digitally encoded information in a purposeful and structured way.

Scientists at the American *Massachusetts Institute of Technology (M.I.T.)* in *Cambridge* recently discovered that bio-molecules can be addressed and influenced by radio waves – that is, generally speaking, by "radiation". They intend to use this new knowledge technically and will try to integrate biological material into electronic components in future. No biologist ever spent much thought on the notion that probably nature has manipulated or even combined biological material in the same way from time immemorial – a theory which could easily explain the generation of living cells.

Furthermore, American chemists of the *Oak Ridge National Laboratory* of the American Department of Energy in *Tennessee* discovered only recently that certain synthetic material forms chains and webs of tiny pearls when drying out. Such micro-pearls are resonance bodies which store light. They are especially effective when magnetic particles are enclosed in their cavities.

These latest results of research thus confirm in a very impressive way the theory that cells as well as certain organic macromolecules, such as red blood pigment, haemoglobin, chlorophyll in plants or the three-dimensionally structured *DNA* of our genomes, are also suitable resonance bodies for the storage of information such as light. And what is so special about haemoglobin and chlorophyll? Well, both molecules contain a magnetic metal which may be possibly acting as an antenna, iron in the first case and magnesium in the second. Is this the way that plants pick up information from their environment and does this enable blood to transport immaterial information throughout the body? It is indeed imaginable. And the genes of living cells also seem to be an ideal container for storing information received by means of weak and especially *coherent laser light.*

This would point to an additional and completely new role adopted by our genes in the hereditary process over and above their already well-known function of passing on characteristic features in a biochemical way: their three-dimensional structure would enable the macromolecule

DNA especially to pass on characteristics such as character, instincts, behaviour, etc. in a physical way.

I find it astonishing that the great diversity of the human species is attributed to the mere 25-30 thousand human genes. Even if we assume that there may be more due to errors in counting or due to the possibility that the proteins encoded by genes are also relevant for passing on certain features – even a combination of all these factors would only produce just one more drop in the ocean in respect to the amazing human variety. However, the quantitative and qualitative variety could grow into shear infinity if it were not just the finite number of biochemical, i.e. physical, genes which is being drawn upon, but also quantities of infinitely many immaterial, possibly digital, units of information emanating from a kind of world spirit or – expressed in a more modern way: from an omnipresent spiritual *internet* – would play an additional role.

It is clear anyway that the number of genes involved and thus their biochemical influence can only be of secondary importance: there are some types of plants – e.g. rice – which have significantly more genes than do humans. Furthermore, the genetic differences between two species, which seem to be worlds apart, are in fact unbelievably small. For example, from a genetic point of view, we humans are in fact unbelievably closely related to worms, or yeast.

Of course, for certain reasons this must be so; considered in respect to pure substance all organisms, including us humans, are ultimately made of the same matter.

However, with respect to very nearly everything which distinguishes them as individual beings or species, the organisms grew apart in a most dramatic way in the course of evolution. Should the genetic differences between the different forms of life and us humans ever be so insignificant, then the only rational conclusion would be that genes and their biochemistry cannot be the only carriers of hereditary information. It follows that in addition to the known physical form of heredity, which seems to be more or less responsible for pure physical appearance, other forms must exist: e.g. the transfer of information on a level which corresponds with the character of the information itself, i.e. on an immaterial level.

When humans appeared on the stage of evolution, they too had specific physical characteristics: features that distinguished them, which made them fundamentally different from animals and which seemed to be a kind of perfection in physical specialization. The most important innovation was probably the human hand. It provided humans with a unique instrument for performing finely-tuned manual operations. Furthermore, especially in combination with the newly acquired upright posture, which enabled them to watch and observe their immediate surrounding more effectively, this gave them a great advantage over any animal. Today most scientists assume that the upright posture and this fantastic tool, "the hand", made it possible to introduce and accelerate the intellectual development of humans and their cerebrum.

I believe, however, that the order of things was really the other way round: the complex brain was developed first which was then able to accelerate the development of humans, including that of their hands, and their upright posture. With respect to the speech centres already developed and active in babies, I have been able to demonstrate this.

The very development of humans seems to be a clear indication that evolution must work in a different way. I already pointed this out in my book entitled "Life" while basing my argument on the presently more than 80-year-old ideas of the German naturalist *Edgar Dacqué*:

It took many millions of years before hooves or leaves on plants were developed, whereas, much later, it took only a fraction of that time to create such a complicated and fantastically complex cerebrum as that found in humans and to develop it to such anatomic and functional perfection.

When man first appeared on the stage of life his cerebrum was, from an anatomical point of view, practically speaking already fully developed. From the beginning of its existence this cerebrum acquired hardly any new significant features – if any at all, as the smaller volume of brain in modern humans may suggest. Shortly after, the immense variety of neuronal anatomic structures and their interconnections came into existence. Even if the complexity of the human brain, which can only be measured when scrutinized under the microscope, indeed grew by a few percent over the last few hundred thousand years – we have to admit that, in principle, the development has practically come to a standstill in comparison to its original quantum leap from mammals to humans. Nevertheless, humans with their almost finished cerebrum were then only at the very beginning of an absolutely amazing development in their spiritual, emotional and cultural diversity which is still proceeding today – in a positive but also, unfortunately, in a negative sense.

After significant morphological innovations ceased, the following started to happen in humans: with respect to brains, which are practically of one and the same type and which are equipped with comparable features, a development set in, very slowly and gradually at first, but accelerating later, until it rapidly reached an astronomical increase of spiritual diversity and individual variety. This was especially the case over the last few centuries.

The variety of life and its individual forms – and thereby also the inseparably connected spiritual variety – depended solely on the number of differing species for hundreds of millions of years. Each species was an isolated unit and developed its species-specific, yet collective, perfection. Now, however, for the first time in humans, both, the variety of life and the spiritual diversity have become something purely individual.

After humans appeared the striving for variety in life changed into a striving for spiritual variety and perfection in this one species "humans" and here in every single individual. Evolution had changed horses.

The immense spiritual differences between various single human individuals with practically consistent brains are no longer comparable to those of different individuals of the same species of animals. The spiritual, emotional and cultural competences of single human individuals are sometimes worlds apart and the differences are constantly increasing. This must lead us to the conclusion that spiritual abilities and understanding, emotions, culture and much more are non-physical items. They become apparent in living beings very slowly and gradually. Much later they increase dramatically. In the end, they take over the actual command in humans and shape the future life of the human individual. This process depends directly on how far the development of the brain of all living beings has progressed, i.e. it depends on the maturity of the necessary physical interfaces. The human brain has been perfected to become the physical *interface* to that spiritual world of information. Any further maturity takes place on a purely spiritual, informative level and not by changes in the physical brain this being the necessary hardware.

Most animals, all birds probably and certainly all mammals, however, are already in constant interactive contact with the omnipresent spiritual field. In contrast to human beings they are not aware of this fact. The supposition that these contacts do indeed exist is supported by many experiments which, for example, also convinced the biologist *Rupert Sheldrake* to assume that a purely spiritual world exists in the background.

The amazing fact that some animals, even if they are of different species, learn more easily if somewhere at some time the knowledge has already been assimilated, caused Sheldrake to establish his thesis of *morphogenetic spiritual fields*. Most brain scientists today, however, employ ever more complicated methods to discover traces of spiritual activities *within* the brain –without success up till now.

And they may never succeed. Whatever they have discovered up to now is only of a descriptive nature. In fact they can only state that certain regions of the brain have *something to do with* certain functions and behaviours. The discoveries of brain research up to now, therefore, only permit the assumption that *correlations* do exist, but nothing more. The interpretation of such correlations culminates today in the opinion expressed by some brain scientists that even the free will of humans does not really exist. The brain is merely assumed to lead humans to believe that they indeed possess their own free will. In fact the brain has already instigated specific activities shortly before the human being takes notice. And the individual perceives the intention as being his own free will. Such opinions, which are certainly described here rather shortly, are based on observations made by brain scientists. But these observations could also be interpreted in a completely different way if scientists were prepared to take a little more effort. Sadly, scientists are not willing to go that far because they are from the start orientated to a materialistic view of the world to the exclusion of all other possibilities.

The assumed lack of free will in humans, who are thus degraded to mere recipients of orders issued by their brains, culminates in the – in my opinion – almost perverse perception of some brain scientists that humans are not free with regard to criminal responsibility. In other words, they are saying that no one is responsible for his deeds, and, therefore, that punishment and atonement are superfluous.

Should this ill-founded opinion become accepted in our society, it would be fatal and we would ultimately all be doomed to failure sooner or later. Based on today's very extensive measurement of activity in various areas of the brain we can only conclude that they are involved in actions but not that such actions are instigated or even "ordered" by this area. And the fact that electrical currents are detectable immediately before a conscious action is effected and that the point in time when, depending on the test structure, test persons determine as being the moment of their decision taking, does not mean that the decision to carry out this action is made *in* the active brain area, e.g. the frontal lobe (prefrontal cortex). It is also imaginable that, at this moment, the action is only initiated by the relevant area since, according to my model, spiritual interactions can only occur simultaneously. After all, they are merely the obverse of one and the same coin. On the other hand, well-known and perhaps already automatized as well as routine and simple actions may be initiated by the brain itself since they are based on a learning process. They were probably planned in advance and were only standing in line similar to a print job on a computer. The computer determines the point in time when the print job is carried out which will be unknown to us before it is carried out. We might become aware of some simple actions after they have already been initiated. I already discussed these rather complicated possibilities in detail in some of my earlier books, especially in the second volume of my trilogy entitled "Life".

The micro-anatomy of the cortex is especially unusual, as the famous brain scientist and Nobel Prize winner *John Eccles* demonstrated. Its remarkable structure tends to support the notion that an information transfer takes place here, as John Eccles himself always strongly believed. A body-independent spirit provides the device "brain" and uses it at the same time.

Brain scientists may be correct in saying that patterns are actually stored in the brain itself, but only for those completely automatized and recurring, routine or simple, predictable actions and abilities. This applies also to knowledge activated by training. However, inexplicable complex phenomena such as consciousness, self-awareness, the personal free will of humans and their ability to decide, or indeed the phenomenon of deeply felt love, seem to be *no mere products* of our brain.[61] Also, logic cannot be stored *in* the brain as the German brain scientist *Olaf Breidbach* believes. He very clearly states in an interview: *"We register logic relationships with our brain but it does not produce them."*[62]

I believe, they are more likely rather expressions of an immaterial and, in principle, brain-independent spirit using the brain perfectly for its own purposes. It is the spirit that possesses control over what happens *with the aid* of the brain. Unfortunately only a small number of renowned scientists support this notion.

---

[61] This, unfortunately, does not prevent scientists from reducing the complexity of love to inadequate attributes such as "caring for and feeding the offspring" and discerning the responsible programs in the brain.
[62] Interview with the science magazine GEO, 01/2003

In such a scenario, as I already pointed out, the classical dualism is no longer needed. Once the brain has reached a certain complexity it simply participates in its capacity as a transmitter and receiver – like a simple radio – in the spirit of the world which in itself is a form of real existence, symmetrical and diametrically opposed to the physical world.
Depending on the level of its own development, the brain can, like a computer with an internet connection, interact with the spiritual field – the spiritual internet – and utilize part of it, mould it and differentiate it from its own intranet. From a certain level of development onwards a human being becomes aware of these abilities. Due solely to its physical existence every single atom of the brain transmits huge amounts of information into this omnipresent web, the spiritual field of our world, and – in combination with the personal intranet – the individual gradually develops his very own, distinctive personal sector which becomes an exact mirror image of the individual, of his past, present and also his future BEING, of all his actions, his words and his entire behaviour.
Each and everything becomes a distinguishable part of the interconnected whole. It becomes an independent intranet within a gigantic spiritual internet which creates the entire world, envelopes and permeates it.
At the same moment as any individual achieves the ability of self-awareness it will recognize itself as an independent personality within this internet. This is exactly what humans are able to do, and they are the first on earth to have realised it. From that moment onwards a human being no longer has any doubt that he himself is his own personal intranet. He can recognize himself with all his personal attributes since he, as a completely depicted spiritual personality, is, without any doubt, an integrity. This is the most important key which will enable us to understand how we survive our own death.
Perhaps you consider this only a small consolation for the previously so strong physical presence in this world? On the contrary: as I have already explained in detail in several of my previous books, our physical existence is also – viewed objectively – in fact more appearance than substance. Matter only appears to us so strong and solid because everything, including ourselves, is made of the same "material".
All matter really consists of 99.999% empty space. Each of us consists of an incredibly large number of atoms. Each one of them possesses only a

few tiny components which orbit each other over huge distances. Between them there is void – really nothing at all!
If we accept that the solidity of matter is only a question of perspective it is no longer difficult to imagine ourselves as being an "organism of information consisting of information units" of equal number and consistency, of course, and which account for hardly less matter than those tiny particles of material.
For us nothing has changed in principle. However, suddenly there is a real possibility of integrating the various imaginations and sometimes even confirmed sightings of "spiritual, ethereal and astral bodies", of "transfigured persons" or "apparitions of transparent matter" into a new, understandable context. At long last it would become possible to reduce natural science and metaphysics to a plausible common denominator.
Humans exist in duplicate right down to the last details of their selves. Here, in "this world of our physical universe" they are a combination of matter and spirit, in which the spirit matures slowly and, oddly, many humans do not want to become aware of this fact although they experience the opposite in their everyday life.
When the body dies at some time, it just falls away from the spirit since the spirit is the real core, the spirit and the human being go on living unblemished in a purely spiritual form – without at first subjectively noticing the slightest loss. The other world is by no means another place to which the spirit goes. The other world is merely another sphere to which this world is subordinated; it is the symmetrical and polar counterpart of all existence in this world.
In this way, we all live under "one common roof" with our dead brethren. Few people recognize this. Some do not want to know. However, at some time or other, everyone will experience it.
And their deeds here in this world are followed by the echo in the other world. How we behave today will come back to us later.
The echo of our life here will be branded as heaven or hell in the world beyond.
These age-old concepts are certainly not just inventions for manipulating people. Neither heaven nor hell are *places* of existence in the world beyond, like some institutions still maintain today, but they are rather *conditions*. And nobody can avoid them. Everyone is already creating them for himself – by his actions here and now in this world.

6. There are two sides to everything

In the last five chapters I attempted to show that there is a continuous unbroken red thread by which I clearly orientate my notions of the world in which we all live. Only if I succeed in integrating all observations and phenomena in my theory can I be on the right track.
Lao Tzu, the great Chinese philosopher, already distinguished between BEING and SENSE as two symmetrical and simultaneously polar realities of our world.
In a sense we might today also name them MATTER and SPIRIT.[63] During the 5th century BC „BEING and SENSE" became the two basic categories of Chinese cosmology, the well-known symbols of *Yin und Yang*.

Being symmetrical and polar to each other Yin and Yang are in constant interaction, they intertwine and merge. In this way all changes in heaven and earth are symbolized.

Mathematics is accepted as being an objective science. If we believe, as I do, that simple geometrical forms and also the numbers derived from them, which are themselves based on the first four ordinal numbers, are determining the most important and really existing pre-conditions in our world, then we may as well introduce some simple laws to support my theory.
This is why I use basic mathematical principles as analogies for explaining our world.[64]

---

[63] From Lao Tzu: Tao Te Ching: Translated as "The Book of Meaning (Tao) and Life (Te)"; H.G. Oswald (see List of References).
[64] See also my books: "'Arguments for a Life after Death and a Slightly Different View of the World"; " Key to Eternity"; and the trilogy "A Better History of the World" (Volume 1, " The Universe", Volume 2, " Life ", Volume 3 "Death").

First of all, there is the nothingness, in mathematics the zero. Although there are indeed two symmetrical and polar realities to the zero, namely the sequences of positive and negative natural numbers, neither of them emerges from the zero; they do not appear from nothing.

However, for both realities we can describe another common origin. Logic will help us here. We all know that we can take the square root of "+1".

Logic tells us that we should also be able to take a root of "-1". However, this cannot be expressed mathematically.

Mathematicians, for whom logic is the Holy Grail, recognize this and calculate therefore with an imaginary value. They call this number *"i"*, which means as much as: "We know, there must be a number, but we cannot clearly define it."

They now establish: the square root of "-1" is "i".

If we consider the occurrence of ordinal numbers from a purely logical point of view we find two different realities which are symmetrical and simultaneously polar to each other, they are of opposite nature. *Neither* emerges from the nothingness, but rather from something which, without doubt, exists and must exist but which we cannot clearly define.

I believe it is possible to explain the whole world in such a simple and apt way. And it is actually congruent with the tenets of all religions and myths and with the notions of the most famous philosophers in world history. The example of Lao Tzu and the principles of *Yin und Yang*, based on this philosophy, elucidate this beautifully.

Already the *Bible* indicates with the first of the Ten Commandments that we *"shall not make an image of God for ourselves"*. This probably does not mean that it is really forbidden as many strict believers would have us believe, but rather it suggests that we should not even try because it is impossible.

My simple mathematical analogy shows this in a rather plausible way: the *"i"*, the smallest indescribable point and quite incomprehensible to us yet still compellingly existing, represents "God" and everything equivalent to God in other religions.

In my opinion the whole world consists of two opposite realities, symmetrical and polar to each other, which – similar to Lao Tzu's BEING and SENSE – are spirit and matter or spiritual world and physical universe.

Just as "-1" and "+1" do not emerge from „zero", i.e. from nothing, so the two realities of our world do not emerge from nothing either. The

spirit is, as I assume and will substantiate, the primary, the first reality which develops from the indescribable but compellingly existing unit.
From it and with it are created the first components of matter and, slowly and gradually, the cosmos as we perceive it. At this point, the parable of the mustard seed comes to my mind in which Jesus very succinctly demonstrates the physical insignificance of the spirit on the one hand while emphasizing on the other hand its fundamental importance[65]
"And Jesus said: How shall we picture the kingdom of God, or what parable shall we use to describe it? It is like a mustard seed; when sown in the ground it is smaller than any other seed, but once sown, it springs up and grows taller than any other plant, and forms branches so large that birds can roost in its shade."
Both, spirit and matter influence each other and merge into each other as the imagery of Yin and Yang shows so succinctly.
Interfaces such as light or, generally speaking, electromagnetic radiation, and the brain give support. Matter emerges from spirit with whose help spirit is created again.
The spirit itself matures from an originally fallow, spiritually unused field, the *pluripotent* spiritual field (PSF) as I call it. A previously undifferentiated spiritual field is moulded to various extents by matter and its interfaces, such as the brains of its organisms, thereby being gradually but constantly developed further. The previously undifferentiated spirit is now increasingly differentiated. Matter and spirit are two sides of the same coin.
The law of symmetry and polarity is universal. We will find it everywhere in the physical world. Let us imagine for simplicity's sake just the creation of humans. Humans exist in a symmetrical and polar form, as man and woman. From an anatomical point of view everything was initially denominated female. Later on "the male develops from the female" so to speak; they both do not develop from two different basic forms.
Of course, symmetry and polarity as universally valid law support my perception that space and time are not combined in a mere four-dimensional space-time continuum, as *Albert Einstein* assumed: they are also two sides of the same coin.
Time is, in fact, a continuous quantity. If this were not so, nothing in this world could exist. Everything would disappear within a fraction of a second and be regenerated again for the same period of time. The

---

[65] The Holy Bible, e.g. The Gospel according to Mark, 04,30

conditions of the physical universe, however, require that time is clocked. Physical time becomes discontinuous. We measure time as the number of strokes or oscillations.

Space too is a continuous quantity, but we perceive this only in its manifestation, since primarily it is the product of all ordinal numbers by which it is formed.

Numbers can be distinguished, they are discontinuous – and they give a structure to and clock space. However, numbers are a purely spiritual reality. As many single in**tra**nets do not jeopardize the continuity of the entire in**ter**net, so do numbers not jeopardize the continuity of space.

Light is an *interface* between the spiritual and the physical world.

On the one hand it contains pure information on LIFE. We know this from computer technology in which we use the commands "light on" and "light off" or the numbers "1" and "0" for "information" and "no information". This is known as a binary code. The world operates in this way even if it organizes things along the lines of the decimal system.

On the other hand, light is matter since it is energy. Light is quantized, i.e. it consists of single particles which have, alas, no mass of their own.[66] Therefore, light is actually visible information.[67] "Pure" matter is created by light, by the collisions of mass-less energy particles or, much better, just by information.

Matter is thus not formed out of nothing. Neither does light, the "source material" for matter, appear out of a void since it is pure information. Therefore, light is also a part of the other, the spiritual reality. We keep finding two sides of one and the same coin, which are built on to one another like cascades and which are intertwined with each another.

Since any kind of matter possesses its "spiritual side", i.e. the simple information "to be" – always with the most exact instructions about position – it has on the one hand only a finite existence, while on the other hand it has simultaneously an infinite and eternal existence: its physical side is always finite, its informal and immaterial side, however, is not.

My previous intellectual model regarding the growth and proliferation of a smallest finite point, the (unit-)circle, starts with the spiritual, the informal and immaterial aspect; **3** pieces of pure information determine perfectly the circumference of the circle and thus the smallest physical

---

[66] Photons have no rest mass at all
[67] Photons/light are not luminous themselves – only when they collide with physical matter, e.g. the retina of our eyes, are they perceived as a luminous spot.

(finite) speck. When this is mirrored several times, which means as much as "maintaining symmetry and polarity", a two-dimensional infinity is created and, by further mirroring, a four-dimensional infinity. *Within* this infinity, three-dimensional objects, i.e. physical bodies, crystallize. (See Chapter 4 and Appendix)

Viewed from this more evolutionary-historical vantage-point, any kind of matter also possesses two sides of one and the same coin:

One is the finite three-dimensionality, which lends it the quality of a closed body, and the other is the infinite and, therefore, eternal four-dimensionality which is automatically formed around it by numbers, whereby it pronounces in eternity the actual "being" of this matter – even if its physical character no longer exists.

Time can be objective, but it is nevertheless relative, as we know from *Einstein's* theorem. In my book entitled "Life" I discussed 24-hour rhythms. They are found in all mammals and, of course, in humans and they always cover approximately **24** hours.[68] In rats and mice the rhythm covers 24 hours and 16 minutes, in humans it is nearly 25 hours. These rhythms are completely independent of the day-rhythm or the lunar cycle, or any other fixed marks. In my opinion they are another example of the influence exerted by really existing numbers behind the scenes in our world.

Time is, however, also perceived subjectively. Some psychologists say that our own feelings tell us that we have already lived half our life when we are 18 or 20 years old. We do not have the feeling that the remaining 50, 60 years or more will be a period of time as long or even longer as the first 20 years.

It seems that the measurement of time under objective criteria and identical environmental parameters do not really have much significance. For example, you book your three-week summer holiday in August in January already and you are really looking forward to it. During the waiting period three weeks seem to pass "infinitely" slowly. However, as soon as your holiday starts it seems to be over in a flash. Time flies by.

There is also a biological time. Different people grow old at very different speed. One person may be fifteen but looks like twenty, another is in his mid-forties and his hair is already grey. I belonged to both categories:

---

[68] $24 = 1 \cdot 2 \cdot 3 \cdot 4$ (= a combination of the first four ordinal numbers)

When I was only 16 I had no difficulties being admitted to movies which were not recommended for persons under the age of 18, while a friend who was already 18 always had to show his ID card. And a girlfriend once deserted me when I was 15 years old upon discovering that I was her junior. She was already 17 and it seemed quite unthinkable for her to have a friend who was only 15 years old. Today (unfortunately) people much older than I am sometimes think I am about their age. So now, I no longer relish what previously may have served my purposes.

It may be expedient to subdivide the biological age into an "external", an "internal or functional" and a "spiritual" age. Many people still feel young, spiritually and internally – even younger sometimes than persons ten years their junior – although externally they are already rather old. Unfortunately our society has not yet recognized that the spirit can grow with age, and that it does grow regularly as long as we grant it the opportunity to do so and as long as no diseases interfere with or even destroy the brain, that important mediator facilitating the growth. Erroneously, this is often described as a mental illness, whereas we really mean a brain disease. In the next chapter I will discuss in detail how humans mature by spiritual growth.

Every human being is capable of learning things and of widening his horizon even in old age. Everybody should aim to do this.

Recommendations to the contrary are simply nonsense. It does not matter at all if some things take a bit longer. Many things will be done more thoroughly.

The two sides of time, which I have explained here in detail, are the logical follow-up based on the symmetry and polarity of spirit and matter as the two sides of the same coin. Humans are the first creatures on this earth who are able to recognize their own existence, and they are able to measure time objectively and subjectively, to experience it and to assess it. In our dreams, time may be extremely distorted in all directions. Subjective experience and objective duration are often worlds apart.

In a similar way, the concept of time needs redefining for a spiritual world. It cannot be comparable with our terrestrial objective perception. In a purely spiritual world the subjective sense of time alone is important.

An objective sense of time will fade even more into the background than when experienced it in our time and life.

When, during the mid-seventies of the last century, the famous philosopher *Karl Popper* and the great brain scientist and Nobel prize-winner *John Eccles* discussed the question as to whether there was – or even must be – a life after physical death, Popper was strictly against the hypothesis. In his opinion the prospect of eternal life was unbearable.[69] This argument, however, becomes unimportant if we look at all this from my point of view.

Everywhere in the world we find symmetry and polarity: Spirit and matter, space and time, objective and subjective concepts of time, three-dimensional finite and four-dimensional infinite space – all this, and much more, are fundamental and existential examples for this theory.

There are enough examples in our physical world also: I have already mentioned some of them. For reasons of symmetry and polarity it is inevitable that we keep finding the numbers **10** and **24** as **2·5** or **2·12** respectively. We possess, for example, 2 x 5 fingers and toes, and if we count the bones in those fingers and toes with three extremities on each hand and foot there are 2 x 12. Why else should the thumbs and the big toe only have 2 extremities and not 3 like all the others? I prefer not to go into too much detail again here, I have already mentioned it in other places often enough – yet, everywhere we are continually confronted with exactly these same numbers.

Symmetry and polarity are also essential components of the spiritual world. While on the purely physical side or in physical counterparts of basic spiritual principles they always seem to be "stark" symmetrical opposites, on the purely spiritual level they are in fact rather like two poles with blurred transitions.

Therefore, blatant contradictions could be experienced within one physical manifestation if in addition the spiritual side is also very pronounced. A typical example is man and woman: apart from rare intermediate forms, which are usually caused by defective genes, there is only either one or the other. They are two equally entitled (but not identical) symmetrical and polar forms, of one and the same species, i.e. humans in this case. – Unfortunately, equal rights have not yet been fully implemented in all civilizations and on all social levels.

The two poles, man and woman, are again the two sides of the physical side of the coin "human being". As humans they possess, of course, an especially highly developed spiritual side. And this is why they no longer display such stark polarities on a spiritual level. On the contrary, we find

---

[69] see Karl Popper and John Eccles, "The Self and its Brain – An Argument for Interactionism, Springer (1977)

a plethora of transitions which reflect the various facets of human behaviour.

Sadly today's society has in general still not matured enough to recognize this and to assess it properly. As a result, humans who feel bound by the physically induced "polarity" of their gender and thereby become dissimilar to the great majority are very often unjustifiably discriminated against or compromised.

For me personally it seems absurd, for example, to keep discussing the obviously normal sexual variants of human existence, of which certainly homosexuality is one, since in such debates I must continuously put up a fight for the acceptance of those concerned.

It is about time, and would be a sign of spiritual maturity, to consider them as complete equals and to accept them as a matter of course. This might even restrain those who try by means of especially strange and sometimes unnecessarily provocative behaviour from emphasizing their peculiarity, which is not really a peculiarity at all.

Exclusively spiritual terms, such as love and hate, good and evil, justice and injustice, beauty and ugliness, harmony and disharmony can only be vaguely defined as opposite poles. The poles themselves are already rather vague and nebulous concepts. Only the Absolute, God (or however we choose to name this ideal) who, as the ultimate creator, must fully penetrate our world, can claim for himself to possess absolute love, justice, grace, beauty or harmony. This Absolute must exist for the simple reason that it alone enables the opposite poles to exist in their own flowing transitions. However, the opposite spiritual *Absolute*, i.e. hate, injustice, evil, ugliness or disharmony or in short, the devil, cannot exist.

The reasons are obvious:

On the one hand, symmetry and polarity are the result of the physical world developing from the spiritual whereby its solid and absolute forms are developed. At the beginning the spiritual world is undifferentiated, i.e. without such sharp contrasts.

They develop in the physical world where they are needed for bringing about a maturity which will eventually take us back to our own true self. This becomes ever more clear on the level of the individual. The result is the highest possible and widest variety of spiritual differentiation. Without the previous purposeful development of symmetry and polarity this would never have been possible.

On the other hand, this world can only exist if the original Absolute, based on absolute good, indescribable grace and immeasurable love, is the *only* Absolute. If an opposite Absolute existed as well, nothing would ever have had the chance to develop. Something absolutely evil would eliminate right from the start not only everything positive but also any other form of existence. Nothing could exist alongside the absolute evil, otherwise it would not be the absolute evil.

Would we really bring children into the world if we did not believe in the positive and in love?

Furthermore, based on all previous observations it seems logical that all development in the world follows one direction. In the physical universe this phenomenon is known as the tendency towards increasing chaos ("positive entropy", "second law of thermodynamic"). In the spiritual world this would mean striving towards an increasing maturity and order. The physical and the spiritual development are again both, polar and symmetrical to each other.

It follows that the world as a whole is striving for further spiritual growth, or maturity, and order while simultaneously physical disorder increases until it completely disintegrates.

Pierre Teilhard de Chardin called this degree of maturity the Omega Point.

I mentioned the awakening of humans to God, or that mankind itself is a God in emergence. There could never be a unilateral development towards the absolute good, to God, if the absolute evil also existed, since between two Absolutes[70] a mutually neutralizing or exterminating tension must always develop, otherwise they could not be called absolute.

Finally, the perception of something absolutely evil would contradict the laws of mathematics, which indicate that **two** polar and symmetric realities develop from only **one** indefinable factor, the *"i"*. Symmetry and polarity – **two** characteristics of this world, developed from only **one** *first* reality.

Evil, hate or the devil are the consistent and inevitable results which can be solely ascribed to the spiritual expansion into the physical. The biblical Fall of Man possibly refers to this and is thus a *symbolic* reality. Everything, and this unfortunately includes the evil, is necessary so that in the end something good is developed. If this were not true, the absolute good, God as the first reality, could never have emerged. Good and evil are thus necessary fundamental conditions for our general

---

[70] Not taken into account here is that something "Absolute" is a superlative which, from a logical point of view, can only exist as a singular anyway.

development. The existence of evil, therefore, by does not by any means allow God to be brought into question.

However, this does not mean that we must simply accept the negative excesses in our society.

On the contrary, it is an indication of the growing spiritual maturity of all human individuals and, therefore, also of all individual human society, provided rigorous and strict measures are taken to combat evil. There are clearly different degrees of evil: worst of all are the crimes of violence directed against the body, but– with reservations – also against the soul of others. In the Christian Bible we have the holy commandment "Thou shalt not kill". In the Koran, the holy script of the Islam, written down by the prophet *Mohammed*, it says: *"The first judgement on the day of the resurrection will be over the blood that was shed"*. Unfortunately, in both religions these commandments are frequently forgotten and in the most shameful way.

In my opinion, manslaughter and murder should as a matter of principle and almost without exception be punished with the maximum sentence, irrespective of the *perpetrator's* or his *accomplice's* pleaded unaccountability, be it real or only pretended. For me it is quite intolerable that in our country, for example, a so-called satanic couple, who tortured and killed a human being in the most horrible way, escaped with a sentence of *only* 13 and 15 years in prison – based on a psychiatric report, the defence counsel even demanded acquittal on the grounds of diminished responsibility. Or another example: in 2002 a twenty-year old man killed a girl called Vanessa in Southern Germany during the celebration of carnival. He was disguised as "Death". He broke into her bedroom, frightened her and killed her in the most barbaric manner. During his trial at the beginning of 2003 he admitted the killing but he tried to make excuses and explained that he had never wanted to kill the girl but that he just wanted to scare her. When the girl started yelling, he killed her without premeditation in the heat of the moment. This explanation was rightly not taken into account when the sentence was pronounced. Nevertheless: he was sentenced to only 10 years in prison because in Germany people are of age and are allowed to vote when they are 18 years old, but are still treated as adolescent in court until the age of 21 if an expert opinion confirms their immaturity.

This actually happened. I am strictly against reduced sentences in such cases.

Basically, I am in favour of a minimum prison sentence of 25 years in *all* cases of manslaughter or murder unless somebody is killed due to gross negligence. In the cases mentioned above, however, and especially in a case of murder very single case should be reviewed to establish whether a life sentence would not be more appropriate. In the case I mentioned above, only a life sentence for the *perpetrator and his accomplice* could be considered a suitable punishment.

Nevertheless, I believe that the death penalty, unfortunately still imposed in some countries, is quite simply the *wrong* way. Death is not a punishment. However, in my opinion the deliberate killing of a person can only be justified in exceptional cases when a direct threat to the life of another innocent person is thereby averted.[71]

Allow me in this context another critical remark concerning the proceedings in our present judicial system:

For my mind, it is a scandal that those committing offences against authority, often as a result of disagreement in ideological or general political questions, are often sentenced to harsher punishments than others who have inflicted bodily harm on other people, or even killed them. However, I intend to discuss such issues and other social-political problems in more detail in a later book.

Whether it is the fixed aspects of symmetry and polarity resulting from the production of matter which are manifested, or rather the more flowing, indefinable, transitional aspects of the spiritual, depends primarily on the period of time over which the influence is exerted by matter or spirit, and also on the specific level of spiritual development. The longer the period of influence and the higher the level of spiritual development, the more significant is the expected process of transformation. Purely physical things which appear spontaneously are not subject to a long-lasting spiritual influence and are, therefore, always manifested in either one of the two possible symmetrical and polar forms. This is why only matter can exist and not anti-matter, or, if at all, only in insignificant quantities. And this term "anti-matter" should be understood in a different way, as a special form of matter, similar to humans who are either left-handed or right-handed. And for this reason, *nearly* all amino acids are optically active, etc..

In contrast, spiritual, emotional, ethical-moral or aesthetic values can only develop or alter if they are influenced spiritually over a longer

---

[71] In our language we have the unfortunate term "Finaler Rettungsschuss", which translates roughly as "ultimate permission for the fatal shot to be fired in order to save lives".

period of time. In this way they undergo a continual *process* of development. This is why we humans can look into the future with optimism and hope in spite of all the dangers and horrors present in our world. We can assume with justification that evil will be turned into something good and injustice into justice, etc., in the course of time.

This applies to mankind collectively as well as to every single individual: since every single individual is important for the evolution of mankind, every individual must and will finally recognize this, so that mankind as a whole can benefit.

Humans as physical creatures do not live long enough, however, to reach this stage. It may become easier for later generations if the process of maturing were to progress in more humans than is the case today. Nevertheless, the harrowing experiences made over the last few thousand years, seem to support this: in spite of the still widespread suffering in the world, there have never before been so many people who are enjoying a good life as there are today.

But this is not enough: all humans, including ourselves, the "ancestors of the future", must get there. Only then will mankind be "redeemed" in the true sense of the word.

In order to enable mankind to achieve this, every single individual's survival of death is an absolute necessity.

Life and death are also two sides of one coin and they are symmetrical and polar to each other. And as any physical order develops towards an increasing chaos (positive entropy) in the course of time, so – in turn – the other side of the coin is developed, the opposite mirror image: an ever more complex, increasingly organized and constantly higher developed, more differentiated spirit.

The world needs the increasing disorder of the physical universe to enable it to attain the increasingly improved organization of the most highly differentiated spirit.

In the same way as the spirit is superior to matter and infinity is superior to finiteness, good will conquer evil and love will triumph over hate, since a world of such dimensions and of such overwhelming, indescribable beauty which is revealed to us humans slowly but inexorably, can only be the result of indescribable kindness and immeasurable love – otherwise it would not exist.

In this case the precept of non-creation would have overruled the precept of creation – in the same way as we can only bring children into this world if we love this world and our life and look with trust and

optimism into our future, in spite of all the difficulties with which our life and the world confront us. I already mentioned this.
This is exactly the message which religions propagate if we were only prepared to look closely.
Life and death are two sides of one and the same coin:
Death represents the inevitable finiteness of any three-dimensional body. Just as the polar mirror image of infinity exists for any form of finiteness, so is eternal life the infinite counterpart of death. Life in general is something spiritual and not the product of a body.
Therefore, life is infinite and eternal.
Death is just the fate of mere finite bodies.

7. Progressive Spiritual Maturity

Young people especially do not like to hear the remark "Maturity comes with age". But it is true.
The life of every human being is dominated by constant learning from the day of birth onwards. To be sure, there are some higher developed mammals, e.g. elephants, whales and primarily, of course, various kinds of primates, who *also* learn as long as they live. But in comparison to humans there are tremendous differences which as a matter of principle and without reservation permit the conclusion that animals are characterized by the term "to be" and humans by the term "to become".
One very important criterion is the comprehensible, completely individual, unique and thus distinctive biography which every human has. No species – not even primates who are closely related to us – possesses anything equivalent. The lives of individual animals are, generally speaking, rather interchangeable. Of course, in the subjective view of a person who has a close emotional relationship with an animal this may not seem to be true. But that is not the decisive factor here.

In all animal species the individual as such has in general a rather low status compared with that of the individual human. It is the collective group as such which counts – the entire species is always most important. This fact as well as the theory of evolution according to which humans and animals have common animal ancestors, are mainly responsible for the disregard and the suppression from which the human individual so often had to suffer and over the last hundred years especially.

Nevertheless, a number of more highly developed mammals are indeed able to show amazing spiritual efficiencies – and probably some of them even have distinct emotions. Who ever saw an elephant mother desperately trying to shake her dead calf back to life, in the end throwing it to the ground and then staying close to the dead body for a long time as if in sad mourning, can believe this. Elephants even recognize the bones of their brethren in a jumbled heap and they put them carefully to one side.

All too easily, however, such stories become the origin of legends and myths which are blown up far beyond the facts. Of course, elephants do not have a feeling of reverence or even a distinct perception of death itself as humans have. Nevertheless, they can still show a kind of mourning when they notice they have lost a calf or a partner. The ability to recognize the bones of their brethren is probably due to their extraordinary olfactory sense which is superior to that of all other mammals. To separate the bones of their own species from those of other creatures seems to be an act of pure instinct. Elephant graveyards, however, as places where the animals "consciously" go to die belong to the realm of myths.

Elephants, to keep to the nice example of an intelligent mammal, certainly have emotions and possess a consciousness.

But no animal will ever reach or even come close to the level of humans with their extremely versatile intellectual, emotional, social and cultural facets.

This becomes especially apparent with regard to the two basic values of "good and evil". The last hundred years have shown us a formerly unequalled evidence of the broad possible range between these two antipodes, something of which only humans are capable of.

I do not think that I need to quote more examples since many, especially the evil ones, are still in our sad memory and not only in the history books.

In contrast to the individuals in all animal species, there are tremendous differences between human individuals, i.e. between individuals of the same species. The evolution of life changes its direction in humans: from now on evolution happens among the individuals of only one species, the humans. It is not the species as a whole which strives toward collective perfection but every single individual itself that has to follow this path in future.

Evolution has changed the horses which does not make the "work" it has to do any easier. On the contrary, the development is now to a greater extend and even more often accompanied by devastating setbacks – in former times as well as today and possibly even more so in future.

The new direction of evolution is clearly defined and is now directly bestowed upon every single human being. The "new" kind of evolution is no longer physical. The human brain has been finished for the last few thousand years and between a genius and an imbecile, between good and evil, between people in love or in hate there are no relevant anatomical differences.

The field of activity of the "new" evolution is constantly expanding. For the first time ever there are significant differences between the single individuals of the same species and they are increasing all the time. There are intellectual, emotional, social and cultural differences which are drifting apart dramatically. No single human being is comparable to another – we can all rest assured that we will all remain for ever a unique and absolutely unmistakable character, the only one of this kind in the entire universe.

Exactly this is the result of his "becoming" and not of his "being". The absolute uniqueness of a human personality *develops* in the course of its lifetime. We could compare this again to the positive entropy in thermodynamics which also irreversibly leads to distinctive conditions.

From the very beginnings of life, it has always been the species as a whole with its subordinated individuals that continually strived for the greatest degree of perfection. The group as a collective has always been the most important factor.

Mankind as a whole, however, can only be perfected gradually through the progress of every single individual. The group thus depends on the development of each individual.

For evolution, changing horses meant encountering a previously unknown, quite considerable risk. At the same time a tremendous opportunity is opened up which otherwise would not have happened. On the one hand evolution now runs the risk of failing on a very high level after billions of years because it is humanity itself – the success model of evolution as we believe – which is the only species on Earth capable of destroying the entire achievements of evolution in one crushing blow. On the other hand evolution now has the unique chance of achieving ever more perfection in an immeasurable and incredible degree of variety.

Evolution must obviously have "known" the risks and opportunities because it has not and cannot have all been pure coincidence.

Evolution "chose" this way because the chances were calculated and the advantages outweighed the disadvantages. Evolution will succeed because it must succeed. The aim of all evolution is success.

But what is the objective, the success? Well, it can no longer be a mere physical aim since all physical matter is limited, is finite and countable. The new factor introduced by evolution, which has first become apparent in humans as a change in paradigms, arises from a completely different dimension: in the case of humans, evolution clearly revolutionises the field of the infinite and uncountable, since it no longer produces great physical but tremendous spiritual diversity. Physical differences are of minor importance. Spiritual facets, such as good and evil, love and hate, beauty and ugliness, justice and injustice, genius and idiocy, harmony and chaos, are all unlimited in quality and quantity and potentially infinite. In the course of his physical life, every single human has, in principle, the opportunity to absorb the largest possible portion for himself. Within the limits set by inherited or acquired physical traits, by the prevailing environmental conditions and also by the social and cultural environment he experiences later, the human being is free to choose which facets of life he wishes to adopt.

And, if he so chooses, it is the positive which can prevail.

However, all these facets are of a purely spiritual nature.

Although nothing here is really tangible and everything is subject to direct sensual experience, these are in fact the important attributes and characteristics which decide the direction our human life takes. The human being is able to utilize them all because, as *spiritual* possibilities and ideals, they obviously exist *in reality*.

After all, it is the human spirit alone which recognizes a beautiful symphony in the physical chaos of vibrating air surrounding him – the vibrations themselves could not convey this impression.

And again, it is the immaterial human spirit alone that can interpret a jumble of various light frequencies as being the fantastic colourful splendour of a beautiful sunset.

Since humans, for a certain period of time, are also physical entities, they need certain tools, e.g. sense organs, with which they have in the meantime been adequately equipped. Their signals, however, must always be "translated" and interpreted. Although some of these signals are individually encoded by specific conditions in the brain itself, much of it is a purely spiritual function. In our physical universe beauty or ugliness do not exist. Neither do bad and evil, justice or love.

All these are purely spiritual qualities which life itself will be unable to *experience* and to *discover* before it has attained a certain maturity. And, similar to the evolution of physical matter, which has obviously always strived for perfection, we may assume that the evolution of the spirit is doing the same.

It was the evolution of physical matter which brought about such large numbers of the most diverse species. They all developed to their own specific optimal functional perfection. Exactly this is the basic principle of the Darwinist term *selection* – a great achievement which was correctly recognized as such by *Charles Darwin*.

The evolution of the spirit must no longer take care mainly of whole species – no, it is confronted with every single person.

It must deal with every single spirit and no longer with various groups. As a result, we all find ourselves in the midst of an evolution of each single spirit with the inexorable aim of developing the spirit of every single human being towards its very own, best functional and best possible perfection. From this perspective, the evolution of the spirit has no interest in the physical body – it does not need to take the body into consideration.

The greatest disadvantage of the physical body is, of course, its finiteness, which sooner or later will inevitably result in its death.

Taking all this into consideration, death cannot be considered as an obstacle for the evolution of the spirit which itself must survive death since it has nothing at all to do with it.

Death only affects the finite, that is the physical body.

In almost all animal species the collective group, the species, receives foremost priority. Individuals within the same species are all placed on a comparable spiritual level which is, in comparison to humans, rudimentary. Even those mammals most similar to us, e.g. primates, possess by comparison only a poorly developed consciousness and self-awareness. Nothing in the world could turn the spirit of a primate into that of a human. The spiritual level of humans is the result of an almost incredible quantum leap with regard to quality and quantity.

This becomes especially apparent if we consider not only the absolute time but also the small number of descendents. We may safely assume that the spiritual appearance of humans who lived 10,000 years ago did not differ significantly from those who lived 100,000 or even 200,000 years ago. They were all simple hunters and gatherers.

This means that the acceleration in the spiritual development of humans has taken less than 10,000 years. Considering that this covers merely 400 generations[72], then the entire, all-important spiritual development of humans took place within a breathtakingly short period of time.

An ever increasing individualization was, without doubt, a development which ran parallel to this incredibly dramatic process. Thus the evolution of the human spirit is, as I already mentioned, simultaneously the evolution of the individual human spirit. If physical death is not a barrier to this evolution then it follows that every single human being should comprehend the process of his own spiritual evolution as something going beyond his physical death.

In principle, the same applies to animals: the animal spirit also survives physical death, of course, but it is part of the collective spiritual entity of its species and is not aware of its self. In other words: only someone who is able to recognize himself as a spiritual creature "in this world" will also be able to recognize himself after his physical death and will thus be enabled to further the progress of his own spiritual development.

Evolution for us is no longer something that has to be suffered passively. On the contrary, humans become active participants, cooperative partners of evolution who can and will accelerate the process enormously. The spiritual level of all organisms which are not yet able to participate in the process is also preserved, of course, but in this case as a collective or species-specific memory.

My theory can be used to explain many biological phenomena without difficulty and other theories could be supported which are still completely inexplicable or which are often even criticized as being absolutely unscientific. These include certain phenomena such as

---

[72] A human generation is calculated as the period of 25 years.

convergence and *mimicry,* the *coordination of behaviours between different species* and also the *morphogenetic fields* of the British biologist *Rupert Sheldrake.*
Each human individual first becomes the centre of his own evolution. It is primarily a spiritual process of unlimited infinite possibilities. At the same time individual evolution becomes the necessary prerequisite for a successful evolution of mankind as a whole.
What is needed, therefore, is altruism, i.e. the giving of assistance in the successful evolution of our brethren. And the ability to recognize this is a sign of spiritual maturity. Each of us needs only to become aware of this.
It follows that all egalitarian ideologies are fundamentally wrong.
They are the result of an obsolete materialistic view of the world, which we should now be overcoming at long last. It would actually be a reactionary process if we were to adhere to them any longer. In doing so, we would be committing a crime against mankind and obstructing our own development. Of course, once started no development can be terminated unless, that is, we seek our own destruction since every individual as a construct of evolution may one day advance and demand the rights granted to him by evolution. However, this may unfortunately cost countless lives. The last hundred years have shown this often enough in its alarmingly barbaric excesses.
Every single human being must be given the chance to perfect himself within the possibilities inherent in his own unique form.
Inseparably connected with this is our duty to help our brethren to seize their chances. This individual responsibility of every human should not be limited, far less forbidden, by any kind of institution. Each single human must learn to recognize himself as the engine of his own meaningful evolution and to convey this knowledge to his brethren.
Every human being possesses immense chances which even in any remotely similar form are denied to all animals on Earth.
It follows directly from this that every human being carries an immense responsibility for himself as well as for the well-being of his brethren. Therefore, it must be the duty of society to ensure with the utmost strictness that *both* are realized. This is exactly what is meant in the Bible, as I already explained earlier, by the terms *"love of God", "love of oneself"* and *"love of one's neighbour"* – and in exactly that order.
The "love of God" includes the above mentioned recognition that humans are not in this world by accident but that they are highly developed, conscious and self-aware spiritual creatures which *"God created*

after his own image". This biblical statement is directed, of course, to the completely new spiritual, i.e. intellectual, emotional, social and cultural, dimensionality which has become apparent only in humans and which distinguishes every single human being for all time as being unique in this world.

"Love of oneself" develops from the recognition of "one's own self", its status and its responsibilities – and "love of one's neighbour" follows on inexorably from that.

Only he who recognizes himself as what he really is, namely a non-interchangeable, spiritual and lasting – even immortal – being, will be able to summon the necessary amount of selflessness (altruism) which will finally result in his readiness to take over responsibility for all of us. All of us, mankind as a whole, and also our beautiful Earth with all its living creatures urgently need this responsibility now more than ever to be saved from the threat of destruction.

At birth humans are the most unfinished creatures on Earth. In contrast to young apes, children remain unable to procure their own food for years and years after they have been weaned off their mothers' milk and are unable to survive without help. Unlike any other creature, their development takes many years, practically two decades, before they are fully grown up adults who, in comparison to animals and in relation to their remaining life span, are still not quite finished. When animals reach adulthood there is nothing that could sensibly be added, whereas humans still find themselves at the beginning of an incomparably more exciting, purely spiritual development.

Compared with this the physical development of humans is hardly worth mentioning while for animals it is of the utmost importance.

The spiritual development of humans can be subdivided into the intellectual, the emotional and mental, the ethical-moral, and the cultural and social development. Each individual experiences these developments with regard to quality as well as quantity in completely different ways.

But irrespective of the priorities engendered by the development or the character it adopts, and no matter whether more good or evil remains, there will always be an immense increase in purely spiritual attributes and, with growing age, they will obviously seek to attain their (temporary) zenith. Although humans like animals become weaker in old age, their spirit keeps growing – and thereby potentially their wisdom also. Wisdom has not necessarily anything to do with intelligence!

As a physician I have very often noticed how wise old people are – even if their intellect is somewhat limited. They possess the ability to watch and judge the world from a different angle, I could almost say from a more distant and higher but more relaxed and generous point of view. The key to their wisdom is often an amazing level of tolerance which they did not possess while they were young. In all unspoiled primitive civilizations old people still have the greatest say. People like to be near them and to ask their advice. In many illiterate societies they are furthermore an encyclopaedia of lifelong experiences, essential and indispensable for the survival of the tribe.

As long as diseases of whatever kind do not damage or incapacitate the communication device brain, humans remain indefinitely capable of learning as long as they live. Some functions may slow down and become more difficult, but this is always a purely physical problem and never a spiritual one.

In theory, unlimited spiritual growth is possible for everybody. It seems that only death can apply the brakes. However, according to the explanations mentioned above this can only be fallacy. While death puts a natural and even a sensible end to the physical body, it does seem initially as if it also puts an abrupt and needless end to the lifelong spiritual endeavour to achieve ever higher perfection.

For logical reasons alone this must be utterly absurd, especially since the former physical body always played a secondary role which moreover continually lost significance with growing age. This becomes especially apparent in those humans possessing a conspicuously astute mind who suffer from a physical disease and who are ailing as long as they live, as the example of the British physicist *Stephen Hawking* demonstrates.

This is approximately what the famous German poet, philosopher and naturalist *Johann Wolfgang von Goethe* meant when he said to his intimate friend *Peter Eckermann*, who was also a writer in his own right:

"I draw the conviction of our survival from the definition of activity; when I remain active till the end of my life, then nature is obliged to provide another form of existence for me if the presently adopted one can no longer tolerate my spirit."[73]

The physical death of a human being is not his spiritual end.

It cannot be. Every single person has it in his own hands during his (still physical) "lifetime" to render himself immortal in a positive sense. Each one of us only has to recognize that it is in his power to differentiate the

---

[73] Johann P. Eckermann: "Conversations with Goethe", published between 1837-1848.

"spiritual potential" available to him in the most efficient way, i.e. to perfect himself in a positive way within his possibilities.

All his chances but also his shortcomings, all the good and all the evil, his kindness and his love, but also his greed, his hate and his misdemeanours – everything, everything without exception, remains preserved and in eternal existence since nothing of spiritual nature will ever vanish from this world.

Humans may have given much pleasure to other humans or they may have killed them, they may have helped this world or damaged it. None of it will ever perish.

This world-embracing, all-encompassing and all-penetrating "spiritual internet" sees and remembers everything for ever and ever.

The time will come for all of us sooner or later when we can be either very proud of our behaviour or perhaps deeply ashamed of it. There will be nobody passing judgement on us –each of us will judge his own demeanour himself – and that is even worse. Everyone will repeatedly have the chance to do good, to learn how to love and not to do evil – and to reconcile where necessary.

But never will the new deed make the past one sink into oblivion. In the end, however, the new goodness will suppress the old evil and will make it fade.

We must gradually learn to recognize this so that we may cope with our immense responsibility for this world and its evolution, for which we are now the spiritual carrier of hope. The path to the human species was immensely long, thorny and stony to the extreme. It was full of detours and demanded a great deal of indescribable sacrifice for our predecessors.

This path could only succeed because it has always been the obvious result of comprehensive love which will for ever remain incomprehensible to us humans: the love of God, however we wish to define him/her.

In the last instance, all attempts at imagining God must inexorably fail. It is as impossible to create images as it is – using a mathematical comparison – to extract the root from "-1", although logic tells us that it ought to be possible.

This is exactly the reason for the biblical commandment that we should not make for ourselves an image of God and the reason why the Islamic world has no depictions of Allah at all – not because we are not allowed but because it is impossible to do so.

If we should wish to draw another conclusion from the above with logic and consequence then it should be that, irrespective of who or what God is, or whatever the nature of "He+She" might be:
"He+She" in one (!) must simultaneously be something extraordinarily individual and personal.

8. Sexuality reflected by Evolution and Spirit

My ideas concerning the evolution of all life (see Volume 2, "Life") focus on three key theses:
1.) Alongside the evolution of life itself there is an evolution of its evolutionary mechanisms at work. It is only at the beginning that mutations are of such immense importance as an ignition device while natural selection always remains as a control factor.
Cooperation and communication together with instinct, consciousness and self-awareness are newly added independent influencing factors which slowly take over a more important role and more and more control of the process. The original, pure Darwinian selection theory remains unaltered by these.
2.) It soon becomes apparent that the most important element of physical evolution is the generation and the consistent and constant further development of effective communication systems under a hierarchically structured and downwards-compatible control, i.e. the central nervous system (CNS) in this case.
3.) Evolution is simultaneously also a body-independent spiritual process. In this case the central nervous system (CNS) becomes the mediator between a spiritual and a physical evolution. The development of species is increasingly influenced by the ever growing *emergently* differentiating spiritual field supported by continual interactive feedback.
At first there are certain fundamental, i.e. number-controlled and geometric principles of development according to which all forms of life

are moulded. Mutations are incidental ignition devices which cause direct biochemical changes in the genotype.

Over long periods of time mutation and selection are the most important motors producing an array of new developments and selecting the best suited organism. However, from the very beginning an influence is already exerted –unspecific at first – by an all-encompassing spiritual field. Purposeful information, e.g. by light quanta or general electromagnetic radiation, is the reason that complex mono-cellular and multi-cellular organisms are generated at all and that they cluster. Information is the spark that brings dead matter to life provided it has attained the appropriate conditions. A permanent exchange of information by interaction with the spiritual field is set in motion.

The biochemical basis for this and thereby for life itself, are complex three-dimensional structures – large molecules and cells. They act as resonance bodies and antennae for the "information material" which determines certain directions and outlines within which mutations may work.

The best suited survives. Everything, and that includes every new structure which is "tried out", exerts information which is stored in the spiritual field. In this way the spirit itself is slowly further differentiated; for a very long period of time this happens "unconsciously".

Gradually, new species appear – at ever shorter intervals each being better equipped than its predecessor due to the ever more efficient informational feedback.

In addition, the pre-determined patterns, the endless mutations and the permanent mutual adjustments, facilitated by a continuous feedback, become perfected by comprehensive communication systems which develop at an early stage.

These too undergo further refinement and are constantly improved in the course of time. In this way an ever more complex nervous system, the central nervous system, is generated in a strictly hierarchical structure.

The quantity and quality of communication is thereby slowly improved – the communication between single structures of one and the same individual as well as that concerning the level of interactions with the spiritual field. The CNS develops parallel to an ever more efficient mediator between the spiritual world and all physical creatures. It follows also that the spiritual world is differentiated at an increasingly fast speed and more comprehensively. In fact, species-specific memories are developed which determine and adjust instinctive behaviour. Over immense periods of time an early kind of consciousness develops which facilitates an even more efficient feedback. Finally, with the appearance of humans a comprehensive self-awareness emerges like a phoenix from the ashes. This enables mankind to become a valuable partner in the evolutionary process and to participate actively in forming it.

From this point on the spiritual field, being increasingly differentiated, becomes personalized and individualized. Coincidental mutations are still possible and occur frequently, but their influence decreases constantly. The enigmatic phenomenon of *congruence* can be simply and plausibly explained: it is due to the access evolution has to a pool of information which has been in existence for millions of years.

With the awakening of consciousness and self-awareness developments are now induced and supported for the first time which do not primarily serve to support the preservation of the species or ensure its bare survival but rather start to diminish the previously robust influence of selection. Both, consciousness and self-awareness, are luxury goods, so to speak, whose purpose in life only becomes apparent if we assume that a constantly active, controlled feedback exists whereby they are upgraded to become new and valuable mechanisms of evolution.

It is amazing that evolution apparently always endeavours to perfect all new attributes. Mimicry, i.e. the imitation of certain characteristics or behaviour, is, I think, a very good example.

All advancements towards perfection are usually aimed at ensuring the preservation of the species and its propagation.

In the case of the human sexuality, however, the anatomy of the essential organs exceeds the bare necessities.

In short: perfection is quite obviously no longer the mere "unrestricted performance of natural requirements" alone; something completely "un-evolutionary" has been introduced, namely pleasure and joy! This becomes understandable only if there are other reasons for "inducing" evolution to introduce this novelty. I can only imagine that a "purposeful spiritual demand" is responsible. Religious taboos imposed, for example, because certain sexual behaviour is rejected as it does not serve propagation, proves thus to be absurd. I will explain this in further detail. Apparently there are only three animal species, bonobos, dolphins and humans for whom, as a matter of great certainty, sexuality is not only a means of propagation. The females of all other animal species go courting, for example, only during the fertile period of their cycle and it is only then that they permit sexuality. Only humans are sexually active without the restrictions of firm rutting seasons or seasons of heat. One biological reason for this seems to be the hidden ovulations of women. This happens very rarely in the animal world, although it can also be found in some primates, but not in chimpanzees which are the closest relatives to humans (the difference between their genotype and the human genotype is only about 1%).

A woman is one of the few female living beings who generally does *not* notice when exactly her ovulation takes place and she becomes fertile. Therefore, the object of human sexuality cannot merely be reproduction. In contrast to nearly all female animals a woman is always *sexually* receptive.

Unlike a female primate and all other animals a woman has a clitoris – "from a purely reproduction technical point of view, a strange attribute" – the reason for which can only be the pleasurable experience of sexuality.

Something similar can be said for the male penis.

In an erect state it has an average length of 12-13 cm. Gorillas only have a length of 3 cm and orang-utans only 4 cm. This is surprising since both species are closely related to humans and they are both much taller.

For intercourse, the length of the penis is irrelevant as it is for complicated coitus positions. In spite of their short penises gorillas and orang-utans can even manage it in trees.

Nor does the size of the penis have any bearing on the length of time taken for the coitus: the average time for humans is, according to the American physiologist *Jared Diamond,* 4 minutes, orang-utans take 15 minutes. There is no important physiological reason for this.

Meanwhile, we know that the comparatively long human penis is much less attractive for a woman than for the man himself. *"Women,"* so Diamond, *"usually report that they are more attracted by other male attributes, and that they find the sight of a penis, if anything at all, rather unattractive."*

Over a long period of time Jared Diamond observed tribes in New Guinea.

The natives there use a decorated tube, the so-called penis case. They possess several variants which they put on according to their mood. Without this case they feel naked. And Diamond adds: *"The penis case is really a conspicuous erect pseudo-penis and it makes perfectly clear how men (!) like to be endowed."* (the exclamation mark is mine)

Clitoris and penis are without doubt two attributes which neither possesses direct significance for propagation and thereby for the preservation of mankind, nor any necessity in their existing form and design necessary. They provide no direct advantage for the survival of mankind either. Their use could, of course, be explained – for example with the observation that, due to the pleasure it gives them, men and women come together sufficiently often to serve the preservation of the species. And here again we approach a higher spiritual level. And that is exactly what I was getting at.

We may assume with some certainty that the sexual anatomy of modern humans differs little from that of our ancestors. It probably developed parallel to the evolution of mankind and was the same then as it is today. We have to ask ourselves therefore, why it is that a sexual equipment was developed in humans which targets spirituality and consciousness and triggers a purely spiritual feeling, namely pleasure, while for almost all animals the unconscious-instinctive program for the propagation of the species is the main objective.

Jared Diamond also articulates his doubts in all purely materialistic theories.

For humans sex obviously does not merely mean propagation, but seemingly, since the beginning of mankind, it has always been a source of pleasure as well and that without any seasonal limitation. This makes humans different from all animals. It is an inexplicable fact according to presently known and confirmed evolution theories.

Humans build their own species-specific collective spiritual field with the aid of individual spiritual fields. These together provide the physically manifested individuals with information.

These perceptions are congruent, at least partly, with the "collective unconscious" or the so-called "archetypes" as the psychoanalysts *Sigmund Freud* and *Carl Gustav Jung* postulated.[74] Information of „general interest" or of fundamental meaning are constantly fed into this spiritual field and can thereby influence the species-specific process of evolution.

Another absolutely amazing phenomenon also raises questions. It only exists in humans and pothead whales and in a few other, comparatively *primitive* animals:

---

[74] This includes the human experience as a whole.

I am referring to the menopause, the sudden and lasting disappearance of the female menstruation cycle which usually takes place between the woman's 40th and 50th year.

In contrast men stay fertile all their life, even if with a slowly decreasing tendency. Usually the fertility of female animals also decreases only very slowly. With regard to the mere preservation of the species, it would really make more sense if women would also remain fertile until they reach old age. Of course, there are good reasons that this is not so. But again we notice an amazing aspect: all these characteristics seem to have already existed at the time humans appeared on the stage of life, since the menopause of women had not been developed by evolutionary trial and error over immense periods of time. It has probably always existed.

A good reason for the early menopause could surely be the life expectancy of women, which should be long enough to enable them to take care of their children for a sufficiently long period of time until they become independent. And later, as the life expectancy increased further, they were able to take care of their grandchildren. By analysing population data of the 18th and 19th century, the German scientists Eckart Voland and Jan Beise, both from the University of Gießen, established that children whose grandmother is still alive seem to have a better chance of survival (interestingly, however, this applies only to their mother's mother).

As Jared Diamond wrote, a woman is obviously better able to increase the number of people who carry her genes when she is prepared to care for her potential grandchildren and other relatives instead of giving birth to another child herself; bearing a child, it is reasoned, is more complicated and dangerous than it is for an animal to give birth, because in comparison to the size and the weight of the mother a newborn baby is unusually large due mainly to the size of its cranium. And each additional birth immediately endangers the older children as the mother could die in childbirth. There is hardly any animal species where the risk at birth is so comparatively high. The older the mother is at birth, the higher the risk for the child of being born in poor health or of dying early. Men do not have any of these problems. They do not die at childbirth and very rarely while fathering the child. And their degree of exertion is in comparison to a pregnancy negligible.

This is why men do not need a change of life.

Now there is, of course, a counterargument: it is not only human females who have a secret ovulation and a menopause and not only human males who have a large penis. And possibly some biologist could prove to me that animals exist or existed which have or had something similar to a clitoris. But would that contradict my argumentation? No, I do not believe it would.

On the contrary, I think it would rather add further support to my theories as a whole:

Without restrictions and *emergent*, evolution constantly develops something new within the bounds of its possibilities (determined by spiritual information). It is not only mutations but also the growing spiritual forces which play important controlling roles here.

With specific mechanisms the "best suited" is then selected.

Parallel growing feedback mechanisms create a kind of steadily increasing "spiritual information pool" on which the emergent evolution can draw while its process is progressing. But this always happens in a very expedient way. Following this plan evolution provides human with reproductive organs which are also very expedient and useful in their functions. However, that happens suddenly and probably all at once.

All the reasons supporting the theory that it happened "like this and in no other way" are of spiritual nature. The purely physiological devices necessary for reproduction and preservation of the species – evolution could have achieved the same by simply *further* developing the tools which our human ancestors, the primates, already possessed. However, humans are completely new, *mainly* spiritual beings – and, therefore, spiritual reasons also played a role when they were being endowed with their equipment. It seems obvious that from the very beginning evolution intended human sexuality to give pleasure and not to be merely a means of propagation. Unfortunately, a number of social groupings have not recognized this yet.

Evolution also seems to have shown rather far-sighted planning, if we consider the plausible but less materialistic explanations for the female menopause.

An immaterial spiritual force seems to have influenced the moulding of sexual organs and functions in a sensible, useful and far-sighted way. This force exists although we cannot perceive it with our senses. However, it helps us to gather wonderful sensual experiences – and I claim that it was exactly this that had always been the actual aim. In this context even the menopause can be considered to be a conscious gift to women since their life expectancy has increased slightly in comparison to that of their forbears.

I believe that this example of human sexuality makes it very clear again that any kind of evolution, even if it appears to be a merely materialistic one, is in reality embedded in a spiritual and obviously intelligent basic concept which evolves simultaneously and is constantly improved. All forms of life – physical and spiritual – are developed by evolution.

9. Extraordinary: the Psychogenic Death

Using the example of human sexuality I explained in the previous chapter how it is that the higher the level reached by the spirit the more qualities and characteristics evolution produces whose meanings and purposes can only be plausibly explained if viewed from an immaterial spiritual perspective. This becomes especially clear for me when the intention of human evolution seems to be to maximize pure pleasure. In this context, another aspect is also especially significant, in my opinion, i.e. the fact that all these new developments first appear in humans and, furthermore, that they are completely and immediately manifested.
None of these new inventions seems to be the result of a long evolutionary process.
Nor has there ever been an evolutionary test phase which one might expect for such complex combinations. Only the right combination of all these devices makes sexual pleasure perfect.
A completely different example of spiritual influence being exerted on evolution seems to be, in my opinion, the *"psychogenic death"*.
Unlike all animals, all humans know that one day they will die. Many people, especially today, believe that death is the definite end of their existence. If that were true then it would also be the end of an absolutely amazing, life-long process of spiritual maturing. The fact is that our body starts to deteriorate only a few years after we have reached adulthood. Its substance grows old and, of course, this process will inevitably end in

death one day. However, our spiritual and emotional abilities are not subject to this easily understandable process. This significant discrepancy, which I already discussed in detail in Chapter 5, makes for the difference between humans and animals. From the viewpoint of a (still) living person, death is surely a sudden and brutal interruption in the process of our spiritual maturing. I see it, however, as merely a short interruption at the most. *Pathologists* have known for a long time that there is a whole range of cases in which death cannot be attributed to a long illness, an accident, to homicide or suicide or to any other organic reason.

In many cases an acute cardiac arrest is suspected, although in the post-mortem the heart shows no adequate, pathological syndromes.

The physicist, psychologist and psychotherapist *Gary Bruno Schmid* examined some of these cases very closely.[75] In the preface to his book the pathologist *Professor Thomas Hardmeier* wrote: *"Psychological factors especially play an important role and determine without doubt the time of death."* The so-called "psychogenic death" seems to be induced by mental influences alone and is accomplished by the human powers of imagination. *Schmid* sees here the *"most dramatic example of the power imagination and language exert over human life.* And Habermeier says: *"The trigger mechanisms for a psychogenetic death are valid at all times and are anthropologically universal, they can also be called archetypical."* In the end comes the simple cardiac arrest. In the meantime, the American scientists *Phillips* and *Kwok* were able to confirm this cause of death by a study in which they analysed more than 200,000 such deaths, as even the renowned "Deutsche Ärzteblatt" *(the most important German Medical Magazine)* reported recently.[76]

If you go for a walk around a graveyard and you study the dates of death on the gravestones you will notice that very often spouses or close relatives died one after the other within a relatively short period of time. This happens especially often with elderly partners who were very close to one another in their old age. In popular belief people like to talk of a supernatural cause of death, in these specific cases of being *"drawn by the previously deceased."*

---

[75] G. B. Schmid, "Tod durch Vorstellungskraft" (2001), (*Death by the Power of Imagination* not translated), see List of References.
[76] Deutsches Ärzteblatt, 45 (2002)

We often see people who had, as I would like to call it, a deep emotional and intimate relationship with one another dying within a short period of time.

Somehow different is "a series of deaths" in which persons who are celebrities, for example, or who belong to the same kind of profession, e.g. famous politicians or actors, die within short periods of one another. This phenomenon can also be observed relatively often. After such a series there may be a long interval. Statisticians may consider this as an incidental accumulation and dismiss it as the law of sequence. And they may even be right in such cases.

But was it just coincidence, for example, that my father died on Valentine's Day 1996 and that several of his closest friends, bowling partners and skat partners and former colleagues died shortly before or after that date? It simply appeared as if they had "arranged" it previously. At least we should ask ourselves, *"whether death could not originate* (also) *in a supernatural, spiritual level of being"* as Gary Schmid puts it (I added the word "also" since Schmid himself quoted several possibilities in this context).

Some people died immediately on the day of a special anniversary, e.g. the birthday of a loved person who is already dead or on the day he or she died. Schmid talks of a typical "anniversary reaction". I believe that we saw two classical examples of this theory in the British Royal Family: On 7th February 2002 Princess Margaret, the sister of Queen Elizabeth II, died. Her dearly beloved father, King George VI, had died on 6th February, 50 years previously. Margaret died officially of a stroke. But why did it happen so closely to an important anniversary for the Royal Family, probably even on the very same day? We gain an insight as to how close Princess Margaret was to her father from her last will in which she laid down the terms of her funeral: Margaret was the first member of the Royal Family to be cremated.

The simple reason for her wish was that she also wanted to be buried in the royal vault. There was only enough space for one more coffin and that was reserved for the Queen Mother who was 101 years old at the time. Margaret, however, wanted to be in death as close to her father as possible and that was only feasible in an urn.

Her funeral was 50 years later on the same day as her father's. And only a few weeks later, on Easter Sunday, 30th March 2002, the Queen Mother, 101 years old, also died. Of course, at her age you have to reckon with death any day. However, the close temporal proximity to the death of her daughter was probably no mere coincidence.

Here are some more examples also belonging into this category of so-called anniversary reactions of probably psychogenic deaths which I experienced and which happened out of the blue without warning:

A few years ago the 100th birthday of my brother-in-law's uncle was approaching. He planned a nice party and he even insisted on preparing all the important details himself. However, the stress was too much for him. Two days before his birthday he died of sudden acute heart arrest. He had never been seriously ill before.

A lovely old lady from Essen told me a similar case. We met her and her husband in Brazil in November 1995 and we remained in friendly contact with them. Towards the end of the 2nd World War she had been saved from marauding soldiers and hidden for some time by a farmer's wife in the Bavarian mountains. A close friendship developed later between the two families. Some years ago when the farmer's wife was very nearly 100 years old she was asked whether she was looking forward to her special anniversary. Her laconic reply was: *"Not really, it won't do anything for me, it'll just cost my money."* Three months before her 100th birthday, although still relatively healthy, she died suddenly without any recognizable reason.

Another example I experienced is a psychogenic death due to "hopelessness in a desperate and helpless situation": In early 2002 my friend and colleague's brother-in-law, Mr W., died at just over 60 years of age. He also died suddenly. It happened during a tennis match in Africa where he had worked for a steel manufacturing company for several years. The typical diagnosis was heart attack. A routine check-up of the heart only a short time previously had not shown any heart problems. Certainly, something like this happens almost daily – but it only tells us that it might sometimes be worthwhile to study the exact attendant circumstances in a case of death. In this case the circumstances seem to point to a psychogenic death.

As long as Mr W. worked for his company he must have put a lot of effort into his work. He had been abroad for this company for many years in various places in Asia and Africa. Over the months prior to his death the company's economic performance deteriorated constantly. There were already rumours going around about staff cuts, although W.'s own future in the company did not yet seem to be jeopardized. Around the end of 2001 W. visited Germany. Without anybody consciously noticing – only after he had died did his relatives realize – W. made a complete round of "farewell visits". He even went to places he had not visited for years, in some cases for good reasons. He visited several relatives, his wife, his two grown-up children who no longer lived at home, friends, his house in Spain, he went everywhere – as if he did not expect to see any of these places ever again. He probably did not consciously notice his own strange behaviour. A few days before he died he received a peculiar fax. It seems as if someone of his company played a mean practical joke on him by informing him that he was fired as well. When he made inquiries the management told him that this was not correct. Whether this denial was true or just a temporary mollification I do not know. He himself did not live long enough to find out.

In this case the deceased seems to have lived over a long period of time in a state of unconscious and subliminal hopelessness and was tormented by fear. He probably felt helpless in a situation which possibly only appeared to be so desperate so that in the end he died a psychogenic death.

By the way, something else is remarkable: about fifteen years previously W.'s father had also died of a sudden heart attack while playing tennis. And only shortly after he died, his younger brother died. Shortly after W.'s death, his younger brother died too…

A well known phenomenon is certainly death due to homesickness from which, for example, many a soldier died during the last world wars at the front. The same is meant by the old adage: "You should not uproot and move an old tree." Often, old people die shortly after they move to a different place. This was the reason for the deaths of two of my three grandmothers[77]: They both died within a few weeks after they had deciding to move from their own home to a nursing home. There was no forewarning of their unexpected sudden death, they did not suffer from any kind of physical disease which would have indicated their imminent deaths. I suspect too that the death of my "third" grandmother was due to this phenomenon.[78] However, she died in 1962 and I was too young to become deeply involved with the circumstances of her death. Of course, I remember her well. She lived alone in her flat in Berlin and used to visit us in Cologne once a year in the fall for three months. After Christmas and New Year she usually went back. She never liked to say

---

[77] One of my grandfathers married twice, so that in addition to my two real grandmothers I had a third one whom I loved no less.
[78] My grandfather on my mother's side was married twice.

good-bye to us. Maybe that was the reason why she decided to retire from life. She died a few days before Christmas in our house.
The psychogenic death seems to have a mental cause.[79]
The question arises as to whether there could be a *"Darwinian perspective"*, as *Gary Schmid* calls it, or as I like to call it, an evolutionary reason or connection. Schmid explains it even further: *"What would be the advantage of a psychogenic death for the survival or for the propagation of Homo sapiens?"* In reply to this question he relates to the same reflections as I already did:
We may assume that modern humans possess the same neurophysiological and neuropsychological constitution as their ancestors who lived approximately 10,000 years ago as hunters and gatherers. All in all this adds up to about 400 human generations which is far too short a time for mutations to cause significant changes in the human constitution – which evolution biologists would expect.
This means that the psychogenic death must have already existed in those days. *Schmid* now concludes that in the prevailing social conditions in which the family groups lived, taking into account authority, prohibitions, the unity of the society and intuition as well as the anticipation of various social regulations and perceptions, the psychogenic death was a kind of conflict management. The compliance with certain rules and regulations and the subordination of the individual in almost symbiotically dependent relationships with, for example, the tribal chiefs or the magicians by avoiding taboos or by remaining behind in the clan's home region, etc. – was in Schmid's opinion necessary for the survival of the whole species. If disruptions occurred in these symbioses, so *Schmid*, the "profound human spirit" was free to separate itself from or defend itself against the death archetype and unconsciously force itself to choose death instead of life.
I cannot entirely follow *Schmid's* reasoning simply because he ignores or seems unaware of the new orientation of evolution which, in my opinion, is well verifiable:
As I already explained, we can show that, with the appearance of humans, evolution constantly strives towards individuality. With increasing clarity and succinctness it is the single human being alone, i.e. the individual instead of the collective group, which becomes first priority. And it is exactly this which defines the evolutionary advantage

---

[79] I also consider everything connected with "soul" or anything "mental" as originating in the spirit. For me the soul is the spirit of a human being which is finally differentiated at the time of his (physical) death.

of the spiritual creature "human being", as I explained in previous chapters. Only by individualization can evolution proceed on its way towards perfection and achieve such an otherwise unattainable variety. Each human individual strives for personal perfection while formerly this was the task of the entire collective species. This means that, with regard to humans, every possible Darwinian (or evolutionary) advantage is judged by the benefit the individual derives from it now. From this point of view *Schmid*'s ideas are of no importance.

Therefore, I believe that we must be consistent and draw a completely different conclusion: The psychogenic death of a human being – and we may be sure that such a thing exists – must offer an advantage to the individual since that is the actual aim and objective of "modern" human evolution.

The question arises now as to what advantage such a death could bring for the individual. Furthermore: to comply with the motives of evolution, such a death must offer an advantage in survival! However, this seems paradoxical:

Can death, the dreaded end of the human personality, really be an advantage in survival?

In my opinion the only plausible answer could be the following:

The death of a human being is not, as commonly assumed, the actual end of his personality. On the contrary, the life of every single human goes on after his mere physical death – immediately and directly!

The psychogenic death could thus be considered as a kind of conflict management in a situation which seems hopeless to the affected person at least, for whatever reason that may be.

It serves primarily the individual himself and not the species as a whole, and in the case of an overwhelming psychic threat it could even be considered as an evolutionary advantage for the survival of the individual.

Viewed like this, the psychogenic death is, I believe, an important indication that we survive our own deaths "by dying".

10. In the Shadow of Death

"I asked Jacob how he was. Without any hesitation at all he looked at me, smiled and said in joyful astonishment: 'I do not exist!' We smiled at one another; he squeezed my hand. His son, however, came closer and put his hand on Jacob's shoulder: 'Oh yes, you do exist. You are my father.' Jacob smiled at his son: 'Yes, I am your father.' 'You can be both, can't you, Jacob?' I added. His smile broadened and grew more radiant. 'Exactly!' he said."

The American hospice counsellor *Robert Sachs*[80] held this conversation with a desperately ill patient shortly before he died. These few words seem to be typical and significant for what happens to a person facing death if he is permitted (!) to experience consciously the last phase of his approaching death. You think it must be a punishment to look your own inexorably approaching death in the eye?

According to statistics the majority of humans would prefer to die suddenly, without prior notice, preferably while they are asleep. However, I believe that this wish is too short-sighted and we would be depriving ourselves of important experiences.

Those of us who have already accompanied a person on the last leg of his journey through life – in most cases this was presumably a close relative – will surely have experienced that, towards the end, the people had changed somehow: their personality clearly changes shortly before they die. Days, or at least some hours, before they die they seem to recognize *clearly* that they will soon be leaving their bodies behind.

"The suitcases are packed", said Martin to his mother only a few hours before he died at the far too early age of 31 due to a horrendous cancer disease.

Weeks before he and his family had learned that there was no hope of survival for him. His doctors had given up. When I heard about this by coincidence, I asked whether he would allow me to accompany him during his last few weeks. And so it came about that in many conversations I was able to convince him and his family that he should not be afraid because he would not really die.

---

[80] from: Robert Sachs, "Perfect Endings. A Conscious Approach to Dying and Death", Healing Arts Press, Rochester (1998), see List of References.

Martin passed away in 1996 with this absolute conviction. As an impressive example for me he proved that his approaching death was more like a kind of graduation for the human spirit and not its imminent destruction. Over only a few weeks he accumulated great wisdom. He saw the world in a completely new, different light – it was the view usually adopted by old people, supported by great composure, inner calmness and strength.

In January 1996 when my father went into hospital in Cologne, because his doctors had told him he urgently needed heart surgery, everyone in the family was convinced he would come home after a few weeks in good health. A few years previously he had already had to undergo surgery several times and his death seemed imminent. When he died 4 weeks after his heart surgery, we all recognized that, unlike the last time he had to go to hospital, this time he had carefully ordered and completed all the matters that seemed important to him down to the last detail before he left for the hospital. Furthermore, he had written a moving and deeply distressing letter of farewell to all of us in which he expressed his meanwhile *grown* deep conviction that we will all see one another again at some future time.

On the last Sunday before his operation all the family members came to the hospital to visit him as if by command although we had made no prior arrangement to do so. It was very rare even if it ever happened at all that my father was so spontaneously visited by all of us at the same time.

When I left him that day I suddenly felt a cold shower run down my spine while walking along the corridor. *"That's it!"* I thought and was at the same time shocked by my thoughts. Unfortunately I suppressed my thoughts in the same way as I had already disregarded the other strange signs which I had experienced during the previous days. In hindsight I am still convinced today that I had ignored a number of subtle indications which should have warned me about what was about to happen.

Due to a complication my father had to undergo surgery twice that same day, both within only a few hours. In the weeks that followed he only woke up a few times and, unfortunately, he was seldom, even for short periods, able to take up contact with us who visited him frequently. Since he was unable to breath of his own accord he had to be connected with a respirator. But even when he seemed to be in a deep coma and it appeared as if he were unable to notice anything – he registered everything as he often proved to me by the smallest movements of his eyes following direct questions.

In a fascinating book *Jean-Dominique Bauby*[81], formerly the chief editor of the French magazine "Elle", describes some of the time he spent in a coma before he died at the age of only 43. Yes, you have read correctly: he wrote a book although he spent more than a year in hospital and seemed unable to perceive his environment after having suffered a stroke in 1995 which seemed to have deprived him of all means of expression.

After having been in this condition for a long time it was only the attentive observance by some close relatives that made them aware that he was actually conscious and was able to register everything that was happening around him and, by weakly blinking his eyes, he finally even succeeded in responding to direct questions. With the help of a *speech therapist* an alphabet was agreed upon based on a new sequence of letters adjusted to their frequency in the French language. One blink meant the first letter, two blinks the second, and so on.

With a huge effort and utmost patience he was now able to describe his thoughts which made this book possible.

I was especially impressed by some paragraphs in which he mentions the behaviour of the nursing staff that did many things wrong because they were unaware that he was indeed fully conscious. There was, for example, an interesting football match on TV, but a nurse came in and just switched the TV set off. Of course the nurse thought the patient was unable to follow the match and as *Bauby* was incapable of telling him otherwise – he just became very angry.

In a similar way I was able to hold a "conversation" with my father. On his last birthday, only a few days before he died, he was obviously wide awake although he was still intubated[82] and unable to speak. Simply by blinking his eyes he gave me to understand he would probably not pull through. Since I had already devoted a lot of time to studying the subject of death and had long since become convinced that death was not the personal end of a human being, I asked him about his feelings and perceptions. I had to put the questions in such a way that he could answer with "yes" or "no".

By blinking his eyes and pressing my hand very lightly he answered my questions – albeit with great effort – rather unambiguously. It seemed to

---

[81] J.D. Bauby, "The Diving Bell and the Butterfly", Wheeler Pub (1977) see List of References.
[82] A tube in the windpipe for artificial respiration.

me that he had somehow gained an insight into his possible future. He even seemed to have a *choice* as to whether he wanted to go on living but remain handicapped, or to die and follow his parents, his two brothers and his many friends who had died before him. During this "conversation" it became clear to me that he had already decided for the second option.

However, I did not want to accept that at the time and during the last week of his life I took up my own fight against the unavoidable. I saw to it that he was moved to a different hospital and I asked a friend and specialist to help my father. In the end I had to give up.

On that last birthday tears ran down my father's face when I showed him a letter and a picture of my two sons who congratulated him and begged their beloved grandfather to get well again soon. That in this difficult decision he probably took the better of the two options became very clear to me later in a completely different way:

Two days before he died quite out of the blue I heard a melody for the first time with my inner ear. The tune was completely unknown to me – at least I did not know it consciously – it was as if I had composed it myself. I kept "hearing" this melody for the next two days but it always seemed to come from far away. The strange thing about it is that this melody for me always seemed somehow closely connected with my father. I still do not know how and why, but I seemed to have no choice. Later I learned that this melody was the chorus of a song which at that time was the latest hit. I "heard" the same melody again on the day my father died. But this time it suddenly seemed very loud, almost at full blast and very persistent...

On a table in the nurses' room which was only partitioned off from the intensive care unit by a curtain, stood a big radio. I was not the only one to notice during my visits that it was always tuned into the same radio station. My father's bed stood right next to it. As enquiries later showed, the radio station must have played this song, which I did not know previously, almost exactly at the same time when my father died and I "heard" without sound the song so penetratingly. It seemed as if it had reached me in Aachen...

It must have been about the time when my father's spirit drifted away.

I ask myself now, whether he tried to prepare me for this moment with this song and to inform me. He was still connected to the mobile kidney dialysis machine and the artificial respirator was still working. However, there were no longer any detectable signs of life when I visited him that afternoon. It was as if a long dead shell was connected to the life-support systems. Shortly afterwards the machines were switched off and his death was officially announced that evening.

The very next day the family met again in Cologne to prepare the funeral. I told my mother and my brothers and sisters of the song which I had heard so often only mentally during the last few days and I hummed it to them. But no one knew it. When the same evening my youngest sister telephoned her girlfriend she was almost transfixed when she suddenly recognized the song I had only hummed to her: her friend had a record playing in the background while she was on the phone. By this coincidence we all came to know the song *"Anywhere is"* by the Irish singer *"Enya"*, a name which at that time did not have any meaning for any of us.[83]

During the eight days between my father's death and his funeral whenever I *got into* my car to go to Cologne or back to Aachen this song was playing nearly every time on the car radio but only then. When some days after my father's death somebody gave me the record with this song, I read the words for the first time and the blood ran cold in my veins. The last words are:
"I took the turn and turned to – begin a new beginning – still looking for the answer – I cannot find the finish – it's either this or that way – it's one way or the other – it should be one direction – it could be on reflection – the turn I have just taken – the turn that I was making – I might be just beginning – I might be near the end".

Many people who are about to lose someone to whom they are very close experience strange phenomena around the time of the approaching death and a similar dramatic and sometimes confusing flood of feelings which they often find unbearable as *Robert Sachs* describes in his book. Death announces its approach – not only to the affected person.
In the same year 1996, only 7 months after my father had passed away, our "Auntie" died. For more than 40 years she had been part of our family. First she had helped to raise me and my brothers and sisters and, later, my own children. She loved us all and we all loved her very much.

---

[83] Meanwhile Enya has become famous especially with her song "Only Time", which has become the sad hymn of the barbaric terror attacks on the World Trade Centre in New York on 11th September 2001.

Of course, she was already 86 years old and her old age and health problems made life increasingly troublesome for her. But it was only when my father died, whom she had worshipped for such a long time, that her will to live broke.

Often enough I caught her mumbling to herself, why it had not been her who had died instead of my much younger father.

As she had already done for the last few years she wanted to spend the autumn holidays of 1996 again with us in the Bavarian mountains.

On the last but one Sunday in September 1996 I spontaneously went on my own to visit her. She asked me to open a certain drawer in which she kept her many photos. We looked at all her photos and suddenly I became conscious again that the atmosphere had become very strange in a way which can hardly be described.

Never before had we looked at her photos. To each one of them she told me a story now and together we remembered so many occasions we had experienced together. She also told me details of her childhood, her parents, her husband, whom I knew well, but who had been dead for 17 years. She also talked about his family and the details which decades ago had caused her nieces to emigrate to Uruguay and later to Australia, and two of her three children to emigrate to America. She talked about everything as if this were the last time that she would have the occasion to talk about such things. Actually, it was indeed to be the last time. And I had the same feeling that I had had months before when I left my father in his hospital bed just before his operation.

Later, when I said goodbye to "Auntie", she sat down in her wing chair. I hugged and kissed her. I briefly mentioned again our autumn holiday in Bavaria. I felt as if it was some kind of incantation which could quieten my inexplicable uneasy feeling, as if by talking about it I could already create facts.

She looked up at me inquiringly and just said: *"Who knows?"* *"What do you mean?"* I wanted to know and I can still see myself standing in front on her. She just shrugged with her shoulders, she did not say anything but with her left hand she pointed to the floor. It is clear to me that she seemed to have felt her own death approaching.

Two days later a neighbour found her lying on the floor in her house after she had not, as she usually did every morning, called on her that day. About lunch time in hospital she regained consciousness once more. Her son, Michael, and my wife were with her and she seemed, as they told me later, very relaxed and almost full of joy. She thanked both of them and smiled.

It seemed as if she saw things nobody else could see. When I finally arrived she unfortunately had already passed away.

In 1975 my father's mother, my beloved grandmother, died at the age of 81. Only a week previously she had moved to a nursing home near Cologne. Over the last few months she had been suffering from a horrendous old age dementia which sadly caused grotesque malfunctions at the very end.

My parents had last visited her the day before she died. I remember very well how my father told me enthusiastically that same evening that she had seemed so mentally clear this time. She thanked my parents for everything they had done for her. She asked them to pass on her thanks to us, her grandchildren and talked about a number of things that were important to her and which she obviously wanted to settle.

Alzheimer's disease and dementia are not mental illnesses but rather the result of destruction in the brain. Passages are blocked and instruments in the brain are damaged, those very devices of the brain through which the spirit communicates with the body and its external surroundings. I supposed that there are really only very few real mental illnesses exist, one of them is probably a bad character.

A person with an advanced brain disease had after all succeeded in settling important things at the very last, decisive moment. Many of us may have experienced something similar. With regard to the facts and the timing it is incomprehensible how (too) many brain scientists can presently still consider the human spirit as a mere product of the brain, a so-called epiphenomenon.

I cannot help but think that a brain-independent spirit under time pressure had searched desperately for a possible way to settle open questions and unsolved problems with the defect tool "brain" while there was still time.

Just imagine, the engine of your car breaks down on the motorway at night. The car is rather old anyway and a new one has already been ordered. All you want is just to get home with the old car. Well, you know a bit about cars and you take a look at the engine. You feel sure it can be fixed in a makeshift way without much trouble so that it would at least take you the last few kilometres home. All you need is, maybe, a nylon stocking to replace the fan-belt. So you fix the engine and drive home under your own steam.

What happened? *You* yourself succeeded in repairing the car; your car did not repair itself! Maybe this example is a bit too bold and simple but in principle it is correct. But let us go back to my grandmother.

There were several strange circumstances which bothered me on Wednesday, 20th August 1975. During the night before already I experienced a number of strange coincidental happenings just when I wanted to visit my grandmother. I could not get into my car because I had forgotten the key inside and had slammed the door shut. Then I was unable to get hold of the second key. When I had finally borrowed another car I found I could drive off because the neighbouring house was on fire and the fire brigade had blocked the road. In the end I managed to get hold of the second key to my car. I sped away, but just then the engine of my car broke down and I had to be towed away. It was impossible; I had to postpone my visit until the next day, the 20th August 1975.

At the time I was still completing my practical training in a hospital in Cologne. For the first and only time my radio alarm clock let me down that morning although it was set correctly. It is still doing its job very reliably today, by the way, and this one single failure is one of the main reasons why I still use it today, 30 years later.

Understandably, I overslept for several hours.

I finally arrived in the nurses' room of my ward, clad in my white cloak, rather flustered, in a hurry and – as my father liked to say – "far away from home". The very first thing I did, inadvertently of course, was to knock over a tray loaded with dozens of carefully sorted pillboxes containing various pills and medicines.

Everything ended up as a huge mess all over the floor.

The room full at the time with nurses and doctors all having their breakfast break and I got it from all sides almost in chorus: *"My God, Walter!"* There was a hit at the top of the German charts at the time with exactly that title. [84]

As I had started late I had to work longer that day which seemed very hard to me. I could not concentrate on my work and I kept thinking of my grandmother and godmother. Although she had been quite well the day before and her life did not seem to be in danger, I was intuitively

---

[84] "Mein Gott Walter" by the German singer and comedian Mike Krüger

very concerned and I wanted to go and visit her immediately after I finished work. Shortly before I finished my longer working hours I received the sad news by telephone that my grandmother had just died.

These few incomplete and very private examples show how approaching death can cause a whole host of strange phenomena, in the dying person as well as in his direct environment – and especially in those persons who have been very close. All these experiences are of a purely spiritual nature.

The thoughts and the behaviour of the affected persons but also the whole atmosphere is influenced in a strange way. I would even talk of unusual atmospheric tensions. Many things obviously happen subconsciously and very often we only recognize with hindsight how strange some things were. Other processes are consciously experienced and realized early on, especially by those persons affected by the approaching death. When the actual end is near, even those who had been terrified of this moment all their lives seem to have lost their fear.

Yet, this is by no mere sign of resignation or of submission to an inexorable fate. On the contrary, towards the end almost all dying persons with whom we can still talk shortly before they pass away show neither fear nor pain. Often they perceive bright lights which are approaching, they see people who have already died and they talk about them or with them or they relive events of times long past. For them, however, everything seems to be absolutely authentic, as if it was happening now. They thank their relatives and friends and usually they cannot understand why everyone looks so sad.

They avidly want to settle still open matters and they are mostly calm and composed, often even relaxed and cheerful.

For me it is also amazing that the direct environment of a dying person is very often subject to a number of events and processes which are usually of a subtly atmospheric nature. And this applies not only to cases when, due to various circumstances, one might expect death to be drawing near.

By the way, this is not the exclusive privilege of *humans* who are close to the dying person; very often pets are the first to notice something.

11. On the Threshold: Near-Death Experiences

"I knew a man in Christ above fourteen years ago, (whether in the body, I cannot tell; or whether out of the body, I cannot tell;
God knoweth;) such a one caught up to the third heaven.
And I knew such a man (whether in the body, or out of the body,
I cannot tell; God knoweth;)
How that he was caught up into paradise, and heard unspeakable words, which it is not lawful for a man to utter." [85]

These lines appear in the second Epistle of the Apostle Paul to the Corinthians. They probably describe the experience which converted him to Christianity. Originally his name was Saul and he was a bitter opponent and persecutor of Christians. After the vision he experienced, known as the Easter experience, he famously and quite suddenly reformed himself completely changing his personality and his behaviour. No one can tell us exactly today what it was that he saw in his vision. However, there is good reason to assume that Paul had a near-death experience (NDE). He is one of a long list of those people who, based on such extraordinary borderline experiences between life and death – or better: between the physical manifestation and the purely spiritual existence – have founded practically all religions in this world since the beginning of mankind. In the course of his NDE, Paul had an out-of-body experience (OBE). During this experience, to his complete amazement, he had been absolutely convinced of his own physical integrity. At the same time, however, this completely contradicted his beliefs and his experience of life which cast him into serious self-doubt. Paul was obviously unable to comprehend his condition. His great confusion is reflected, I believe, by the repetition – *"whether in the body, I cannot tell; or whether out of the body, I cannot tell; God knoweth."*
His personal experience enabled him to glimpse a paradisiacal world beyond.
Between a third and half of all people who have escaped death by a hair's breadth say they have experienced an NDE.

---

[85] The Bible, New Testament, II. Corinthians, 12.2-4

Over the last 30 years such cases have been examined systematically by various researchers. For this work we have to thank some very courageous scientists, such as *Elisabeth Kübler-Ross, Raymond Moody, Melvin Morse* and *Kenneth Ring.* They can certainly be described as courageous since, in extremely difficult times, they dared to contradict the purely materialistic perceptions of natural scientists of the time. Their examinations made clear that such materialism must obviously be wrong. They experienced the same as many "exotic" scientists before them: at first they were completely ignored and were not taken seriously. Even today, their findings, although confirmed in the meantime by thousands of reliable studies, are at best met with dismissive smiles but, often enough, with ridicule.

While for some the survival after death has already been proven by NDEs, others try to show that they are some kind of protecting reflex of the brain, practically a conciliatory farewell gift of evolution. Such people tell us that, just before we pass away, NDEs delude us into believing that there is a paradisiacal world beyond, thereby taking away our fear as our existence draws to its inexorable end. However, the question is never put forward as to *"why"* evolution should create this delusion – if it is one – which is so completely unnecessary for the survival of the human species.

In this chapter I will restrict myself to merely describing the phenomena of near-death experiences (NDEs) and will only discuss them superficially, if at all.

A more detailed and critical study will follow later in the second part of this book in the discussion with my two sons.

As we know, humans are the first creatures to be aware of their own "death" and that the inexorable consequence thereof is the total destruction of at least their bodies. Therefore, we could say that humans suffer the worst fate of all, compared to animals which live completely "carefree" and unaware of this fact. Being the only species with knowledge of their own "death", humans are already punished from birth.

The above mentioned "parting present" would not change anything since it would always come too late.

Or is it not rather as I claim: that one cardinal aspect of human evolution right from the beginning is the intuitive knowledge that death is not the final end.

Thus humans are treated justly. Yet, they are not prepared to accept this knowledge because they did not engender it themselves.

It was probably the knowledge of the inexorability of our own death which in truth lies behind the original sin claimed by the Catholic Church. With the act of christening, people are freed from this sin because they join the Christian congregation of *believers*. To be a believer means, however, to believe that our soul will go on living in eternity. Thus we are freed of our originally insurmountable *burden* which only humans inherit solely because they are human. So the original sin is not so much a real sin as a burden. Religious thought is again meant to help us so long as we can accept the possibility of intuitive experience as being a source of knowledge and as long as we are prepared to accept a kind of "balance of power" between religion and science, as being a world of sensory perceptions and the source of knowledge.

Philosophy being the world of conscious thought, would regain the status it was meant to have as a reasonable mediator between the two antipodes of religion and science. This is supported by the following remark made by the German poet and theologian, *Johann Christian Friedrich Hölderlin: „Oh, man is a king when he dreams – a beggar when he thinks."*

History is full of NDEs, but at the present time the number of experiences seems to be increasing. There are various reasons for this. On the one hand the world is becoming smaller and the media are disseminating information – preferably sensational news – within the shortest time – which for a long time included NDEs. On the other hand, modern emergency medical care is much more adept at bringing people "back to life".

Those affected, however, are usually very careful when reporting their experiences. And in most cases that is the better choice, after all, even today, they still have to reckon with scorn and derision and, more often than not, they are dismissed as exotic nut-cases or mentally disturbed, hallucinating fools. In any case, the fear that they may be disadvantaged during their future physical life is usually intense and they often keep quiet about their experience. Many a professional career could otherwise be wrecked prematurely.

The scientists I mentioned above, who have studied NDEs over the last decades, all live in the USA. This is certainly a good indication that we evidently find more openness and tolerance in that society in general and especially for such inexplicable phenomena. There is an association in the USA known as IANDS[86] which facilitates the systematic collection of vast quantities of detailed data on NDEs and to coordinate the findings of various programs all over the country in which these phenomena are studied. There is also a branch of IANDS in Germany. Its president is the Heidelberg psychiatrist *Michael Schröter-Kunhardt* who kindly wrote the foreword to the third volume of my last series.

In 1992 *Kenneth Ring* estimated that 8 million Americans have had a near-death experience. In Germany the estimated number is approximately 3.3 million.[87] Some estimates are much higher.

Almost all scientists agree that, although each single near-death experience is different and there are great variations, a number of their key issues are identical, almost stereotypical, which enables comparison. Furthermore, they are universal and completely independent of the age of those experiencing them or of their cultural or religious backgrounds. Even children experience the same as adults. Blind or deaf people who have experienced NDEs could hear or see the same acoustic or optical phenomena as those without such handicaps.

Not all experiences are equally complete. Many of them contain only some, or sometimes only incomplete, elements of a complete "ideal-NDE".

I would like to quote a paragraph from *Raimond Moody's* book in which he describes a complete NDE. This will give me a basis for further discussion. This paragraph describes all the elements which typically occur during an NDE:

" A man is dying and, as he reaches the point of greatest physical distress, he hears himself pronounced dead by his doctor. He begins to hear an uncomfortable noise, a loud ringing or buzzing, and at the same time feels himself moving very rapidly through a long dark tunnel. After this, he suddenly finds himself outside of his own physical body but still in the immediate physical environment, and he sees his own body from a distance, as though he is a spectator. He watches the resuscitation attempt from this unusual vantage point and is in a state of emotional upheaval.

After a while, he collects himself and becomes more accustomed to his odd condition. He notices that he still has a "body", but one of a very different nature and with very different powers from the physical body he has left behind. Soon other things begin to

---

[86] IANDS = International Association for Near Death Studies. Established in 1981 at Connecticut University by Kenneth Ring, Bruce Greyson and John Audette. Meanwhile, branches of this association exist in other countries.
[87] H. Knoblauch et al., "Todesnähe: Wissenschaftliche Zugänge zu einem außergewöhnlichen Phänomen", (not translated yet: *Proximity of Death. A Scientific Approach to an Extraordinary Phenomenon"*, see List of References).

happen. Others come to meet and to help him. He glimpses the spirits of relatives and friends who have already died, and a loving, warm spirit of a kind he has never encountered before – a being of light – appears before him. This being asks him a question, nonverbally, to make him evaluate his life and helps him along by showing him a panoramic, instantaneous playback of the major events of his life. At some point he finds himself approaching some sort of a barrier or border, apparently representing the limit between earthly life and the next life. Yet, he finds that he must go back to the earth, that the time for his death has not yet come. At this point he resists, for by now he is taken up with his experiences in the afterlife and does not want to return. He is overwhelmed by intense feelings of joy, love and peace. Despite his attitude, though, he somehow reunites with his physical body and lives.
Later he tries to tell others, but he has trouble doing so. In the first place, he can find no human words adequate to describe these unearthly episodes. He also finds that others scoff, so he stops telling other people. Still, the experience affects his life profoundly, especially his view about death and its relationship to life."

Not all near-death experiences contain all of these elements. However, in general the following phases can be systematized:

1) Leaving the body: At the moment of his "clinical death" a human being leaves his physical body. This is known as an "out-of-body experience" or "OBE".

Such OBEs can also occur, as well as other elements of NDEs, in non-life-threatening situations. This has in the meantime been proved in experiments. Therefore, they are not a definite sign of approaching death. In the case of a real NDE, however, OBEs are typical and are experienced regularly. They have still not been explained in a plausible scientific way, especially when a change of locality is involved. They can be easily verified so that we may consider them as being some of the most important indications for an NDE.

During an OBE, the affected person sees the body he has left behind from the outside, while sometimes "floating under the ceiling". Usually the people can describe exactly and in great detail their environment and the doctors and nurses who are treating them and their actions. Very often they are even able to repeat the exact words of those who were helping to save their lives.

Especially impressive are those cases in which the affected person has moved away from the place of the actual event. He usually notices that physical objects, like walls or people are no longer obstacles for him.

Later, he can usually give exact descriptions of objects in another room or objects in general that are far away from his body, which proves that he must have seen them or heard about them.[88] Often he seeks to console or comfort mourning relatives. He tries, for example, to influence doctors and nurses, and he sometimes even tries to hinder their attempts at bringing him "back to life". But he notices soon that they cannot hear or see or feel him, and he becomes rather confused.[89] He considers everything he experiences during his excursion as being absolutely real.

He has not the slightest doubt in his own physical integrity, i.e. he is convinced that he is still in his body.

The fact that he can also see his (physical) body, confuses him and gives him a feeling of insecurity. He notices that the consistency of his present body is completely different from his usual body.

In esoterism the term "ethereal matter" has been established. I think this term describes the phenomenon perfectly.

The most famous and authentic example for such an out-of-body experience was reported by the famous heart surgeon *Christiaan Barnard* from Cape Town, South Africa, who has died in the meantime:

While undergoing treatment himself in hospital, an old woman came to his bedside. She seemed rather confused. He could describe her later in detail. Everything was absolutely real for him. A short time later she disappeared. It was established later that this woman had died shortly before she appeared at Dr. Barnard's bedside. This was a rare example in which the "spiritual body" of an already deceased person is perceived by someone who is "still alive".

Normally, a person experiencing a near-death experience is invisible for "still living" humans. On rare occasions, an OBE is at first accompanied by a feeling of disorientation and sometimes even by fear. In most cases, however, this passes quickly.

2) The tunnel experience: While an OBE is often accompanied at the beginning by unpleasant noises this soon changes. The spiritual body stays in the room for a while observing his (physical) body and all the activity taking place around it. After some time it may glide through a

---

[88] Of course, there is also the possibility to make contact by so-called extra-sensory perception waves (EPWs), as animistic parapsychologists believe. More about this in the next chapter.
[89] This could explain the words of the Bible which I quoted at the beginning of this chapter and which are so strangely repeated twice.

kind of long and dark tunnel or corridor. In some cases this is described as an unpleasant experience. Usually the gliding is experienced as being very fast, sometimes even extremely fast. Furthermore, the unpleasant noise often noticed at the beginning may be heard during the passage. Not long after, however, beautiful and harmonic melodies can be heard. People then feel light, carefree and almost relieved. They are no longer in pain.

3) The light after the tunnel: After the person has passed the tunnel or corridor, he usually sees a radiant bright light which, however, is never unpleasant. He is irresistibly attracted by it. When he reaches the light he is almost always overwhelmed by a feeling of unbelievable happiness. Sometimes people describe the light itself as being a kind of personality. Therefore it is often called a "being of light". Depending on the cultural or religious background, the being of light is interpreted in different ways. Some people see Jesus in it or Mother Mary, others see the gods or prophets they worshipped all their lives.

Always the being of light is absolute love personified. During this encounter most people feel in absolute harmony with themselves and their environment. They feel peace, overwhelming joy and an indescribable, deep happiness.

4) The reception or welcome: Usually the person now sees close relatives and loved ones who passed away before him. It is quite amazing that people seen in this phase are without exception already dead, "still" living people never appear. This is a fact confirmed in all studies.

The person is usually met and made welcome by relatives, friends and acquaintances. In a number of well-investigated cases, the person was actually met by people who he assumed to be still alive when embarking on his near-death experience. Only later, after his "return" to his body, was it established that the person he had encountered had indeed died in the meantime completely unbeknown. *Elisabeth Kübler-Ross* describes such an example: Two befriended girls were taken ill with a bad infection when still children. One of the girls died of this infection. Shortly afterwards the other girl had a near-death experience and saw her friend who was already dead. Nobody had up till then informed her of her friend's death in the hope that her recovery would not be jeopardized. She found out about it by her near-death experience.

Sometimes the person recognizes people only because he has seen pictures of them; long-dead ancestors, for example, whom he could never have met during his earthly life.

It also happens that persons are received by obviously very kind people none of whom they recognize. Only after their "return to life" are they able to identify them from old photo albums, probably covered in dust, as being long-deceased close relatives.

5) The panoramic review of ones life: After a short time (subjectively speaking), often in the presence of the being of light, the person sees a kind of three-dimensional display of visual imagery in which all the important events of his former life are recapitulated (life review).

While this film is being played the person realizes for the first time which events in his life were really important. Often they are incidents which he himself had not regarded as being especially significant.

During this process the person himself is at the same time both actor and observer. He sees scenes of his life in which he was especially good and helpful to others, but also events to which he had reacted inappropriately, behaved in the wrong way or even badly. He is embarrassed about his bad behaviour but pleased with the good deeds he did. However, he alone judges and must judge his own deeds. Furthermore, he not only sees what he has done but he also recognizes the consequences of his deeds for others. He obtains thereby a grand overview over all the consequences of his earthly activities. At no time does he have the feeling of being "condemned" by someone else, by the being of light, for example, who is present. The person concerned always judges himself. Furthermore, he is especially receptive to experiencing the feelings of others who had to suffer the consequences of his earthly actions as if he were experiencing them himself. He will experience all the pain he caused others in his "life time". While watching the film the being of light stays with him and, with its love, it helps him to enjoy his successes and to come to terms with his failures. The aim of this process seems to be not so much the person's punishment, but more his rueful regret followed by the promise to mend his ways.

6) The feeling of overwhelming love: Anyone who has experienced at least some of these stages or phases is deeply impressed by the perception of an omnipresent overwhelming love. This is especially true when he must relive unpleasant or even the most dastardly events in his

own life. Raimond Moody wrote on this: *"Have you learned to love? Almost everyone is asked this question during their near-death experience"*. I can confirm this from my own experiences. And Moody adds that after their return to our world nearly everyone says that love is the most important thing in life.
It is the most important reason for our being here in this world.

7) The terminal phase of an NDE: After this deeply moving experience, which is always perceived as being absolutely real, although not usually of traumatic character, something else happens which is usually experienced in very different ways.
In general, these events herald the commencement of the final phase of the NDE: the person may see a kind of "City of Light". It may also be beautiful paradisiacal landscapes. The most striking detail about these images is that they are always seen in vibrant colours which are usually described in great detail. The persons even agree that in their previous lives they had never seen such beautiful and clear colours.
Therefore, they have difficulty in describing the images in their entirety. This applies especially to the City of Light. The beholders emphasize again and again how the brilliant light is always present but never unpleasant.
Many people discern bustling activity in this City of Light. At the same time they have the impression of being able to understand everything and also of knowing everything. They recognize that they are part of this immeasurably great and harmonic whole without being able to describe it in more detail later. The knowledge obtained during their experience is usually lost when they return to their earthly life. Only the feeling remains that they once possessed absolute knowledge.
Soon after, the person reaches a kind of border or limit. It could be a fence, a hedge or a river. He may notice familiar people on the other side waving to him or even beckoning him over. The person seems to "know" intuitively that there can be no going back if he once crosses the border.

8) The return: Some people report later that, when they had reached the border in the final phase of their NDE, they were absolutely free in their decision to cross it, thereby leaving their former lives truly and finally behind them.

Others report that they would have very much liked to cross the border, but their resolve to do so was weakened by some power "beyond". Others again report that they were prevented from crossing to the other side in a rather rough way. A number of persons asked for permission to go back because they had young children waiting for them to come home, for example, although for themselves they would have preferred to stay.

In most instances the return itself is very abrupt and happens rapidly. The person instantaneously finds himself in his physical body again and feels the same pain as before.

For every person this experience feels extremely real and is in no way comparable to a dream. Carefully the person tries to talk about his experience with friends and sometimes with doctors or nurses.

In most cases, however, he receives the impression that nobody really believes his experience was real. He is told that he had been in a coma and that he had hallucinated. Therefore, people often prefer to keep quiet about their experiences.

9) Life changes: A near-death experience by no means ends with the return to the physical body. On the contrary, it usually has an enormous influence on the subsequent lives of those experiencing them; this is another amazing and very important fact. Hardly anyone who remembers his experience right from the beginning[90] will ever forget it. It is a deep incision in the life of an individual. Almost without exception the people concerned are absolutely convinced that they crossed the threshold of death and that they really did glimpse the world beyond.

Hardly anyone can be talked out of his absolute conviction – no matter who tries to persuade them. Such people look benignly upon the current theories of natural science, according to which there must be one or more strictly materialistic explanations for all these events. They remain quite impartial. Those who have experienced an NDE almost always take a distinctly changed attitude or approach towards their physical lives: they remain much calmer and more composed, even when they experience bad knocks in life. They feel closer than ever to nature and to other people and often their character changes drastically. This closeness

---

[90] Between a third to a half of those persons who have been very close to death can remember their experience. In the dialogue I will discuss the reasons why 50%-70% cannot remember anything.

makes them develop a greater responsibility towards everything in their environment.

Their wish to attain greater knowledge and wisdom, and to impart it and use it to help others, increases noticeably. However, they do not try to convert other people in an importunate manner. They rather leave it to people to decide for themselves whether they want to join them in their new outlook on life or not. They know that everyone of us will go through the same experience one day. They are no longer afraid of death which they know will actually come their way one day. They are convinced that they know how it will be --- namely exactly as they were already allowed to experience it once.

They no longer strive egoistically for power, money and success. This does not mean that these attributes have become absolutely unimportant for them, but they consider the way towards these aims in a more composed, relaxed manner and with much more patience than before. They abstain from joining the prevailing "me-first" mentality and they see everything with much more love.

After several decades of research dedicated to the subject of NDEs *Elisabeth Kübler-Ross* was sure that physical death is not the end of a human life.

During an interview[91] in 1998 Elisabeth Kübler-Ross said the following: *"Yes, I still say: death does not exist. Death is only a transition into another frequency and a wonderful experience. Life is much more complicated than death. There is no reason for being afraid of death."* Later she stated that nobody dies alone.

For every person passing away there are people waiting *"beyond"* who have been closest to him or her. *"We can do research on this. Many dying people have told me about it. This is no fantasy. But doctors are afraid of this truth."* She also gives advice concerning the general attitude to life which reflects the composure of people who went through a near-death experience: *"Enjoy your life, dance more often, eat Swiss chocolate[92] and do not just work all the time. In Switzerland I was educated according to the principle: work, work, work. You are only a valuable member of society if you work a lot. That is absolutely wrong. One half of your life you must work and the other half you must dance: that is the right mixture! I myself have danced too little and played too little!"*

---

[91] Her interview partner was the television presenter and author of books Dr. Franz Alt.
[92] Professor Elisabeth Kübler-Ross was born in Switzerland and – upon her marriage to an American – emigrated to the USA.

I believe that this is a very important and wise cognition of a wonderful scientist who unfortunately died on August 24, 2004. I had the pleasure to have a telephone conversation with her myself a few years ago.

12. Mysterious Phenomena

A great number of books deal with inexplicable phenomena. Before going any further I refer to relevant literature on the subject. You will find some interesting examples mentioned in the List of References to this book – none of which should be construed as any kind of evaluation on my part; not everything seems to me to be reliable.

In this chapter I will therefore only report of some phenomena I experienced in my own personal environment. Most of these events were closely related to the deaths of close friends or relatives.

I assure you that all the events I describe here are authentic. However, this can only mean that everything happened in the way I describe them and that, even after careful consideration, I myself cannot find a different explanation for them.

Parapsychologists differentiate between *telepathy* and *telekinesis*, often also known as *psychokinesis*. Telepathy describes the full range of purely spiritual communication, while psychokinesis or telekinesis covers all forms of spiritual influence on matter. *Animists* among the parapsychologists believe that the spirit is traditionally connected with the brain. A not yet exactly defined area in the brain, which animists like to locate in the right hemisphere of the brain, sends *extra-sensory perception waves (EPWs)* which are meant to travel to another person.

Animists assume the existence of an – as yet unknown – effect produced by a physical organ, the brain.

The question remains open as to whether this effect is something physical itself for which scientists have not yet found any proof – similar to gravitons which are assumed to exist but which have not yet been found.

Or is it something of a completely different quality, namely something immaterial? For animists, however, the brain remains the sole domicile of the human personality. When the brain dies, therefore, the personality is lost and with it the ability to send EPWs. In fact, precognition does indeed seem possible and explainable: such EPWs are assumed to travel into the future and to bring information back from there.

Spiritualists play only a secondary role today.

They believe traditionally that real, purely spiritual powers which are not linked to matter, such as a brain, exert an influence. Spiritualists believe that spirit and brain are two completely different issues. For them the spirit of a deceased person remains in existence after physical death and may continue to influence events in the physical world.

The opinion of modern physicists and biologists completely contradicts all these perceptions: non-physical causes for unexplainable phenomena do not exist.

A number of these experiences are not verifiable anyway. Others are misinterpretations, and many are just due to the imagination running wild. Often they are based on blatant fraud, sometimes perhaps with the objective of impressing other people. Any connection between a verified but still implausible phenomenon and, for example, the simultaneous death of a person, are considered as being of purely coincidental nature. The Swiss psychologist and psychiatrist *Carl Gustav Jung*, a student of *Sigmund Freud*, coined the term *coincidences* for this phenomenon.

In the opinion of scientists, phenomena, even if inexplicable as yet, must at some time or other become explainable on the basis of the confirmed (materialistic) view of the world – if not now, then later.

Psychologists like to explain these phenomena as projections of one's own subconscious or as an access to the *archetypes* of a collective unconscious.[93] Without expressly admitting it, they are poles apart from the current materialistic view of the world with their explanations, since the very foundations on which their theories are based are just as unproven.

In my opinion, these explanations are no more advanced than those put forward by the purely spiritistic camp. That would leave only the following two alternative hypotheses:

Either, we fully accept the current scientific view of the world, in which case all discussion about spirit, soul, survival after physical death, etc. are

---

[93] The theory of the "collective unconscious" was introduced by the Swiss psychiatrist Carl Gustav Jung, see Glossary. It means the entirety of human experience.

ludicrous and without serious foundation. Should anyone experience inexplicable phenomena, then they should be filed away under the categories of dreams, imagination, misinterpretation or coincidental temporal parallelism (coincidence). It would be best just to forget all about them in order not to become unnecessarily irritated.

Or, we believe that these phenomena could indeed happen as immaterial but real events and we refer to the historically known and still existing limits of natural science.

Has it not been demonstrated often enough in the past that most theories and perceptions of the world have had to be revised again and again, i.e. they are subject to constant changes or adjustments. Why should this be any different today?

In this case, however, psychological and parapsychological theses should, in principle, have the same value without falling prey to arbitrariness; they are both based on unconfirmed foundations – and in all cases immaterial dimensions, such as spirit, soul or psyche, collective unconscious, etc., are involved.

Therefore, the question arises which of these theses seems to be more *rational*. In my opinion, we can only arrive at an adequately well-founded decision if we consider the whole context. First of all, we have to inform ourselves of the limits of single fields of science and to leave them behind us. For this reason we must try to gather all the really confirmed knowledge available so that the basis for our explanations is made as broad as possible. We should not be afraid of trying to reconcile the various fields of science without constantly keeping an eye on the purely materialistic explanations of contemporary natural science.

This is the basic intention of all my previously published books. I am convinced that a spiritual dimension exists in this world and that it is independent of any physical manifestation, is all-encompassing and omnipresent.

Furthermore, the physical world is absolutely essential for the self-awakening of the spirit. In other words, it is due to the assistance of the physical world alone that enabled the previously totally undifferentiated and unstructured spiritual "waste land" to finally develop into a differentiated, fully structured and highly complex spiritual entirety, and to be distributed over as many, and as great a variety of individuals as possible.

In this way, due to the cooperation of us all, a new "God" develops, as *Pierre Teilhard de Chardin* expressed it. Since, under this premiss, the individual diversity is a basic requirement, a *conditio sine qua non*, we are constantly surrounded by self-confident and individual "spiritual beings". In my opinion, therefore, a *spiritualistic* explanation seems to be the most reasonable one. Based solely on this argumentation I believe that I am right when I assume that there are *causal* and not only coincidentally parallel *(contingent* and *correal)* connections between an unexplainable event and the simultaneous death of a person who is very close to us.

Of course, I want to make clear that other explanations are indeed possible if we base our consideration on a different view of the world.

As regards my own experiences I invite any physicist to offer plausible explanations which agree with his own current view of the world. Should the answer, however, indicate that such phenomena are dubious or non-existent, then I would reject it.

I am certainly no clairvoyant. On the contrary, my family is usually rather amused when I try to forecast the weather for our next garden party. They think that in all probability the weather will be completely different from my forecast. Unfortunately, I also tend to buy shares at the wrong time. If I were a clairvoyant that would not happen. By carefully observing some of the basic rules of the stock exchange and by holding on to certain shares long enough I have, thank goodness, usually been able to compensate my bad timing. In this way I made the same experience as the famous Hungarian stock-market expert *André Kostolany* who died in 1999 at the age of 93: when he was asked how he managed to earn his fortune on the stock-exchange he answered that 49% of his speculations ended in a loss, but 51% brought a profit – and the difference was sufficient.

Without claiming to be especially mediumistic, I must admit that often and spontaneously I have had momentary impressions which remained inexplicable. I will discuss some of them in this chapter.

Early one morning, when I was 13 years old the doorbell rang at my parent's house in Cologne. I woke up, got out of bed and saw my father opening the door. I heard voices but was unable to understand the words. When my mother saw me standing there she came to me and took me into her arms. Spontaneously I said to her: *"Uncle Alfred is dead."* And I was right. My father's younger brother had had a car accident and had died that night. A policeman had rung the doorbell to let my father know the terrible news. What was the matter with me?

At the beginning of the seventies of the last century I spent my holidays as I often did on the Dutch North Sea coast. One day I was swimming alone in the sea off the island of Noord-Beveland. In the distance I could see some huge concrete pillars which were intended to carry a causeway between the islands of Noord-Beveland and Schouwen-Duiveland. Later on it was decided to build a gigantic flood barrier which for many people is the "Eighth Wonder of the World".
Although I was a good swimmer, I realized that I had swum too far into the open sea. I realized too late that the current was carrying me towards the concrete pillars. I remember that I tried frantically to swim against the current. But my efforts seemed to be in vain. The current was stronger than I was. Suddenly I very clearly heard a calm, strong male voice. I still do not know from whence it came since I was quite alone.
I did not just hear my own thoughts, what I heard was a real acoustic perception. A psychiatrist would call it an acoustic hallucination. But this term explains nothing since it gives no information about the source of the perception. However, this voice calmed me down instantly. It advised me not to keep trying to swim back, but to swim diagonally to the current and to use the current to take me back to the beach before I reached the pillars. I did exactly as I was told and was thus able to reach the beach a long distance away from the point from where I had set off. I was extremely relieved that nothing untoward had happened to me and I walked all the way back along the deserted beach. In the course of my life I have heard this voice several times (!) each time when finding myself in situations of mortal danger which I was then able to master. What causes such "hallucinations" occurring at the right time and offering the right solution?

In March 1993 Hannelore, a daughter of our beloved "Auntie", died at the age of only 56 while undergoing heart surgery. She had lived in the USA for the last 30 years and already had children and grandchildren of her own. Our families were very close.
We had often visited one another. It was already evening in Germany when she was taken to the operating theatre.
There was a program showing on TV with Uri Geller who became famous during the eighties due to his claims of being able to bend silver spoons and to repair broken clocks solely by the power of his thoughts.

In the course of the program he asked the viewers in front of their screens at home to place broken clocks in front of the TV-screen. My wife and I watched the program and we laughed about it. I remembered that I still had a wall clock and an old radio set which were both broken and had stubbornly and successfully "resisted" several professional efforts to repair them. I had meant to throw them away long since. For a laugh I fetched them and placed them on a chair in front of the TV-set. By the end of the program, as expected, nothing had happened – both, the clock and the radio remained broken. About two hours later I went to bed after having taken a last look at the two defective items. Still nothing had happened, as was only to be expected.

At about three o'clock in the morning, we woke up with a start because the telephone was ringing. Bill, Hannelore's husband, had phoned to inform us of the sad news that his wife had died during the operation. Since I immediately promised to attend the funeral service I had to see to a few things before leaving for the USA. So I got up and dressed right away. I went into the living room where the clock and the radio where still lying on the chair. In passing I gave them a short casual glance. And lo and behold! Suddenly both devices worked perfectly. The clock ran for another three or four years, the radio which we had already taken to two repair shops – to no avail – is still working more than ten years later! This is a fact. Coincidence?

I am absolutely certain, however, that this was not due to a long-distance effect executed by Uri Geller – and I do not wish to discuss his assumed telepathic abilities here.

However, there are several reasons why I tend to believe that there was a direct connection with the passing away of "Auntie's" daughter in the USA. Therefore, I will come back to this.

In Chapter 10, I already mentioned some of the strange incidents surrounding the death of my beloved father in 1996. Apart from some other events which I prefer not to discuss there are two which I would like to mention:

My father once gave my mother a pair of earrings with a diamond in each. The night before my father's funeral she put these earrings on her bedside table just as she always did. When she came to put them on again the next morning, *both* diamonds lay neatly arranged *beside* their settings which did not show any damage.

Two months later our son Alexander celebrated his 13th birthday here at home in Aachen with us. We were all sitting in the living room round a table having our coffee when all of a sudden the door of an old cupboard, which, although unlocked, was firmly shut, sprang open and a copper kettle which my father had given to us fell out – although it had been standing behind some other items right at the back of the cupboard on the top shelf. No one had been near the cupboard or touched the door. My father had loved this copper kettle and had often used it for preparing his famous burnt rum and red wine punch for special occasions.

In the three days between the death of our friend Heidi in Vienna and that of our "Auntie" on the 24th September 1996 – I already reported on this in Chapter 10 – something strange happened. The water-main for our house are in the washhouse in the cellar. Some devices such as the metre and the decalcifier are installed there. Originally they were all standing upright – quite normally.
At some time or other during these three days, the solid water-pipe together with all the integrated devices had tilted forward by exactly 45 degrees. Neither the plumber nor the experts from the water works could offer any explanation for this.
They had never experienced anything like it and they all agreed that it could only have been done by a brute force. But why? There was no sense in bending the water-mains. The installation was never touched by anybody who could have exerted such force – at least not such physical force. A little later, however, prompted by another incident, a sound phenomenon, I realized that the inexplicably bent pipes were probably connected with the imminent death of our "Auntie" and that the already deceased Hannelore had played a part in this. By the way, the entire installation went back to its normal position of its own accord – in December 2000, directly before my "third" grandmother died at the age of 97.

In mid-October 1996 I had a borderline experience which touched me deeply. One night, for no specific reason, I woke up with a start. Before I knew where I was I felt as if I were sitting in a roller-coaster. Actually, it was rather like a park-deck in which one has to go round narrow bends to the upper floors.

However, I was not sitting in a car but was flying myself at high speed. I was actually feeling rather dizzy. Suddenly I found myself in a broad street where a parade took place. I was dressed completely in white clothes. Everyone else was also dressed in white. I myself was leading one section of the procession, but I was unable to recognize anybody. After having marched on for a short while I suddenly saw my late father standing a little way away to the left.
He was just standing there. I turned off and immediately went to him.
We embraced. Everything seemed so very real to me at this moment, not like a dream. I felt every single one of the scars in his face, the hair on his head and the stubble on his cheeks. I noticed everything down to the last detail, with much more intensity and clarity than I had done it while he was still alive.
Neither of us said a word – we just embraced warmly. I experienced a feeling of utter happiness and *both* of us had tears on *our* cheeks. How long this meeting lasted I cannot say. For me, however, it ended far too soon.
As suddenly as everything had started I was back in my bed and I was wide awake! The tears were still on my cheeks and I was completely beside myself. My wife had also woken up – she must have noticed something. I do not remember what I told her, however, I did not tell her the real story. That was the only time that I had had the feeling to really see and, moreover, feel my father again after he had died. Even today I still feel an indescribably huge difference between this experience and everything I have ever dreamt. No dream, however oppressive and deeply distressing it may be, is comparable with this experience which still is so subjectively real for me and which I still remember in full detail.

A colleague once told me of a similar experience. She worked as an assistant surgeon at a large hospital in West Germany. Her boss was Dr N., a lady's man and very convinced of himself. However, she gave him no opportunity to try his charm on her. Nevertheless, they must have had an almighty row about this, which clarified their positions. In the end **Dr N.** became her main sponsor while she trained to become a surgical specialist. Later she moved to a different town. However, she felt the need to thank him again for his support. Because he was well known for directing his charms towards many female colleagues, she had always kept the necessary distance from him and had thus forgotten to express her thanks adequately. A good friend, a doctor herself, told her

one day that Dr N. had suddenly died when he was barely 50 years old. At that moment she felt that something important between him and her had been left undone and she regretted deeply not having approached him before his death. Some months later, she told me, something extraordinary happened while she was asleep:
She woke up with a start and had the absolutely real perception of rushing along a corridor and seeing a man approaching her from the other end. Shortly afterwards she recognized Dr N.. She kept confirming that all this seemed completely real and not at all like a dream.
They met and embraced very shortly. She was fascinated that during this short encounter she could clearly feel him and his body, his skin and his hair, even, as she told me, his muscles and the twitching of the muscles in his shoulders and upper arms. Then he disappeared and she lay in her bed wide awake.

In September 1998 my youngest sister gave birth to twins – a boy shortly before midnight and a girl just after midnight, i.e. one day later. My wife and I were on a cruise in the Mediterranean at the time. That night our son Alexander and some friends, a couple who stayed in our house and took care of our children while we were away, were awakened by a dull bang.
At first, they thought it was an earthquake, since we have had several small earthquakes in the Aachen area. The couple and Alexander went through the house to see whether anything had been damaged. Everything seemed to be all right, however. Only in the living room a large picture lay on the floor face up. It was a portrait of Alexander as an infant. In his typical manner he is holding a pipe in his mouth which my father had given to him. My father loved to smoke his pipe and Alexander, at the age of one and a half, was so fascinated that my father cleaned up one of his pipes meticulously and gave it to him.
But something strange had happened with the picture: originally it had hung on the wall about one and a half metres high and it had obviously fallen while the nail was still embedded in the wall. The picture was lying face up on the floor not close to the wall but at a distance of almost one metre from it on the carpet – the frame and the glass were undamaged. Was this perhaps also a message from my father?

To end this chapter, another strange occurrence:
This has nothing to do with the imminent death of a close relative or a friend. While still writing my book *"Arguments For Life After Death and a Different View of the World"*, I was searching for a certain quotation from the Bible. It was the biblical equivalent of Lao Tzu's wisdom: *"The way is the aim."* I took a short break, as I do more or less every day, and asked "God above" for help since at that moment I did not feel like searching through the Bible.

The next day, it was Friday, 6th November 1998, I went into my office as I usually do before setting off for my work. By chance, I looked at my fax machine and saw a small slip of paper hanging out. It was part of a typical fax report written on thermo paper. I ripped it off and was about to throw it away when I looked at it more closely: there was no sender address, but it stated my fax number as the addressee and the date (5th November 1998) and the time (22.12 hours) and the following short notice: *"You must seek your good fortune while you are travelling and not at your destination, since there your journey ends. – The Lord has made my journey successful. Genesis."*

I couldn't believe my eyes – this was in fact exactly what I had been looking for. When I printed the fax-journal later, which usually shows all transmissions, those I send as well as those I receive, I was very surprised not to find any transmission documented at that point in time. The previous one was documented on the 5th November 1998, 18.16 hours (sent by me), and the following one on 7th November 1998 (received). And in any case it is inexplicable how, apart from the usual data, these additional words could have appeared on the fax report. Of course, I saved and filed the "proofs" carefully.

Especially the last line, "The Lord has made my journey successful", is an obligation for me today, and at the same time it gives me the confidence to proceed with my philosophical work.

These very personal experiences are only some examples of all the inexplicable events that have happened to me over the last three decades. Some of them are not conducive to being written down. There are others which I will nevertheless discuss in more detail in the chapter "Contacts with the World Beyond – Fact or Nonsense".

Some of them had a close connection with an event of death, while others did not. In spite of some legitimate scepticism, however, I would still attribute them to the subtle activities of deceased relatives or friends

since some concomitant circumstances and indications do indeed seem extraordinarily strange. Of course, in a strictly scientific sense I have no proof at all for this assumption and neither do I consider my own anecdotes as such. However, I did indeed experience all the events I described here myself and more besides and, therefore, I can only describe them as being "mysterious" at the very least.
Some of these experiences I liked and at times I was even overwhelmed by them. Naturally, I am usually unable to decide whether I should believe or doubt them. Nor is it easy for me talk about these things at all in this context. But I am convinced that we survive our own physical death. And the fact that I have had a large number of personal borderline experiences strengthens my conviction. For me these experiences are a further piece of the jigsaw puzzle – in the same way as all the subjects in this book can themselves be merely single pieces of a jigsaw puzzle. But I am convinced that, after they have all been put together, they will form a very harmonious and magnificent whole which I view with the greatest respect and awe.

Finally, at the end of this chapter a small remark:
In 1972 the CSICOP[94] was founded, an association of sceptics, who made it their aim to expose *all* paranormal phenomena as mere hoaxes. Their chairman is the 75 year-old Canadian, *Randall James Hamilton Zwinge*, alias *James Randi*.
His foundation is even willing to pay one million dollars to anyone who is able to prove his or her paranormal abilities under the close observation of scientists. Several hundred people have already applied, but without success. For scientists this seems to prove once again that paranormal phenomena do not exist.
This is not the case, however, and, in my opinion, they have merely chosen the wrong basis for their studies:
Of course, they based their studies on the view today's parapsychologists currently have of the world. As I explained, this is mainly animistic-oriented. Parapsychologists assume that paranormal abilities are induced by as yet undiscovered or unconfirmed functions *within* the brain of a physically living person, i.e. in a physical ESP area. A controlled experiment would be possible only if this indeed were true.

---

[94] CSICOP = Committee for the Scientific Investigation of Claims of the Paranormal

However, I believe firstly that paranormal phenomena usually happen spontaneously, which renders them unrepeatable under scientific criteria. Secondly, I do not see any really plausible reason as to why it should be possible to explain such phenomena in an animistic way.

I believe that many paranormal phenomena at least are of spiritualistic nature and, therefore, the result of direct influences from the spiritual world.

Paranormal abilities of physically living persons are, therefore, the result of interactive contacts with that very spiritual world, i.e. the, in my opinion, global and all-penetrating "spiritual internet".

Serious scientific research should rather concentrate on objectifying, evaluating and controlling such contacts and the methods used. Scientists should collect details of phenomena considered paranormal and, above all, investigate their authenticity. Only when they are sufficiently experienced in analyzing these mostly spontaneous phenomena in a reliable manner (retrospection) will it presumably become easier for them to introduce suitable modalities for experiments through which even phenomena invoked in a laboratory may undergo scrutiny (prospection). Furthermore, scientists must principally open their minds to the acceptance of paranormal phenomena. I do not believe that this is generally the case today, which is why so many experiments lack the essential objectivity. With such a conviction no medical remedy could be shown to be effective since few medicines exist whose effectiveness does not depend to at least 30-40% on the so-called placebo-effect, which is inexplicable in a strictly scientific sense. Only if scientists were to alter their general attitude would such parapsychological experiments make sense and presumably be more successful.

13. Reincarnation in Discussion

In the autumn of last year I found the following headline in the internet[95]:
"Reincarnation proved?" There followed a report about the 13-year old Vietnamese girl, Ha Thi Khuyen. When she was 8 months old she started to walk and at 12 months she was able to speak. She always maintained that her present parents were not her real parents and that she really came from the near-by village of *Van*. When she was taken there one day she immediately recognized her "real" family. It turned out that their daughter had died in a tragic accident 10 years previously. Khuyen also recognized a woman as "her former aunt" and described the tragedy in exact detail: "She" had choked on a peach stone and had died in her aunt's arms before anyone could help her. During her own funeral she saw her "future" mother standing at the graveside full of mourning and sympathy for the dead child who was completely unknown to her. In great haste she had then "jumped into the belly of this woman" which was "like a kangaroo pouch" for her. From then on she lived her second life.

Is this story really proof for reincarnation – or even just one of many? There are thousands of such reports, especially in countries where the belief in *reincarnation* is widespread.

The Buddhists of Tibet select their new religious leader, the *Dalai Lama*, from small children according to defined search-criteria after the death of the previous one. The people are absolutely convinced that only one Dalai lama exists, and that he continues to be reborn.

Without doubt, there are many cases where children especially seem to "remember" other surroundings, life circumstances or people. Furthermore, there are cases where children are even able to speak foreign languages or do things for which they need special skills or even qualified training which they have never had.

The American *Ian Stevenson* has studied the subject of reincarnation thoroughly and in detail. According to his own statement he had collected and analysed more than 20,000 such reports. At the end of his

---

[95] Science page of the internet provider "freenet"

most important book, *"Children who remember previous Lives"* he draws the conclusion that he himself is convinced, based on often most amazing results, that *"... some of them* (the children interviewed) *could in fact be reincarnated ... but I have come to the conviction that we know very nearly nothing about reincarnation."* (underlined by me).

The same opportunities which I so avidly take advantage of myself, namely to support my own perceptions by drawing on the ideas of others from diverse faculties of science, should, of course, also be available to others. This is why I searched for further "proofs" and found the following:

Over the last few decades a grouping of usually well-paid so-called *regression therapists* or *reincarnation therapists* has developed. They claim that under *hypnosis* they can take people back to their earliest childhood or even beyond that to their "earlier lives", thereby enabling their patients to piece together and relive their many earlier lives.

Apart from the fact that the qualifications of these often self-styled therapists vary considerably, there are nonetheless sufficient (apparent) "retracings". I will come back to this shortly and, therefore, I just assume here that their methods and the contents of their reports are in fact correct.

Unfortunately, most religions claim to be the only religion possessing the absolute truth. I reject this categorically and prefer to relativise some of their doctrines.

However, when all are taken together they must contain an immensely significant core of truth and, it is the age-old, intuitive manifestation within us humans which, in my opinion, is the main characteristic which brought forth humanity.

In spite of my critical contemplation, I consider many religious concepts as being very important and helpful. I even use some of them for supporting my own integrative ideas.

Reincarnation is a wide-spread concept in religions of the Far East. Some books, and here I would mention again especially the Tibetan Book of the Dead[96], describe in great detail the journey a soul takes between death and reincarnation.

The most important religions of the Far East are without exception directly or indirectly connected with Hinduism. However, in that religion the belief in reincarnation is not very old. It goes back to the original

---

[96] See Chapter 2

conviction that the *spirit* goes on forever without interruption! For their contemporaries the religious leaders needed an understandable explanation which they thought they had found in reincarnation. However, reincarnation was *not* a dogma when Hinduism was established a few thousand years ago.

By the way, even the early Christians were familiar with physical reincarnation after death. At the beginning of 1997 I visited Istanbul[97] where I had the opportunity to admire the portrayal of such in a mosaic over a portal inside the Chora-Church. It depicts the death of Mary, the Mother of Jesus, and above her a baby already portraying the reincarnated Mary.

The belief in reincarnation was banned from the Christian doctrine by Emperor Justinian[98] at the fifth Ecumenical Council in 553 AD.

Finally, recurring phenomena in our civilization are the so-called child prodigies who – everyone agrees – possess quite extraordinary abilities in early childhood. Some are especially talented in languages, others are mathematical geniuses and others can play musical instruments with astonishing virtuosity – without having really studied them at all.

For me, it is no wonder that some consider this to be almost ultimate proof that such talented people have been reincarnated.

It seems as if there are quite a number of plausible arguments which *confirm* the possibility that humans have been *reincarnated* again *in flesh* after they have died.

Nevertheless, I am *sure* that it is a mere human invention which has nothing to do with reality. Reincarnation exists, but it is quite dissimilar to the popular conception of it: after their physical death, all living beings – and that also includes human beings, of course – are reincarnated into a completely different world, which is for us a spiritual world "beyond", in which everything that has ever been generated in "this world", our physical world, is reflected authentically for ever and ever.

It is only humans who have become aware of all this and will become even more alert in future because of their sufficiently well-developed consciousness and their self-awareness.

In my opinion, a reincarnation (in flesh) is a mere human invention. Why?

---

[97] Formerly known as Constantinople, Turkey
[98] Justinian I (527-565 AD)

1) *"Everything happens in circles"*, is an old American Indian adage already mentioned above. In fact it really does seem as if everything in our world has a circular, cyclic character. I myself work with a simple intellectual model which involves circles, which grow and propagate when I attempt to explain the basic information of our world.

The German chemist *Peter Plichta* and I both arrived at one and the same cyclical space model although we used two completely different routes. Nature shows the cycle of seasons:

If we consider a tree, we know that it will have new leaves in Spring and will lose its leaves in Autumn. The leaves come and go, but the tree remains the same. Why should it be any different for humans? Bodies are born and they die, their very essence, however, i.e. the human soul, remains the same. After all, we accept that every soul has to come from somewhere and, logically, that it has to go back whence it came. But does it really do so?

I think that, on the one hand, people are comparing apples with pears here – on the other hand, a soul must not necessarily come from anywhere:

In my books I put forward the theory that two worlds exist independently from one another, while being simultaneously essential for each other's existence. The spiritual world is the real core of all existence. From that world and with that world our universe, all matter and all living beings are ultimately generated.

A characteristic of all living beings is that they consist of a different, of an organic, matter, which possesses a complicated molecular and cellular three-dimensionality. And this enables organic matter to receive and to store information. Furthermore, it can process such information which is transmitted, for example, by light or other forms of electromagnetic radiation. It follows that information itself must be influencing biochemical processes which, meanwhile, has already been established for radio waves. Therefore, light must be one of several interfaces between the spiritual world which encompasses and penetrates the entire universe and the cosmos as its physical pendant and "field of action".

If we compare the world to a coin with two sides then light (and other electromagnetic radiation) considered from the physical point of view consists of mass-less "luminous particles"[99], from the spiritual point of

---

[99] As I already mentioned, light particles become luminous only when they interact with the retina of the eye

view it is a universal, digital information code, which, similar to the binary code of computers, only emits the information 1 or 0.
Ultimately, the evolution of all life is primarily an evolution of suitable structures which can process the information they receive more and more adequately so that they are enabled to communicate with the spiritual world on ever higher levels. At the provisional end of this evolution on Earth mankind was generated.
The appearance of humans accelerates this spiritual evolution significantly. By consistent individualization a spiritual diversity is generated which shows more and more facets in ever shorter periods of time. Every human being is a prime example of the possibilities of unlimited spiritual growth. This process is terminated, or at least it seems to be, by our inevitable physical death.
This would mean, however, that evolution had finally failed.
Conversely to the laws of thermodynamics according to which all physical matter strives towards more and more chaos, an ever higher spiritual order is achieved here.
Death cannot stop this development. It follows that there can only be a physical death.
This inexorably leads to the conclusion that evolution, which seeks perfect spiritual diversity by means of individualization, must also lead each single spirit sooner or later to the highest level of perfection.
It would contradict all experience and common sense if this goal were to suffer constant setbacks. But "physical reincarnation" would mean exactly that, since the individual would have to start from scratch every time. Experience, obtained over many decades, would be lost again at death. The motto of reincarnation is, in short: If at first you don't succeed, try, try again!
Good and evil deeds would entail an almost endless torment through countless lives, in which the search for the pure *karma* continues. Reincarnation would mean repeating the same year at school over and over again in order to attain at least the first grade. The evolution of the spirit, however, strives for more: it strives to attain the highest possible grade over the shortest possible period of time and with the greatest possible number of school-years.
The evolution of the spirit is a route leading consistently and continuously upwards from one form to the next, which pleases every school teacher. The weaker pupils are inevitably swept forward. However, they will not only need a great deal of extra coaching from

time to time, but they will also have to put in some extra work as punishment, stay in detention or even be confined to the school premises.

The human soul does not come from anywhere. It is formed and grows only *together with* the human being. In the course of a life it differentiates and qualifies itself more and more. When the human being dies the body is severed from the soul which remains behind and – without losing its independence – becomes an independent part of an infinite, world-encompassing entirity. Death is the mere change from one school form to another – and there is still a long and stony path in front of the soul before the final exams are passed.

2) The reason why some religions believe in physical reincarnation lies mainly in the hope for justice.

This is also reflected in the perception of the *karma*. Everybody will experience justice in the sense that we all can and must expect our next life to be better or worse – depending on our conduct during our previous life and on the gravity of our sins. Unfortunately, this perception often leads to degrading and inhuman distortions. Although a *proof* for physical reincarnation does not exist, many people are inhumanely discriminated against in countries in which such religions have taken a strong hold.

Their personal misfortunes are interpreted as the just rewards for a previous life of misdemeanour or even evil deeds.

Their karma, i.e. their sins, with which they are still burdened from their previous life, causes them to be what they are today and make them suffer.

Every human being may indeed be responsible for the degrading circumstances in which he has to spend his current life. To condemn someone, however, who cannot even remember the misdeeds of his former life and cannot regret his behaviour and try to better himself in his current life, is surely not wise nor divine.

I am absolutely convinced that justice does *really* exist in this world, in the same way as love or compassion exist. Each of us may be committing sins for which retribution must, and indeed will, follow. However, this will only have a rational effect when those being admonished are able to recognize the reason for whatever it is they are experiencing at the time they experience it. The call for justice certainly culminates in the question as to what would happen to justice if suddenly mankind had no future on earth anymore. Sadly, we are in a position today to wipe out our species and the entire life on Earth at short notice.

3) The argument of the eternal circles of nature does not apply here either. Even if everything does indeed take place in circles, nothing in fact really comes back. History does not really repeat itself, neither do the same leaves grow again on trees, nor are the seasons ever exactly the same. Each single leave is unique in this world and each springtime also.
If there is a spiritual world, an all-encompassing world of information, then it has a spiritual correlate for each leave and for each springtime: everything is stored and can be "viewed" at any time. The new leaf and the next Spring have only one thing in common with their predecessors and that is their similarity, in the same way as two people are similar to one another because they are both human beings.
If, furthermore, as I assume and as the pattern "life" indeed suggests, the human spirit exists without the physical brain and is generally told to keep growing, then there is no reason to assume that it would need a new physical body to do so.
New reincarnations would involve taking cumbersome long detours.
The evolved nervous system which provides the spirit with an efficient *interface* to the physical world and establishes a highly complicated and complex, perfect communication network, speaks a different language:
Its development always occurred in a direct straight line, it was consistent and it took no such detours. But what may be right for the "instruments" of the spirit should also be right for the spirit itself.

4) Of course, mathematics too must be a strong opponent of physical reincarnation. In my opinion, everything in this world is governed by very simple geometrical or number-controlled laws. Generally speaking, the world obeys six elementary mathematical rules:

1)Nothing comes from nothing: Zero, nothing, is only the opposite of being, but nothing can be generated thereof.

2) No being stands alone: Everything has a polar mirror image. In the same way as "+1" there is also "-1". Matter is mirrored in spirit. Everything is ordered according to symmetry and polarity, i.e. in diametrical opposition.

3) All being emerges from being: We are unable, however, to describe the previous state of BEING in detail and we are incapable of imagining it. Just as we can extract the square root of "+1", which is "-1", so must there also be a square root of "-1". Although it is impossible to quantify it, it must nevertheless exist. We simply cannot imagine it. This root is known by mathematicians as "i". And "i" is thus the smallest *symbol* for the real existence of God.

4) All being is interdependent: In the same way as "i" produces "-1" and "-1" produces "+1" so God produces all spiritual matter and spiritual matter produces all physical matter.

5) Everything develops itself forwards consistently: If something is generated, i.e. it IS – regardless whether it is "-1" (spirit) or "+1" (matter) – then it develops itself further in eternity:
"-1" becomes "-2", then "-3" until "infinitely minus", "+1" becomes "+2", etc. until "infinitely plus".

6) Only physical matter is finite, while spiritual matter is infinite: All physical matter is developed from a primary spiritual, spatial infinity. The (spiritual) information of BEING also adheres to all physical matter. It is the other side of the coin. The information of its BEING is thus infinite and will remain in existence even if the physical matter itself no longer exists: it is eternal.

It follows that there will never be an end to a personality which has once been generated. And, unlike the strange procession in Echternach (Luxembourg) in which people take two steps forward and one back, each single personality will continuously develop forwards as do the ordinal numbers which extend into infinity.

There is *no* place in mathematics for the constant forward and backward movement of physical reincarnation.

Basically, of course, the same applies to animals – in fact to everything in this universe. However, it is only humans – at least as the first living beings on this earth – who are able to recognize this and who are thereby enabled to influence their own future and to follow their own path.

If we accept that for any kind of spiritual information we may symbolically also use the term "word", then the Gospel according to St. John offers an amazing explanation, as does any biblical description of the creation of this world and everything within it, known as Genesis.

The Gospel according to St. John starts with the words (1, 1-5): *"In the beginning was the Word, and the Word was with God, and the Word was God. The same was in the beginning with God. All things were made by him and without him was not any thing made that was made. In him was life; and the life was the light of men. And the light shines in darkness; and the darkness has not mastered it."*
Here I see an amazingly understandable and apt figurative description of my rather simple mathematical rules expounded on the previous pages.
And when the "light", basically just information, is not mastered by the "darkness" it can only mean that information exists for ever and in eternity and in independence of physical effects.

At the end of this chapter we still have to discuss how "recognitions", reports of "regressions" or "child prodigies" as mentioned above, could occur if physical reincarnations do *not* exist. It is not really helpful to simply reject reincarnation – a new and plausible explanation must be found.
Let us go back to the following basic concept:
Humans are not just physical creatures but also spiritual ones. Their spirit is a still developing, i.e. differentiating increasingly in the course of time, part of a global all-encompassing and all-penetrating "world spirit", a "spiritual field" or a "global spiritual internet".
If the human spirit really does exist independently from physical matter, such as the brain, then all of us living in this world today, must be constantly surrounded by innumerable conscious spirits, because – since the beginning of mankind – the spirit of every single deceased person has, of course, consistently developed further.
Imagine these "spirits" as billions of "intranets", i.e. small limited areas of information, within a gigantic internet. Then it should be easy to imagine that information is continuously exchanged between such intranets. Of course, such information can also be exchanged with an intranet still embodied in the physical world. In other words: we humans living in this world can, consciously or unconsciously, contact other spirits including those of deceased people, and can actively communicate with them.
This happens primarily on a purely spiritual basis. When such communication functions extensively, we might conceivably imagine that in this way we could experience perceptions, thoughts, views, knowledge and insights which actually originate from other people.

Especially under exceptional circumstances when under hypnosis, for example, in which we are no longer master of the situation and lock-gates to the spiritual world are opened, it becomes easier to accept that we might consider such strange knowledge and thoughts to be our own.
This would be a plausible explanation for all the phenomena already mentioned without the requirement of a physical reincarnation. Every one of those phenomena could be explained more or less by direct access to the spiritual information available.
More than a few people are able to establish similar contacts, usually quite unconsciously, by means of certain meditation techniques.
A state of tranquillity during contemplation and meditation seems well suited to make us susceptible for a world which is just as real as our own physical world which seems to be the only real one to us.
To attain this state of receptiveness it is first of all essential to reduce our omnipresent and omnipotent consciousness to a significantly lower level. We must learn to switch off and to let our thoughts flow. Our brain, as I already repeatedly explained in detail in my previous books, is a kind of reduction filter. It filters the constant influx of an immense amount of information and merely registers information it considers as being important. It is only when are completely relaxed, when we switch off, that we become susceptible for more subtle influences which otherwise would remain unnoticed. If in doing so we obtain remarkable or even useful information, it appears to us as an "inspiration". We talk of *intuition*.
An unconscious permanent contact might even be established by a kind of "short circuit" between two spiritual intranets.
There may be times when such forms of spiritual networks are even be achieved consciously. This is best imaginable between close relatives or generally between "kindred souls". In principle, we could envisage that a constant information transfer could take place through such connections, which would neatly explain in a plausible, simple way the phenomenon of child prodigies.
It is even possible that everyone in this world has a direct, personally appointed contact to a specific spiritual personality of the other world appointed to them in a way we cannot describe in detail. In this context the belief in a personal guardian angel gains not only a new perspective but much more significance.
I would like to remind you again that at all times and even in cultures in which a belief in metaphysics is not predominant ancestor-worship and

the belief in the possible influences they have on us was always held in high esteem.
Finally, the global spiritual field may contain things of great *general* importance. Basically they are available to all members of the same species, but not everyone is equally well equipped to access them. In the animal world these contents would be identical with the "morphogenetic fields" which *Rupert Sheldrake* postulated.
Of course, mankind also possesses such "spiritual intranets of general importance". Maybe they are the ones we know as "archetypes" or the "collective unconscious"?[100]
It is only when we switch off some of the functions and *reduction filters* of our brain or when we lose some of these abilities due to a disease that we may be able to intensify the connections we have to our "joint human database".
The autistic twins John und Michael[101], whom I already mentioned in my previous books, and who obviously could almost "see" prime-number twins of ten and twelve or even more figures, may be an interesting example for this theory.
To finalize this chapter, I shall risk another speculation which may console the believers of reincarnation somewhat – but first some preliminary remarks:
My thoughts regarding a completely new, alternative and for the first time really integrative view of the world – a perspective which reconciles religions, natural science and philosophy – are based on the following observation: developments which are of crucial importance always seem to take a direct line.
I believe, therefore, that wherever possible, life is generated in the universe wherever this is possible! Our universe should be full of life. And whenever life is created it will always further develop into intelligent life. The hierarchical and extremely consistent construction of a nervous system with perfect downward compatibility clearly supports this theory.
Here on Earth, humans are the first evidence that evolution is taking a new turn: it achieves the greatest possible diversity by means of as much individual variety as possible.
The development of each single spiritual potential is a lifelong process which at its climax (apparently) ends with death. This alone is reason

---

[100] According to Sigmund Freud and Carl Gustav Jung, see Glossary and List of References.
[101] From: Oliver Sacks, "The Man who mistook his Wife for a Hat", see List of References.

enough for me to doubt the finality of death; the process would be utter nonsense and wasteful.

One more everyday experience may also be very important:
If we look back on our lives we will all notice that, over the years, we have changed, not only externally but also spiritually.

We talk about spiritual maturity which is based on personal experience. This maturity, however, is not accomplished by a continual process; it happens rather in phases. Often life is considered to progress in seven-year stages. Traditional Chinese medicine even makes a difference between seven and eight-year cycles for women and men.

Although we all possess a spiritual core which, of course, accompanies us from the cradle to the grave, our spiritual maturity seems to accrue in phases, as if from time to time new development stages, which have matured over many years, are "suddenly" added to this spiritual core.

My feeling is that we enter a new chapter of life every few years, we tinker around with it until, in the end, we incorporate it. As soon as we understand how to handle it, it is added to our treasure of experiences, and we can open a new chapter. Of course, we may sometimes deal with several chapters simultaneously. We ourselves still assume that our personal development proceeds continuously. However, if we take a closer look we can indeed notice the phase-like development. If we follow this train of thought and if we really carry this basic experience with us beyond death, then my speculation is the following:

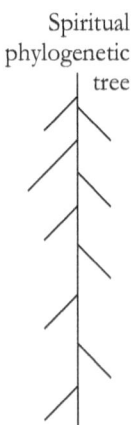

Spiritual phylogenetic tree

There may be innumerable single "spiritual phylogenetic trees", which at some time or other have all been established by humans. Each single human being accumulates a completely new treasure of experiences during the course of his physical life. After his physical death his experience and his entire personality becomes a contribution to the growth of one of these many "spiritual phylogenetic trees", (see the drawing which

Different personalities blend into one another throughout the whole eternal development whereby each new stage on the path to maturity is completed on a higher spiritual level of life unknown to us. Nevertheless, each life contributing to this scheme remains complete as a lasting personal (part of the) whole experience even retrospectively – in the same way as for us a holiday or a relationship represents such a period in our lives.

In this way that which belongs together grows together.[102]

The thesis of so-called kindred spirits fits into this context. However, this idea does not alter the well-known basic principle:

My idea of an integrative world model facilitates spiritual maturity only by everyone's orientation towards the next higher level and not by following an aimless cyclical up and down as claimed by the believers in reincarnation.

Even if clear differences exist between my perception and the current conception of many followers of great religions with regard to our view of the "hereafter", and a further existence of personality after physical death, we are still united by the words of *Tenzin Gyatso*, the 14th *Dalai Lama*:[103]

"I have written the above lines because a constant feeling accompanies me. Whenever I meet even a 'foreigner', I have always the same feeling: 'I am meeting another member of the human family.' This attitude has deepened my affection and respect for all beings. May this natural wish be my small contribution to world peace. I pray for a more friendly, more caring and more understanding human family on this planet. To all who dislike suffering, who cherish lasting happiness – this is my heartfelt appeal."

---

[102] I deliberately use here the words of the former Chancellor of the Federal Republic of Germany, Willi Brandt (*18.12.1913-+08.10.1992).
[103] Dalai Lama, " A Human Approach to World Peace"; Final Words, (1984) wisdom pub. 361 Newbury Street, Boston, Ma, 02 115, see List of References.

14. Where is Justice?

Where is justice when millions of people go hungry every day and when they have no real prospect of leading a life in more dignity?
Where is justice when millions of people are brutally sent to death by the lunatic despots of this world, without a chance of receiving help in time?
Where is justice when a family is eradicated by a car accident caused by a drunken driver or by somebody who wants to commit suicide and does not care whether he kills others when killing himself?
Where is justice when thousands of people are killed in cold blood through cowardly attacks committed by terrorists just because they happen to be in a skyscraper in New York and because their murderers are driven by the absurd believe that they will be rewarded for this deed in the world beyond?
Where is justice when some people die when they are still young children while others die when they have grown very old and when some people are healthy and others are severely ill as long as they live?
Where is justice when there are people who have never known material hardship in their lives, who probably spent their plentiful free time in high-spirits or even with snooty arrogance towards their less well situated brethren – while others are destitute through no fault of their own?

Believers of reincarnation would take up this point and would reply that people are characterized by their personal karma.
In countless former lives on earth they have accumulated a certain amount of debt or perhaps credit so that their present circumstances in life are some kind of punishment or repayment.
But isn't this sheer cynicism?
Does this not rob countless people of the chance to escape their hardship when other people do not even realise that they ought to help them? After all they are solely responsible themselves for their hard lives.
And is it really (pre-)determination – a previously determined inexorable fate – if two hundred people find their deaths in an aeroplane crash – or seven astronauts burn up in their space shuttle as happened for the second time in 17 years?

A good friend of mine who was renovating his house fell with his ladder so unfortunately that from that day on he has been paralysed from the waist down. Is this really a kind of predetermination? Did he possibly receive his just punishment for a crime he committed in his former life? To all these questions I have only the following answer:
The aforementioned tragedies are all incidental and nobody is being punished for anything.
It is also pure coincidence whether we grow up as the child of a poor or a rich family, or whether we are lucky enough to live in a tolerant and free country, or whether we are enslaved under the regime of a barbaric tyrant.
Nevertheless, I believe that, to a certain extent, there are indeed fateful circumstances – however, our basic ways or directions are not predetermined but incidental.
In the next chapter I will discuss this point in more detail.
What is justice then? Is it merely a human invention and thus a rather flexible social convention?
If that were the case then people through the ages would surely have developed different and possibly even completely new perceptions of justice. In that case we would have to concede that all cruel despots of the world are demonstrating an acceptable amount of justice from their personal and subjective points of view and even to the extent of their outrageous treatment of those they hate, such as religious or ethnic minorities, the handicapped or political opponents. Of course, this would be perverse and grotesquely cynical. No, justice is a part of our cultural development. But what is "culture", where does it come from and why does it so obviously strive to perfection as much as the physical development did through the aeons of time?

Justice possesses, as we have to admit, a large number of *objective* attributes which are completely independent of all forms of government or authority, of social norms and rules of conduct and of times and eras and which are universally accepted and similarly defined everywhere.
Justice must be caused, therefore, - at least to some extent – by a deeply felt intuitive human perception which we have all probably carried within us since the beginning of our existence. To me it seems comparable to the countless intuitive religious beliefs in the existence of something divine, of a physically independent spirit and its survival of its own

physical death. Humans have carried these perceptions within them since time immemorial.

There seems to be an "ideal-spiritual" or absolute justice of which only humans have a certain knowledge. No animal has the slightest inkling of this justice, in the same way as no animal has a perception of love. This does not mean that an animal could not develop a caring emotion for its brethren which could equal the *implications* of love. However, an animal cannot understand its own feelings even less evaluate them. Only humans are able to abstract, understand, evaluate and consciously put into practice concepts such as "love" and "justice".

Mankind has been enabled, and this for me is the true evidence for having become human beings, to experience consciously completely new, i.e. spiritual, dimensions. Only humans can feel their own spiritual existence. They recognise real existing spiritual ideals and, in the course of their existence, humans increasingly orientate themselves to them. I believe that this is the actual key to what we call "cultural development or maturity". Therefore, only humans are able to feel intuitively and to objectify justice, and only humans possess the unique chance to keep this ability as long as they live, to refine it and not to let it be continuously watered down by adverse or damaging circumstances in life. Humans recognise or at least believe that this is not based on human imagination alone which they could jettison or manipulate at will should it not serve their own personal gain. However, unfortunately, this does not prevent many of our contemporaries today and in former times from doing so in spite of better knowledge.

If every human being, therefore, from the beginning of his existence onwards, possesses and develops a clear intuitive feeling for objective, ideal or absolute justice (which alas does not necessarily mean that he acts accordingly) then this cannot just be empty words.

Should this not be so then we could easily accept various interpretations. In the last chapter I explained in detail why I am not convinced of an incarnation in flesh, and indeed why I cannot be convinced. Of course, we all create our own karma in the course of our lives, but justice is not dealt out in a new life on earth.

However, justice exists just as love exists and, like love, it is something ideal or absolute. Since it is not subject to human ideas or inventions it is not, and will never be, subject to changing influences caused by time and environment. Therefore, each of us must and will experience justice

sooner or later, no matter what he experienced during his life on earth or what fatal blows he dealt to others.
We will all, always and without exception, experience justice during our indestructible, eternally spiritual life – if not now then certainly in our immediately following spiritual life – after our physical deaths!

15. Coincidence or Predetermination

In the last chapter I mentioned the terms "coincidence" and "fate" or "predetermination". Countless people believe today that their lives and everything else in this world is predetermined. They assume that they are subject to a fateful development which cannot really be influenced.
This is known as "determinism". Natural scientists, however, prefer the strictly "non-deterministic" view, which states that in general everything in this world is "contingent", i.e. subject to coincidence. Taking evolution as an example makes this especially clear: It is still the "golden standard" in science to believe that coincidence alone, i.e. mutations, instigated new developments within species and also the development of new species. This would satisfactorily explain the entire evolution.
As so often before, this question cannot definitely be answered by a simple "yes" or "no". On the contrary: I am convinced that *both,* "coincidence" *and* "predetermination", have been decisive in our world.
Something else becomes easily explainable, I believe, if we follow my line of thought: the evolution of creatures saw the simultaneous evolution of their mechanisms (see Chapter 5).
Not only mutations, selection and cooperation have played an important role here but also instincts, consciousness and self-awareness.
By means of a linear, striving and consistently perfected central nervous system an important central constant of evolution is developed in the course of time: as an interface between spirit and matter it facilitates increasingly interactive ways of communication followed by a purposeful

and, finally, enormously accelerated evolution of all life. Although this effect puzzles many biologists they are unable to offer a really satisfactory explanation.

For me, however, it is easy to offer a plausible and sensible explanation for this evolutionary "accelerator pedal" when I refer to my alternative model of the world. According to my model, coincidence played a significant role at the beginning and for a very long time, it possibly remained the only influence in the evolutionary process. Therefore, it took such an amazingly long time to get into gear and comparatively small changes needed vast periods of time to develop.

When, however, the interaction between the ever more complex living matter and the "spirit" increased, the differentiation of the spirit, which at the beginning was merely a rather undifferentiated spiritual field, started to grow.

Only some basic "spiritual" conditions such as simple geometric structures and ordinal numbers already existed as real spiritual quantities. The more differentiation grew, the bigger and more structured became the influence of the spiritual field on the further development of complex organic matter. At the same time the influence of coincidence was increasingly regulated and, finally, drastically limited. As a result, evolution was visibly accelerated.

Some simple mathematical reflections show, however, that coincidence must still exist. Take, for instance, Galton's famous vertical board of nails:

Nails are arranged on this board in the form of a triangle. Beneath the first nail at the top of the board in the middle, are two nails to the left and the right and beneath them there are three more nails, again to the left and the

right of nails above and another between them and so forth. Each row has one more nail than the one above. A funnel is put above the first nail and little balls are fed into the funnel. Beneath the bottom row of nails there is a row of small open boxes the number of which is determined by the number of nails in the last row. The small balls, which are exactly placed over the first nail, are sent on their journey and fall into the boxes.

This experiment could also be carried out with a sack of rice or sand which is emptied over the first nail.
But let us stay with the small balls which we let fall through the funnel to the board of nails: each single ball has a 50% probability of passing a nail either to its right or its left.
The same probability of coincidence is repeated at each level. The course each ball takes is purely coincidental! However, if we take a look after 1,000 balls have fallen through the nails we find that the distribution of balls always follows the same strict order:
Most balls fall into the middle boxes and the number of balls falling into boxes to the left and the right of the centre decreases considerably at first and significantly more slowly the further the boxes are away from the centre. No matter whether we try this out with balls, sand or rice, the picture, known as the Gaussian distribution curve[104], is always the same. The very same curve can also be calculated by *Blaise Pascal*'s "binomial equation" according to as every student knows today.
During the seventies of the last century the Polish mathematician *Benoit Mandelbrot* broached the highly interesting subject of chaos research. One of the most important findings is that, sooner or later, every chaotic development will find a clear order – and vice versa.
With the aid of so-called chaos games, based on very simple, coincidental processes which can be found everywhere in our universe, I was able to show in my earlier books how beautiful and well-ordered patterns can develop. For chaos research the term *fractural geometry* was coined.
Mathematics, which is certainly completely "unconscious", provides the example: mathematics always demonstrates an active interaction between chaos (coincidence) and order (determination).
Since, in my opinion, mathematics is the real ultimate basis of all existence in this world, and since we already find chaos (coincidence) and order (determination) there, then this must, of course, also apply to all higher forms of development.
Our world is also characterized, however, by the inexorable striving for an ever higher differentiated, perfected spirit, which – by interaction – increasingly influences the development of the world as a whole and which is detectable, for example, in accelerated evolutionary processes.
The clearest signs of this perfected spirit are consciousness, deliberation and self-awareness. These imbue order, which inevitably follows chaos,

---

[104] named after the German mathematician and astronomer Carl Friedrich Gauss, see Glossary

with a completely different but important new quality: order can no longer be determined "objectively" by mathematical operations alone. But it is increasingly determined by purposeful spiritual influences. The new orders are more and more "subjectively" characterized.

Of course, it is still absurd to believe, for example, that a large number of passengers killed in a plane crash means that this was their mutual predetermined fate. It is pure coincidence that in this accident these particular people were killed. The possibility remains, however, that someone may have missed the ill-fated plane because it was his predetermined fate.

Maybe, there were also other passengers, who later died in the crash, who received subtle warnings which they either did not recognize as such or disregarded.

My integrative vantage point allows me to reconcile not only *all* the different scientific observations and the *fundamental* contents of all the different faiths and myths, but also inexplicable para-psychological phenomena or, for example, the widespread belief in guardian angels.

According to a FORSA study conducted some years ago, 48% of the German people believe in a personal guardian angel.

My opinion is that a spiritual field exists which encompasses and completely penetrates the whole world. Each single individual in the universe actively helps to shape and structure it in the course of immense periods of time. Even after death the individual spirit remains integer without any loss with all its former spiritual attributes, its personal characteristics, its biography and its knowledge. The conscious and self-aware spirit also maintains, of course, the ability to further develop its own personal self.

It follows that it must also, in principle, be possible to communicate in a "bilateral" and "inter-active" form between the two levels of existence. Nevertheless, we cannot expect to obtain really exact forecasts "from a higher level" since this would contradict all the rules governing the world with regard to the nature of time and causality. However, it is conceivable that sometimes from such "higher level" certain advice and assistance is emitted since the perspective "there" is certainly superior to ours.

In the next chapter I will discuss this in more detail.

16. Are Contacts with the World Beyond Conceivable?

If we accept that death is only the end of our physical body but not the end of our personality – and if we assume that there is a further existence in another – a spiritual – world, then contacts ought to be possible between these two worlds which we call "the physical world" and the "world beyond".

Many a strict Christian may admonish us now and point out that the Bible says we should not ask questions of the dead. However, according to Christian belief someone is only dead when he is dead "in the spirit". This means primarily that it is not the deceased as such that is dead but rather someone who has failed to live his (physical) life in love.

The biblical admonition can only mean, therefore, that we should not spend time with someone who is "depraved by malice". This interpretation is supported by the following quotations out of the Bible which only seem to contradict one another: On the one hand the Old Testament says: *"Thou shalt not kill."*[105]

On the other hand, a little later, we find the following words: *"He that smiteth a man, so that he die, shall be surely put to death."*[106]

Unfortunately, the latter quotation may even be responsible for the death penalty executed in some states imbued with Christian principles.

The apparent contradiction, however, is clarified if in accordance with the general linguistic usage we appoint two different meanings to the terms "death, "dead" and "kill", namely the "physical" as well as the "spiritual". Only in this way is it possible to understand the two "related" quotations within each of their contexts.

We should better "translate", therefore, that someone who "physically" kills a person should die a "spiritual" death.

Only those who are "spiritually" dead are "really dead". This interpretation is supported by Jesus' words: *'Let the children come to me; for the kingdom of God belongs to such as these.'*[107] The term "children" and the term "Kingdom of God" probably have more symbolic meaning here since it would contradict religious faith if the kingdom of God were only

---

[105] Exodus: Israel at Mount Sinai; The Ten Commandments, 20.13
[106] Exodus 21, 12
[107] Mark 10, 13

open for children. However, children are still fresh, unspoiled and free of heavy guilt. They are not "spiritually dead" and, therefore, they have a future in "Heaven", the dimension of eternal life.

Even Christians, therefore, have no reason to shun contact to the deceased.

In this chapter I will only give a short overview of the various ways of making contact.

I have become convinced that I have already made several such contacts. On the strength if these, I possibly plan to start a new book within the next few years, dedicated to "Trans-communication" together with *Horst Hansen*, a technical engineer, who is the owner of an electronic company in Delmenhorst, Northern Germany.[108]

Such contacts are usually of a very subtle nature, and they must be interpreted. This naturally leaves the door wide open for mistakes and the influx of our own desires and opinions.

However, in spite of critical tests, I think, there still remain justifiable reasons to assume that real communication with the dead has indeed taken place. In general, the specific circumstances which facilitated such contacts support this assumption. I already described some strange and inexplicable cases in previous chapters. These were, however, at best, either one-sided messages from the "beyond" or unspecific atmospheric tensions which might have suggested such a connection.

However, I believe that anyone who really wishes to establish a contact with the "world beyond" could succeed. If a contact is indeed possible it should most certainly not only be possible for initiated persons.

Since I am convinced that our "spirit" doubtlessly also exists without "its brain", I do not believe there to be any kind of "trainable area" *within* the brain where such contacts are constructed and stored. Neither do I think much of the "right-hemisphere mysticism" which has grown into a cult today and fascinates many people involved in psychology and esoteric, even though from different points of view.[109] Again I agree with *John Eccles*, the brain researcher and Nobel Prize winner who died in 1997, who considered the brain to be simply "overestimated" in its possibilities and properties.

---

[108] Diamant-Electronic
[109] To be quite clear: the right brain hemisphere obviously plays an important role in extrasensory perceptions (ESP). But: "to play a role" does not mean that ESPs are located there and start there. When ESPs are experienced, they correlate with activities in the right hemisphere – but that is all. Your computer also blinks when you install a new program. The programmer, however, is not located in the computer!

In the following paragraphs I would like to discuss four forms of contact with the deceased which are especially typical and widely spread:

16.1 Visions of individuals and groups of individuals:

These happen frequently close to the time of a person's death. Physicists relegate these events without exception into the realm of fantasy. Everyone, even scientists who have experienced such visions themselves, are unanimously and vehemently accused of misinterpretations.
Most parapsychologists today are animistic oriented and assume these visions to be hallucinations. Originally this term is reserved for the mentally and spiritually handicapped. When they talk about "otherwise" healthy people, therefore, they call them "pseudo-hallucinations" which in content are no different from "real" hallucinations. However, such terms do not explain the true background of such phenomena.
Furthermore, parapsychologists also consider a "time-shifted development of awareness" as being possible. This actually happens from time to time and many of us have probably already experienced it: parapsychological experiments have shown that some people only really become aware of certain events after the elapse of some time.
Everyone knows the typical "eureka-experience". Although this explanation may apply to single cases it cannot be accepted as a general answer. Some details especially give grounds for justified doubt that these visions are always "hallucinations in the medical sense".
When, for example, a woman, who was evidently already dead and unknown to him, appeared to the heart surgeon *Christiaan Barnard* we might with a high degree of certainty rule out a hallucination (see Chapter 11). An animist, however, would certainly not relent and would argue that by unconscious clairvoyance Professor Barnard had already sent out ESP-waves (whose existence is till unproven) from his ESP-transmitter (which has not yet been located), thereby receiving information from this deceased woman while she was still alive, which were later projected into his consciousness.[110] I cannot believe that!
Fairy tales may occasionally be told with intent to deceive, but are usually perceived as such and can be eliminated.

---

[110] ESP = extrasensory perception. I have already described in detail Professor Barnard's experience in Chapter 11.

Real hallucinations experienced by the mentally disturbed or pseudo-hallucinations experienced by "otherwise" healthy people can be detected with the help of an exact analysis of the events.

Finally, there still remain sufficient examples of visions which should be accepted – as do the persons affected by this vision– namely as a *spiritualistic* reality. I believe this would be the most sensible thing to do.

In the same spiritualistic way we should also accept such phenomena which are experienced sometimes weeks, months or even years after a close friend or relative has died.

Animistic interpretations seem to me to be more complicated and sometimes even give me the impression of being utter nonsense. From the subjective view point of an animist they are no such things, of course, because for him spiritual effects (even long-distance effects) really exist but they are linked with the brain and are lost for ever with the death of the brain.

16.2 Mediumistic contacts, séances:

Here the contact with the deceased is invoked by those claiming to be medial personalities or, simply, to be a medium. Mostly in trance, i.e. in a form of shifted consciousness in the sense of "being spiritually beside oneself", a condition *similar* to being asleep, they make contact with some spirits they already know well and which are then taken to be mediators on the spiritual level.

Meetings with several persons who seek such contacts, whereby at least one is a medium, are known as séances.

Towards the end of the 19th century and even at the beginning of the 20th century séances were quite common and a popular form of social entertainment. It is interesting to recall that the famous inventor *Thomas Alva Edison* was an especially avid participant.

However, as one might expect, there was also a great deal of nonsense, charlatanism and fraud. Nevertheless, it would be a mistake to dismiss all mediumistic contacts and every medium out of hand.

We must assume that there are indeed a number of serious mediums. Of course, the question arises again as to whether such contacts with deceased persons are really genuine or whether animistic explanations seem more plausible.

A medium's gift for telepathy belongs into this category. Animists claim that by "telepathy" mediums first obtain *that* information from their clients which is the most important enabling them to prove their trustworthiness to the client. By "clairvoyance" they obtain further information about things and objects belonging to the person seeking contact or his close relative. By "retrospective telepathy" they are able to make a contact to the deceased – and that at a point in time when that person was still alive.

Finally, by "precognitive telepathy" or "precognitive clairvoyance" they are then able to see the "future" of their "clients" and to give details.

In this way, the clients are led to believe that everything the medium tells them is information directly obtained from the deceased person.

In this case also, I maintain that the spiritualistic explanations are far more appropriate than the animistic ones – provided, of course, that the contacts themselves are genuine. As already mentioned, none of the animistic explanations has been proved up to now. They are all still nothing but hypotheses, based on assumptions claimed by natural scientists that the human spirit is attached to the brain – although natural scientists themselves reject animistic hypotheses.

Of course, under this premise any belief in the individual survival of the human personality after death would be wasted.

Only if genuine indications are found indicating that the human spirit does indeed exist without its physical brain will such animistic notions, e.g. "precognitive and retrospective telepathy", appear as unnecessarily complicated intellectual contortions.

Furthermore, exact forecasts of our future can only be possible to a very limited extent. I have already explained this in detail in my book "Life".

From a strictly natural scientific point of view especially it seems to me that the glass is more half full than half empty. The latter would mean that the odds stand 50 : 50 for a survival after death. In other words: in my opinion the likelihood of a brain-independent spirit and a lasting individual existence "after death" are more convincing. However, that would pull the rug from underneath those animistic explanations which are as yet unproven. Since I have not had any practical experience with "mediumistic contacts" I cannot offer any personal contribution to this subject.

16.3 Dreams and day-dreams:

The Greek physician *Hippocrates* considered dreams to be information the gods send us and he used them to make his diagnoses. One of his methods for curing people was the healing sleep which is occasionally still used today.

However, while we assume today that the body collects sufficient (physical) power of resistance and is strengthened through sleep which enables it to fend off disease, for Hippocrates it was important that the patient had *good dreams*. If a patient dreams that a god touches the afflicted part of his body then this alone would heal him.

The immaterial and unconscious dream itself is thus the real cure. Usually dreams occur several times and periodically during every natural sleep. During dream phases the electro-encephalogram shows specific and especially active patterns which coincide with very rapid eye movements.

This can also be observed in animals, e.g. in dogs. It is a sure sign that many animals and all more or less conscious living beings do indeed have dreams.

In contrast to normal dreams, day-dreams or waking dreams are conscious or at least half-conscious phases which, as the term already indicates, occur not *during* sleep but while the person is awake, sometimes before he falls asleep or after he has woken up. They are an unmistakable indication for how awareness has now changed which can best and most effectively be achieved when we try to create a condition of utter emptiness within us: complete inactivity, when we switch off our own thoughts. It requires that we want nothing, wish for nothing and that we switch off completely. A variety of East Asian meditation exercises have perfected the technique of day-dreaming.

Often these exercises produce an imagination, i.e. a pictorial conscious dream. We could also term it "pictorial imagination" or "fantasy". Advanced masters of meditation claim that they can sever their consciousness from the body solely by adopting the right kind of meditation and allowing it to roam around free from the body.

I believe that real, unconscious dreams as well as the more or less conscious day-dreams could be an effective possibility of contacting the dead and of communicating with them at least on a subtle level. The problem is again how to prove it? Often enough great and splendid "ideas or flashes of inspiration" occur to people in the course of real dreams, i.e. while they are asleep, or during day-dreams. There are many even historically confirmed examples.

I already offered an explanation regarding the nature of "real" dreams in my book "Life": it is conceivable that while we are asleep several physical "receivers" in the brain, the innumerable so-called dendrons[111] in the cortex, are extensively repaired. These repairs are essential, otherwise the connection between the immaterial spirit and the physical brain could suffer serious damage. How else can we explain why the lives of test people are placed at risk when in experiments over long periods of time they are not allowed to dream because they are woken up as soon as they enter a dream phase?

I have explained how we might imagine the immense complexity of the human spirit simply as a kind of individual "intranet" within an infinite spiritual "internet".

In this way it becomes easier to imagine that, especially when our own "intranet sleeps" and is not *consciously* in action, information of other intranets of this internet can penetrate better and more easily into our own intranet.

Dream pictures could then mingle. To illustrate this more vividly, I compared this process in my book "Life", the second volume of my trilogy, to the bustling activity of an international airport. During the "rush-hour" it is flooded with an all enveloping cacophony of sound. When the activity dies down we start to hear the sounds from adjoining halls again or even from the next terminal.

This would be the information from other spiritual "intranets" which carefully "knock" on the door of our "own intranet" and which would otherwise have no chance of making themselves noticed during the "daytime".

In a similar way, this might also happen in more or less consciously induced day-dreams when our attention for such external influences increases because we have learned how to push aside the chaos of our own intellectual world by meditation and contemplation, making our mind free and wide awake for receiving information coming from "further away". This is what normally happens in our "real" dreams. Two completely different mechanisms, more or less, lead to the same mental void – comparable to the quiet airport terminal where the activity has died down.

---

[111] Here: small blind upright nerve endings

During such states of consciousness we may experience incidents that have something to do with the dead. From a purely materialistic point of view these experiences might be nothing but normal dreams. But is this a rational notion? Day-dreams especially are often rather strange and this alone may already indicate that those individuals appearing in our day-dreams are possibly really attempting to "transmit" information to us.

This could include, for example, solutions to certain problems for which we have already long been searching. Or it could be ideas for our future actions so that the term "inspiration"[112] would aptly describe the situation: we "breath in" something or something from the outside is "blown into" our mind.

Day-dreams, as well as "real" dreams, often seem to indicate things we could not have known previously.

I have often experienced day-dreams in which the rough outline of future events is already described.

Day-dreams have also presented me with solutions to more than one problem and they even accompany me sometimes while writing my books. In the course of many years I have learned to provoke day-dreams sometimes. Frequently, I even base important decisions on the inspirations I have had during a day-dream. Often I define my problems or questions and ask for solutions. During a day-dream I might find them – in the past this used to amaze me. And it still does, especially when I originally had a completely different solution in mind than the one offered to me in one of my day-dreams.

An animistic parapsychologist would at best explain this as being telepathy and clairvoyance, possibly embellished with a bit of precognition – and, based on our present knowledge of natural science, this would presumably be the solution which they could most easily "knock into shape" unless they want to declare everything as utter nonsense anyway. However, no proof exists either for this assumption and, as I already suggested here and in my previous books, I do not at all regard the foundations of our natural science to be solid enough for the interpretations which are offered.

---

[112] spirare: Latin = to breath, inspirare = to breath in or to blow into

16.4 Kinetic incidents:

For parapsychologists the term telekinesis, or psycho kinesis, describes the influences the usually brain-dependent spirit might have on physical things. Many of the inexplicable and extremely strange alterations to physical objects which have been observed may be due to psychokinetic causes. In Chapter 12 I described some of my own experiences in this respect.

Should such a phenomenon occur, it could, of course, be put down to coincidence. However, this theory becomes questionable at least when these coincidences occur in increasingly large numbers, possibly in connection with an extraordinary event such as that of a close relative passing away at the same time. Modern natural scientists, who, of course, have not the slightest intention of giving credence to such supernatural phenomena, talk about *coincidences*. In this context the psychiatrist *Carl Gustav Jung* coined the expression *synchronicity*. However, he did not explain whether there are good reasons for two events coinciding or whether it is pure chance that they happen at the same time.

Paranormal phenomena should not be simply ignored, even if things seem to happen which, according to the laws of physics, should not have happened. Of course, we must first try to exclude illusions. This may not always be possible, but sometimes it is not really difficult either.

I consider the phenomena I experienced myself in connection with death to be true **PSI** phenomena which an animist would call psycho kinesis; I myself would prefer the expression "spiritualistic kinesis". I would like to explain the difference again by using the example of the clock which stops when a close relative or friend dies. The *animist* would say: while we were asleep we "saw" the death of this person by means of clairvoyance. It was the psychic energy of our own subconscious which made the clock stop. A *physicist* would not want to complicate the situation unnecessarily. He simply states that it was just a *coincidence* that the clock stopped when the person died. A *spiritist* recognizes the influence of the spirit of the person that has just passed away.

I believe: Once we establish that certain things have happened several times and exclusively in close connection with certain categories of events – never in other circumstances – then coincidence can still not be excluded but it does seem rather unlikely.

The animistic theory is just as unproven – at least up to now – as the spiritualistic one which I favour. Both contradict all previous natural scientific theories and knowledge.

However, should we accept that natural scientific interpretations cannot be correct in some of their basic and decisive points, then both parapsychological schools of thought are strengthened again – which does not necessarily mean that the animists are right.

We should also consider which of these theories seems to be more likely. The animist will lose points especially if his theory is built on a natural scientific basis which, with good reason, now seems questionable.

The interpretation of many PSI phenomena as "spiritualistic kinesis", i.e. the moving of physical matter by the spirit of a person who is already dead as opposed to our own still living spirit, certainly seems reasonable. If this were not the case then the spirit of a still physically living person should cause PSI phenomena much more often – and it should be possible to reproduce these phenomena more often in experiments. With specific regard to psycho kinesis, it has not yet been possible to prove its existence by deliberate spiritual efforts of living persons in strictly scientific experiments.

One special form of unexplainable "kinesis" is the phenomenon of voices on tape recordings. A pioneer in this area was *Friedrich Jürgenson*. Once, in 1959, his tape recorder was still inadvertently recording while he listened to the sounds of nature in his garden; when he played back the recording he thought he could hear voices. Although they were rather weak he could clearly understand them. He kept experimenting over many years until his assumption that they must be the voices of dead people, seemed to be confirmed.

I do not want to go into historical details here, but over the last decades a proper field of research has been established, and it is indeed believed possible to record the voices of dead persons on a tape recorder. To do this one or several faint background noises, which provide as much sound chaos as possible, should be switched on in a room which is sound insulated as far as possible. According to the theory, a deceased person could then modulate words or even sentences by using with these sounds. The best acoustic raw material is provided by several radio sets being tuned into foreign, incomprehensible radio stations. Medium and short wave radio stations seem to be especially suitable. It is essential that the background noise be kept at a moderate level. I have tried this method for years now. At first it was just out of curiosity. In the course of time, however, I have become more successful and have made some quite acceptable and quite unexplainable recordings which give me enough reason to proceed in spite of my own plentiful doubts. I still consider my own results very critically. My experiences show that paranormal voices, if indeed they can be heard on recordings, are usually very difficult to understand.

Scientists researching voice recordings attribute this fact to the hypothesis that the deceased must first "remodel" the raw material that is offered to him. Of course, we have to listen to the recording with the utmost patience if we want to obtain good results. From a purely scientific point of view such voice-recording phenomena are utter nonsense.

The first counterargument is that these experiments are open to delusion. There are indeed various and numerous possibilities for this. For example, due to overshoot interferences we may possibly have received some words or even sentences in our own language. Since we have carefully chosen only foreign and incomprehensible radio stations we might then misinterpret these voices as paranormal recordings. By choosing the appropriate technique we must ensure right from the start that such misapprehensions are avoided.

Another delusion could crop up if we read our own interpretation into a statement in a foreign language which was never actually said. A well-known scientific German TV-series once dedicated a program to the subject "inexplicable phenomena". The presenter, however, tried categorically to expose voice-recording phenomena as being an illusion.[113]

Among others there is a physicist from Wuppertal, here in Germany, who has taken it upon himself to go from one German adult education centre to the next spreading his own personal opinion that these phenomena are mere illusions.

They both refer to the song *"Another Brick in the Wall"* by the British pop group *"Pink Floyd"*[114] to illustrate their scepticism.

In the chorus, which is sung by children in English, they claim that they can hear the German words *"Holt ihn unters Dach und hängt ihn auf"* *(translated back into English it would mean something like "take him under the roof and string him up")*. They then construct an absolutely outrageous story

---

[113] "Quarks & Co.", German TV Channel WDR 3, December 1998, with Ranga Yogeshwar.
[114] From the record "The Wall", recorded 1979.

around this chorus. For the unpractised listener it really seems to prove just how nonsensical it all is. In fact, it only demonstrates how easy it is to deceive and that this approach is, without doubt, bound to deceive. However, this does not prove that the approach is wrong. Any experienced researcher of voice-recordings will not be so easily deceived. Of course, he is aware of the difficulties. His problem lies completely elsewhere: not everybody who uses this technique does so with the necessary critical distance. Only too often the will to hear something is influenced by (understandable) emotions. This alone is reason enough to expect misinterpretations whereby one surely not uninteresting approach is, in my opinion, unfairly and too hastily maligned.

Parapsychologists today do indeed admit that, in spite of the countless misinterpretations – for whatever reason, a number of voices still remain which can be filtered out from these recordings and which could without doubt be described as being paranormal[115]. They do not fit into the context of the relevant radio program, nor could they have been produced by overshoot interferences. Furthermore, they usually give a reasonable and logical answer to a question addressed to a certain deceased person.

A parapsychologist will again attribute this to an ESP-phenomenon: only the experimenter himself by his own "psychic energy" can be the source of the responses manifested on the tapes.

Of course, we must treat the phenomenon of the "voice recordings" very delicately. But in the meantime I have concluded that charlatanism, and even fraud, on the one hand and serious research on the other hand lie very close together in this area.

Nevertheless, in spite of all the misinterpretations many inexplicable, well-recorded and even reproducible experiences remain. Among the many snippets of sentences obtained from experiments all of which require close and critical scrutiny we can usually find in the end an astonishing number of cases which give conclusive answers to previously posed questions.

If I had to decide whether these results were to be interpreted in a *spiritualistic* or *animistic* way, I would tend, due to the logical reasons I already explained, and due to my own personal experiences, to consider them as being real expressions coming from a different, non-physical spiritual level.

---

[115] Special filter software for computers is also ideal for this purpose.

Therefore, I think it is extremely unlikely that the experimenter himself could be in any way subconsciously responsible for these phenomena by way of the physical manifestation of his psychic energy. This gives us compelling reason for assuming that the remaining voice recordings, which have after all been clearly recorded, are indeed the real responses from those deceased persons to whom we addressed questions and from whom we requested answers. I believe that only they would be in a position to give the correct answers.

For these reasons, I believe that a number of incidents and experiences obviously do exist which after critical contemplation could be explained in the most rational way as having been real contacts with deceased persons.

17. Death is not the End of your life

I am absolutely convinced that death is not the end of our personality. I believe as well that the birth of a human being here on earth is the beginning of a completely new spiritual development – no soul, no spirit is born again. Once newly created, the human spirit has in principle no definable end – everyone exists in eternity according to our criteria.

Only our bodies will inevitably die one day – and in death they will go the natural way of all finite matter.

From the beginning of all existence everything and everybody in this world leaves a spiritual trace behind him. In the simplest instance – inanimate matter – this is merely the very information of being – comparable to the "1" in a binary computer code and transmitted through the universe by one light or radiation quantum. The more complex that something becomes in the course of time, the more complex its spiritual trace becomes as well.

The special nature of the spirit is essentially *information*. The same is probably meant in the Bible with the term *"word"*.

"In the beginning was the word and the word was with God"; the Christian Gospel according to St. John starts with these words. For everything and everyone in this world there is an informal mirror image. It is eternal, and as a consequence the entire world must also exist in eternity. In the meantime even some renowned cosmologists believe that our universe is infinite and that it will exist in eternity. I agree – but for a different reason, since in my opinion our universe is primarily a spiritual, number-encoded and, therefore, infinite space.

On Earth we humans are the only ones possessing a high level of consciousness and self-awareness which seems to have developed rather abruptly. No other creature has the ability to attain such a highly structured self-recognition and self-awareness. No animal possesses approximately anything like our ability for abstract thought and imagination, or our potentially fantastically rich, emotional, ethical and cultural potentials.

We humans are the only creatures on Earth who are, to some extent at least, able to discover and to marvel at the countless and indeed incredible wonders of this world.

Over millions of years evolution constructed a strictly hierarchically structured and custom-made, downward-compatible communication and computer system, i.e. the central nervous system and peripheral information systems.

Nevertheless, in its individual parts and functions, this highly complicated nervous system is really rather simple and clearly organized.

It has achieved – at least temporarily – its perfection in humans. At this point in time it was already a mere few seconds before 12 o'clock midnight on the gigantic clock of our earth history.

The short snippet of time between the first appearance of humans and our present time, an extremely short period, saw an unbelievably revolutionary development as never before. There was much positive, but also, unfortunately, far too much negative development. There are two sides to everything.

Over a period of only a few hundred years, mankind has achieved something magnificent, in spite of all adversity. However, everything mankind has achieved is the physical projection of ideas. Ideas are something spiritual.

The sole basis of this revolution is, therefore, the human spirit. It is the distinguishing feature of evolution undergoing change in our time, since the dramatic differences between individual human beings have been

brought about by the human spirit alone. No human being is the same as another – and no ideology can ever make them equal.
All humans are different because, as single individuals, they are the object of another immensely important chapter in the evolution of all life. They are the centre of the new evolution of the pure spirit. Spiritual perfection can only be achieved by following the path of "God", which can alternatively mean the path of "Manito", "Allah" or "Brahman", etc.
Yet the divine path has more often than not little or nothing to do with those paths suggested, or even dogmatically laid down, by institutionalised churches, associations or sects.
The divine path can solely mean:
Love "God" as the incomprehensible creator and background of this world, love yourself and love your neighbour as yourself. Grant the right of free self-determination to everyone in the same way as you might expect it for yourself. Practice the utmost tolerance with everyone since you are not identical with your brethren and, therefore, you cannot exactly comprehend his feelings and emotions. Every human being is different and must be different. Therefore, watch with utmost severity and, if necessary, with utmost strictness that every individual possesses the same rights and that they are not curbed or even destroyed by anyone.

Today the spirit is no longer merely evolving at differing speeds in different human beings. Rather it evolves in different ways and phases with advancing age in the course of the life of each individual human being.
When finally the human body slowly deteriorates, when wear and tear becomes increasingly apparent and the human being becomes aware of his progressing physical inadequacy, the spirit is only approaching the prime of its (temporary) development.
Let us take a look at this clearly tree-like structure of consistent spiritual development in a quick-motion mode.
It starts with the objective information of BEING for each single atom and also of combined, inanimate matter. At this point in time a subjectively evaluating spirit does not yet exist.
This develops only when life appears on the scene and it develops in living beings as a completely new component which is of still low quality at the beginning. The next step is the development of a more subjective species-specific spirit.

Slowly this leads to the development of conscious beings which also includes the higher developed mammals.
Conscious and also self-aware, and in its consciousness unbelievably more complex than any animal, the true nature of the spirit finally matures in the individual spirit of each single human being.
Therefore, it is inevitable that differences arise in the spiritual levels of individual humans. In the end the spirit even evolves in every individual human being and in different individual ways by growing continuously until life is terminated by the (physical) death of the human being.
Thus every single person experiences his own spiritual gradient of development as a natural personal development in his life. And this makes one thing very clear:
The spirit is not cyclical. Each spirit is something consistently and expansively striving for progress. The spirit seeks individuality to optimise the whole in plurality. The spirit is indestructible. Each spirit survives physical death, of course!

18. Optimists have the advantage

It is certainly a fact that nobody has ever returned to this world in the flesh after his death. Therefore, there is no conclusive evidence to prove the survival of physical death. Neither is there, however, any evidence which contradicts this conviction. It would be even more difficult to prove the opposite by applying pure, scientific methods; for as long as the world exists we can never completely rule out the possibility that at some time or other somebody may come back here in the flesh, which I, personally, do not believe, however.
Evidence and counter-evidence are balanced from a purely logical point of view. For either possibility there is a probability of 50%.
Humans are the first creatures on earth who are in a position to think about death and a possible world beyond. Based on this fifty-fifty chance

humans can decide freely as to whether they prefer to take the optimistic view *for*, or the pessimistic view *against,* a life after death.
In line with the spirit of our age most people, at least most of those living in the western world, opt for the pessimistic view of the world. This is why, although in principle either may equally be right, it is only the optimist who is required to prove his notion, a feat which neither of them could perform; the pessimist is permitted to express his opinion without actually having to prove it since it is usually accepted without criticism. This is mainly ascribed to the knowledge of modern science.
In the last chapters of this book as well as in my former books, I made the attempt to explain in detail that I do not share this view and that I consider it to be wrong.
Without discussing the pros and cons, the unbiased observer should really only ask himself which would be the *better* choice:
Sociologists have determined already that humans who are steadfast in their religious beliefs, whatever they may be – and these usually include the conviction of a life after death – are significantly healthier and they usually have a better chance to live longer. This being so, an optimistic attitude seems to be the better choice.
Many "optimists" believe that their choice is the better one because it satisfies their longings and hopes. The criteria for adopting an optimistic view are, therefore, of subjective nature.
But even under purely objective consideration the "optimistic" point of view definitely seems to be by far the better choice. The famous French philosopher and mathematician *Blaise Pascal* made this very clear in his anecdote about a bet:
Pascal changed his life-style drastically after having had a near-death-experience. He became a fervent devotee of God and was convinced that he would survive his death. So he was an optimist and proposed to "unbelieving pessimists" this bet. Pessimists have no chance at all of winning the bet, because only the optimist will ever know whether he has won. Only he will be able to establish whether his choice was right. Should there be no life after death – and considering my conviction I prefer to choose the conjunctive here – then neither the optimist nor the pessimist will ever know, since they would both be irrevocably dead. Should, however, the optimist win the bet, the pessimist would recognize his defeat and at the same time he would resent that he had been unable to enjoy a more light-hearted life. For some people the fear of their own death, often growing with advancing age, is an unbearable burden and

causes depressions in many cases. The optimist, on the other hand, has not only won the bet but he has also been able to enjoy a more conscious, more composed and certainly more cheerful life. The pessimist has no chance of winning the bet. Even if he were right he would never find out about it. Furthermore the pessimist would have to recognise that he did have a chance which he never or only poorly utilised since his pessimistic life-style left him to fall short of his own expectations and of those around him. The optimist will naturally more often than not be inclined to put his own welfare above those of others in critical situations. Nothing would be more natural. Pessimists would also be inclined more easily than convinced optimists to act in ways causing harm to their environment or other people – or even to lure them on to destruction. A pessimist does not fear a punishment after death.

Many pessimists might only try to avoid mundane punishment in time by devious or even unscrupulous behaviour.

Therefore, from a social point of view it is to be recommended to think and live as an optimist.

The victory of optimism is thus a victory all along the line – and at the same time it is the only possible victory!

Part 2:

Near-Death Experiences (NDE) under Discussion

"... finally I knew something, namely that I was immortal, indestructible. I could not be injured, I could not get lost. We have no need to worry. And that the world is perfect; everything that happens is part of a perfect plan. Today I no longer understand this part, but I know it to be true..."
Report of a woman who nearly died while giving birth,
From: *IANDS* – Meeting, Charlottesville, VA/USA (1982)

"At first, when the light came, I wasn't sure what was happening, but then, it asked, it kind of asked me if I was ready to die. It was like talking to a person, but a person wasn't there. The light's what was talking to me, but in a *voice.*"
From: *Raymond Moody*, "Life after Life " (1977)

"That which happens after death is so unexplainably magnificent that our imagination and feeling is insufficient to understand it correctly even in part..."
Carl Gustav Jung (1875-1961), in: Letter to Ms B. 11.07.1944

Once again, I chose the form of a discussion to clarify some of the more important aspects of the subjects discussed in the first part of this book in order to make them more comprehensible and to consolidate our arguments.
And again the discussion with my sons Alexander and Martin is fictional. However, much of what we discuss in this dialogue has actually been the topic of a number of similar conversations we have had at one time or other.

Near-death experiences (NDEs) seem to have always been a fundamental source of intuitive experience as philosophy and all religions show. In the first part of this book I primarily described the character of these strange phenomena. Nature scientists, however, deny that near-death experiences are of reputable significance. Therefore, the second part of my book is dedicated to a detailed and, as regards the contents, controversial discussion.

Is this discussion at all necessary?

"Many people think that all near-death experiences are utter nonsense," Alexander starts our discourse. "Some are just dreams, others are hallucinations and they all are *not necessarily* connected with death at all. NDEs can obviously be provoked in experiments and with people who enjoy the best of health. And if we take a closer look at their contents they are by no means homogenous, as is always claimed. Everyone dreams something different. In the weekly German newspaper *'Die Zeit'* I once read the following article: *'Once to Hell and Back. East Germans die in a different way than West Germans ... . The manner of dying depends on culture and biography.'*[116] I do not think that this whole business about NDEs can help us at all and by no means do NDEs prove that we go on living after death..."
"Slow down," I interrupt him in his monologue, "we have to sort this one out in peace and quiet and then we have to tackle one thing at a

---
[116] Urs Willmann in: "Die Zeit" 29 (1999)

time. What you just said is far too general and not at all tenable in this form ... ."
"But it's true, isn't it," Martin takes the same line, "that not one of those reporting about such NDEs was really and truly dead?"
"Of course, Son, you are absolutely right, not one of them was really dead. No-one has ever come back from the dead ...," I agree and mumble to myself, "... at least not for long."
"Don't say that out loud," Martin retorts, "you will get into trouble with the Church in no time – after all they claim that Jesus rose from the dead in the flesh."
"Well," I reply, "that is a matter of faith, and we do not want to discuss that in detail now, otherwise we will be sidetracked too far and far too long right from the start. But to come back to Alexander's arguments: it is indeed true that NDEs can be provoked in normal healthy people and that something similar can occur in dreams, of course, and that hallucinations do happen. It is also true that the contents of NDEs are not always homogenous and by no means are NDEs *alone* a *proof* of a life after death ..."
"You see," Alexander smiles, "I was right. We can forget the whole issue..."
"No, not at all," I interrupt him this time, "in spite of all your disparaging comments – I am absolutely convinced that 'real' NDEs indeed indicate a real 'hereafter' and that they should be taken very seriously, and I agree with *Michael Schröter-Kunhardt*, when he writes in his introduction to my last book, entitled "Death", that *'similar to a flight simulator they prepare the 'nearly-dying' for the fact that after death they will leave their body'.*[117]
In one of his other publications he says: *'The paranormal performances of living or dying persons and the increased appearances of paranormal phenomena of religious experiences (in death) experienced even by non-religious people, indicate indeed that there is a part in the human soul which is independent of time and space and is thus immortal. The last brain-transmitted activities are NDEs which, as primarily religious-mystical experiences, prepare the soul for its further life after death in a religious world beyond. The experience of a religious-mystical NDE is, as has been proved by NDEs (...,) due to a biologically prepared matrix, (...) which cannot be explained away by any theory and which is an elementary part of the human soul."*

---

[117] Michael Schröter-Kunhardt, psychiatrist in Heidelberg, Chairman of the German Section of IANDS (International Association of Near Death Studies) – see List of References

"Then you have to give good reasons as to why you and others are so certain and why you dismiss all counterarguments." Martin also expresses his doubts.

When are we dead?

"Exactly," I agree. "Maybe we should start with death itself. There is no definite moment of death. Death happens in several phases, dying is, therefore, a process. When the heart stops we talk about clinical death. The brain, however, still goes on living for another few seconds or even minutes..."
"That's what I mean," Alexander jumps in, "only during this short period, if at all, NDEs can happen; when the brain is dead all the lights go out for good. This author of the article in the German weekly newspaper *'Die Zeit'* says: *'Like the radio, which still plays one or two notes with the last remaining electrons after it has been unplugged, the biological being is still active after the blood in the veins has stopped flowing.'* And he gives the example of a rattle-snake in which the bite-reflex is supposed to be still active even one hour after the head has been cut off."
"Possibly," I murmur, rather pushed into the defensive, "but these are reflexes and they are nothing but automatisms. That has nothing at all to do with spirit, as I already explained in detail in my book "Life". But what I meant to say was: even after brain-death the *body* is not yet finally dead, although a return to life is not possible. Final death is now irrevocably initiated by the death of the brain. Even if it is only of theoretical interest: The actual end is marked by the biological death which is indicated by the so-called certain signs of death, such as a low body temperature, rigor mortis and post-mortem lividity.
NDEs can only be reported, of course, if the affected person comes back to life. Nevertheless, there are some cases – *Raymond Moody*, for example, reports on some of them in his books – in which the affected persons described near-death experiences even when no further brain activity had been detected on the EEG[118] - i.e. in the case of a so-called isoelectric EEG."

---

[118] EEG = electroencephalography

"But when the EEG shows a baseline how can anyone still be able to fantasize?" Alexander is rather irritated.
"Exactly," I hurry to explain, "this is an unmistakable indication that these NDEs cannot be fantasies – or let's rather say: hallucinations. I will specify this more precisely later. However, NDEs have been reliably documented to have happened under iso-electric EEGs, i.e. after the entire brain activities had stopped.
In his book *'Light and Death'* the American heart surgeon *Michael B. Sabom,* formerly an absolute disbeliever in NDEs, describes an unusual case. By the way, the same case was also subject of the German movie *'Jenseitsreisen'* *(Journeys to the Beyond)* from the German-French television station *'Arte'*.[119] *Schröter-Kunhardt* also played an important part in the production of this film about NDEs, which, in my opinion, is one of the best and most objective ones yet. The patient mentioned by *Sabom* had to undergo surgery due to a dangerous saccular aneurysm she had at the base of her skull. Her body temperature was lowered to 15.6°C and her entire blood circulation was deliberately stopped. Suddenly, however, her EEG showed a baseline and the activity of her brain stem failed completely." [120]

Are NDEs only hallucinations?

"All right, but maybe the patient had an oxygen deficiency in her blood when her circulation was stopped so that she started hallucinating," Alexander interrupts me.
"I will come back to the oxygen deficiency," I interject immediately, "but first of all let's go back to hallucinations in general…"
"Tell me, Papa, what exactly are hallucinations?" Martin wants to know.
"They are pathological tricks of the senses which are not caused by external stimuli," I explain to him. "They often happen due to certain so-called mental illnesses *(psychoses)*, such as *schizophrenia* and – and it's good that you ask – they happen even when external stimuli are not directly involved: hallucinations can only happen if the sensory organs are generally still in working order. Their sensitivity may be exaggerated or

---
[119] First broadcast on 12.04.2000, 45 minutes.
[120] Failure of the so-called auditory evoked responses of the brain stem.

shifted but they must still be intact. Therefore, the EEG does not show baselines during hallucinations. On the contrary, it even shows especially typical patterns of activity. Besides, the NDEs of children practically show the same basic patterns as those of adults. If the NDEs really were hallucinations, children would have completely different visions of death, since their pool of experience is completely different."

"Hallucinations actually do take on very diverse forms, which...," Alexander wants to go into details, but I interrupt him and continue for him:

"...which are also found in NDEs, you mean?. Yes, indeed, some elements of NDEs could be hallucinations, and some probably are. Nevertheless, there are subtle but clear differences and, therefore, hallucinations cannot entirely explain the contents of NDEs:

For example, there are auditory hallucinations, known as 'hearing voices' which is very often rather disturbing. Only, the voices heard have no real reference to anything happening at that specific moment. The person experiencing an NDE, however, hears a coherent conversation, for example, he hears what people are actually talking about over his body. One of my favourite patients, today he is over eighty years old and is still as bright as a button, is an old hand with regard to NDEs. Mr S. had no less than six heart attacks between 1971 and 1992, two of which caused cardiac arrest. He still remembers exactly what happened during his first heart attack which happened over thirty years ago in 1971.

He was lying in the intensive care unit and, as his wife confirmed, was in a 'coma' for nine days. On the third day he suddenly heard someone shout 'exitus'. At the same moment he heard *'a bell toll'* and he saw himself – or rather – his body lying on a stretcher. He felt like *'a bird sitting in a niche and watching everything that happened beneath him'*. Then he saw the doctors *'giving him electric shocks'*, and he heard these as *'powerful poundings'*. Soon a tunnel opened to the left of his stretcher which was aglow with *'a beautiful warm red-orange light'*. This light *'was soothing and relaxing'* and attracted him very much.

He *'was supposed to go through the tunnel'*, while he *'was torn backwards and forwards'*. Suddenly he opened his eyes and the anaesthetist was bent over him asking what he thought he was doing and whether he wanted to give up the fight."

"But why shouldn't that have been a hallucination?" demands Martin.

"Now, my dear son," I immediately respond to his question, "Mr S. was able to relate exactly what had happened and what he had heard. He was

able to describe exactly all the persons who took care of his dying body. Some of them he had never seen before. He described his experience as having been *'beautiful and wonderful'*. And even today, after more than thirty years, he still sees it as such. Ever since, he has felt *'more relaxed and more contented'*. He claims that he has *'a different relationship with God'* and feels *'even more heartfelt and deep affection'* for his family. His impressions were even intensified when he had another NDE due to a so-called ventricular fibrillation during his fourth heart attack in 1984:
From a kind of bird's eye view Mr S. again saw his body being laid down. Again the doctors and nurses were fighting for his life and soon he noticed again the soothing *'warm red-orange light'* he already knew.
He describes it this time as follows: *'...was conscious that there was a fight going on for my life here on earth and on the world beyond. Suddenly I hear someone say: 'Good bye, Mr Kussmaul'. I had to smile to myself while I imagined the situation in which a gentleman introduces himself to a lady with the words: my name is Kussmaul (something like kiss-gob). Much later, after I had woken up again, I asked the nurse whether she knew the name Kussmaul. She replied: 'Oh yes, Dr Kussmaul was our assistant medical director and he left us to take a better position elsewhere'."*
"Okay, but what about visual hallucinations?" Martin stays persistent.
"Visual hallucinations do not provide us with comprehensive explanations either," I reject his suggestion out of hand. "Visual hallucinations have less to do with 'seeing' than with 'being seen'.
The affected persons have the feeling, that somebody is looking at them, for example, or that hands appearing out of a wall are reaching for them. Delusions are often involved in these cases.
The so-called (he-) autoscopic hallucinations[121] are a special form of visual hallucinations. Many critics of NDEs like to use these kinds of hallucinations and other out-of-body experiences or excursions, OBEs for short, incorrectly as synonyms for one another. But I will come back to this later.
Of course, there are also visual hallucinations in which the 'active vision', e.g. a vision of paradise, are more prominent. Persons experiencing an NDE, however, often see a review of their life like a movie, which always shows coherent and exact pictures of *their* lives. We can almost compare it to video clips."

---

[121] Latin: visual hallucination of one's body image.

"Meanwhile it is believed that NDEs can even be provoked experimentally," Alexander joins in again, "and snippets of their own lives also appear to people during epileptic seizures."
"Yes, even OBEs can be provoked...," I agree.
"But then NDEs and OBEs are nothing more than mere products of the brain as indeed the spirit may turn out to be in the end – and we are just imagining everything about the immaterial spirit and the spiritual dimensions?" He is unrelenting and doubtful.
"No! I am quite prepared to review the whole issue point by point again," it's my turn now, "but not everything at once. – Well then, let us first look at the visual hallucinations in general again: real NDEs have a typical basic structure, a specific pattern whereas in other cases they do not. It is only the content which varies rather a lot, while the pattern stays more or less the same."
"But hallucinogens, the trigger for hallucinations, can be detected in NDEs," Alexander almost bubbles over.
"Yes, and even if so, then they are only correlations, that is the results of interactions." I notice that there is still a lot of convincing to be done.
"We have to be clear about one thing: as long as the affected person is not 'quite' dead his brain will still be functioning. Even if we attribute many influences to purely spiritual causes, the brain is certainly always involved, as we already established in my book "Life" in our discussion on the subject *'Spirit and Brain'*. There are no two ways around. It finally boils down to the question whether something spiritual could exist and take effect without maintaining a connection to its brain, even though we may (unfortunately) not be able to understand how. I am absolutely convinced meanwhile that this is possible. But: as long as the brain is still functioning it will always and invariably show a reaction.
I think that it would be a bad mistake to turn this involvement into a conditio sine qua non. In my opinion it is incorrect, therefore, to say that *only* the brain is functioning and that the spiritual component is induced by the brain and its activity – that it is only a product of the brain.
Therefore it is especially important to go through all these critical counterarguments and to analyse them completely and in detail.
Let's go back to the various kinds of hallucinations: naturally a number of NDE-experiences, especially in some of their vastly diverse details, are very similar to hallucinations.
And some may even be hallucinations as I already admitted. But NDEs show certain typical characteristics which do not occur in hallucinations.

Something similar also applies to your other critical objections; we will come back to that later.

One point, for example, is that persons with mental disorders do not experience NDEs any more often than do mentally healthy people – although by definition hallucinations themselves are a mentally abnormal condition. Please remember that in my opinion even the expression 'mental or spiritual illness' is incorrect in most cases.

As a rule there are brain diseases behind it.

They damage, for example, the interfaces, the synapses. Or the nerves themselves or their sheaths are defective. Often the many messenger substances are involved which have only been known for the last few years and which are necessary for the transmission of impulses from one nerve to the next. Sometimes nothing at all is produced, sometimes too little and sometimes too much.

It follows that there must be certain similarities between disease-induced phenomena and others, which are the direct result of a universal biological 'farewell-program to physical sufferings'.

NDEs could be exactly that: a kind of 'simulator-training' preparing the previously brain-accustomed spirit for a new, a non-physical, existence thereafter. It remains an amazing fact that the basic patterns of NDEs – and I do not mean the great diversity of their contents here – do not agree at all with the typical tenets of western culture or the great religions. In fact, shouldn't we assume that such religious or cultural concepts are given preferential consideration in death?"

Do NDEs show more cultural differences than previously thought?

"Today, some critics are of the opinion that there is no typical basic pattern in NDEs," Alexander objects again, "it is said, for example, that Chinese people never pass through a tunnel – which is supposed to be one of the central experiences – while West Germans usually experience beautiful visions, East Germans (those who live in the former communist part of Germany) usually experience more traumatic visions.

And what is more, OBEs[122] are supposed to be absolutely unknown to them[123]. In short, critics assume that the kind of experience seems to depend greatly on what people have already read or heard about such experiences."

"Well, that OBEs should be unknown to them," I defend my convictions, "contradicts one argument these critics use themselves. They point out correctly that OBEs can be provoked by stimulating certain brain areas or by using certain psychogenic drugs. Why should people of other cultures, in this case an atheistic one, react differently to such stimuli if the reactions were merely natural products of the brain? It seems to me that this issue has not been thought through with the necessary diligence or that a general rejection has been influenced by statistics.

Therefore, every statistic should be regarded with suspicion. Without wishing to offend anybody, the popular 'bon mot' should still be heeded without reservation: *'Do not trust any statistics which you haven't faked yourself.'* The last thing I want to do is to suggest that anyone consciously manipulates statistics, but – in the broadest sense– I want to reveal the possibilities of various research modes being open for manipulation. Any study can be structured beforehand, in accordance with the required results. It is not for nothing that opinion researchers are often perceived as being opinion makers as well. I doubt, for example, that enough documents exist, providing sufficient reliable testimony about NDEs in China because over the last 50 years it has been impossible to study them in a seriously scientific way. OBEs are quite definitely a universal phenomenon – and we will discuss them in more detail later. With OBEs one must also differentiate between those which, due to certain characteristics, belong to the category of real NDE-conditioned realities, and others which are more hallucinative brain reactions.

But let me respond to Alexander's last objection: first of all, the fact that positive as well as negative NDEs are experienced also contradicts the often expressed criticism that near-death-experiences are the mere hallucinative fulfilment of wishes. Since we hope for a life after death, we imagine it 'unconsciously' – especially in life-threatening situations – and we picture it accordingly. Negative NDEs do not at all fit this pattern.

---

[122] OBE = Out of Body Experience
[123] Hubert Knoblauch et al., "Berichte aus dem Jenseits" ("Reports from the Beyond"), see List of References.

It is simply not true to say that NDEs have no homogenous patterns or that they show significant differences caused by various cultures and religions. To say that the patterns change is correct only for the individual embellishments of NDEs, i.e. it applies to the 'how' and nothing else. However, cultural and religious backgrounds can in no way be regarded as an impetus for NDEs and OBEs *to happen at all* nor can pre-information and certain religious expectations.
In this context, *Schröter-Kunhardt* and other near-death researchers pointed out that even children under 2 years of age can have such experiences which are almost without exception very similar to those of adults. This should really amaze all critics since children at this early age do not dream whole stories, at best they dream short sequences but mainly just single pictures, e.g. of teddy bears or of their parents.
Not before children are 9 to 12 years old do their dreams compare to those of adults. And what concerns the positive or negative NDE-contents: Even according to the most sceptic German *Konstanz-Study* made by *Hubert Knoblauch* and his assistants, many East Germans have positive NDEs. It is also true that any belief in 'religion', 'God' or a 'life after death' has almost been exorcized from very many East Germans throughout their 40 years of communist dictatorship – and the same probably applies to the Chinese as well. But then it is even more amazing that in spite of all this, and contrary to the convictions indoctrinated into them, they experience NDEs and OBEs at all."
"Maybe because it is a sort of farewell-program produced by the brain," Alexander gibes.
"But for what purpose?" I counter. "It would contradict all the basic laws of evolution since it lends no advantage for survival."
"It may be that for evolution such a program is a typical issue which it treats with the utmost concern because it always strives for perfection," Alexander remains unrelenting, "these were your own words, weren't they?"
"Your idea is almost the same as the one expressed by the American, *Ronald Siegel,* who – in a mixture of evolutionary perfection and psychological components – banished all NDEs and, of course, any kind of life after death into the realm of human folly. Nature, he said, has constructed an 'unfailing' system which forces us to deceive ourselves about the real nature of death: our neurochemistry works together with all our experiences, our own needs and various cultures which has the effect of supporting and intensifying the deception. The core aspect

behind his idea is his assumption that deep down we resist to accept our own death.

Yet NDEs are certainly no rejection of death. They cannot be, since from a psychological point of view, and that is my opinion, it would be utter nonsense to believe that we would try to escape death by heading in a direction which actually frightens us. If there must be a spectacle at all why not have something more amusing instead, or what do you think?."

"How's that," Alexander is still not prepared to let up, "attack is the best form of defence, isn't it?"

"That does not apply here," I reject the cliché, "the early notion of our own imminent death make us far more fearful than an NDE. The American heart surgeon *Michael Sabom*, who I mentioned earlier, maintained that NDEs occur at a time when the affected person has already resigned himself to death and has lowered all his defences. It wouldn't make sense if a person, who had just found his 'inner peace' after having gone through mental torture, were immediately frightened anew.

And anyway, it has been proved that NDEs are usually prematurely *terminated* by terrifying experiences. This might even be a further explanation as to why it is that East Germans or the Chinese allegedly tend to be confronted with more negative experiences. One of the typical basic patterns of NDEs is the initial tunnel or dark-room experience, often accompanied by acoustic perceptions, i.e. sounds of some kind and frequently combined with horrifically fast motion. I once went through such an experience myself (see Part 1). At first these experiences are more disquieting than pleasant. Those affected will, of course, tend to embellish the contents of these patterns in completely different ways.

We might imagine that during this phase such experiences are far more frightening for someone who has lived in a culturally enforced atheism than for a religious person who in his 'heart' is confident and much more composed.

The purely subjective embellishment of a similar basic experience, such as a "light image" or a "tunnel experience" thus becomes more dramatic for the non-religious person and more often it causes the premature termination of NDEs. In this connection it is interesting, however, to observe that in the end all those undergoing an NDE which started with negative experiences and was *not* immediately terminated, still have just as beautiful and wonderful experiences later, when the NDE is

progressing, as others who have not suffered quite such negative experiences. This fact is supported by historical reports of NDEs which I mentioned in the first part of this book."
"And what else can be said against the thesis that attack is the best form of defence?" Alexander tempts me again.
"Well," I continue, "I find it quite astonishing that NDEs almost always without exception cause people to change their lives distinctly, they become more adjustable and sensitive but also more relaxed in handling death. *Schröter-Kunhardt* underlines this observation and expresses it very clearly when he says that will-power must be called upon *'for taking actual (archaic) action against distressing circumstances in death and to suppress them or to seek death in unconsciousness'*, while *'NDEs and OBEs are - like dreams – attempts to digest reality which has not been suppressed by unconsciousness but which is in both experiences made conscious.'*[124]
In other words: in fear of imminent death we should all really want to escape into unconsciousness, but not into clear consciousness."
"Does that mean that NDEs are just another kind of dream, let's say a more intensive dream?" Martin rejoins the conversation.
"No, son," I reject his suggestion, "nor are they complex day-dreams – even if some day-dreams may indeed facilitate access to spiritual dimensions. These two have no common characteristics such as a different sense of time or a certain sense for reality. As regards (real) dreams, I think I suggested a plausible explanation for them in my book "Life". They are probably the result of repair work at the synapses of the ascending nerve fibres in the cortex. Since these, in my opinion, could be 'physical interfaces' between body and spirit, dreams and NDEs must inevitably have common characteristics.
However, only NDEs show typical basic patterns suggesting the existence of a definite program. Dreams on the other hand are not at all strictly structured and are oriented mainly to day-to-day issues such as fears, problems or hopes.

---

[124] Quoted according to M. Schmidt-Degenhard (1992), see List of References

Are there universal patterns for NDEs?

"But again, Dad, where do you see the recurring basic patterns?" Martin does not seem satisfied yet.
"Well, there are doubtless elements which are especially typical for NDEs. Each of these elements on its own is not exclusive to NDEs, taken together, however, they are actually typical for an NDE and they are always part of the whole picture of an NDE," I reply. "They include especially:
1) The prevailing mood in all NDEs, either all the time or at least at it progresses, is happy and cheerful and people experience the feeling of love and of being loved.
2) The out-of-body experience in which one's own body can be observed from the outside and from a certain distance, in a kind of 'bird's eye view'.
3) The perception of light and even of beings of light.
4) The encounter with other beings all of whom without exception are people who are already dead.
5) The life-movie in which not only positive but also especially negative aspects are shown and which always calls for an evaluation of one's previous life.
6) Often even dramatic, but at least rather amazing, changes in the personality of the person after his return to the body.
As I said, these are typical basic elements or patterns of an NDE which can be embellished individually and with a great degree of diversity. While one person might feel as if he were being transported into paradise, another might find himself in a beautiful meadow and the next in a wonderful city, etc.! All these are purely individual embellishments which are, however, always based on the common identical basic patterns."
"Why do NDEs occur even when the affected person is not really in mortal danger?" Martin changes the direction slightly.
"As strange as this might sound at first, it is exactly one of the major arguments of many critics," I am quite delighted about this objection.
"NDEs occurring in other than life-threatening situations are practically never complete – only single or sometimes several elements are experienced. The real, fully blown NDE only occurs in situations when death is imminent! Critics do not want to believe this, of course, because

they do not regard the completeness of NDEs as being so very important. I think this is a major mistake.
For someone who has experienced a complete 'real' NDE this has very nearly always an almost dramatic influence on his personality which is still noticeable even years and decades after his profound experience. There are some intellectuals who will sometimes suppress these impressions probably because they do not fit their view of the world.
However, intellectuality and intelligence are – in many cases – not necessarily congruent. If I wanted to make a really nasty remark here, I would say that this seems to apply especially to politicians and to some of our media specialists.
Now then, it is a fact that the full picture of an NDE only ever occurs in real NDEs. In experiments or when disease-induced it is only singular NDE-elements which are invoked. The journalist Urs *Wissmann* made fun of this in his article in the German weekly newspaper *'Die Zeit'* (29/1999), quite unjustifiably in my opinion, when he said: *'Our presumed glimpse of the world beyond does **not even** need the proximity of death,'* as if this alone were already proof enough *against* the actual spiritual-religious nature of NDEs and their real significance.
Of course the proximity of death is not an imperative; that which *Wissmann* deliberately avoids mentioning, however, is that this merely applies to single parts of an NDE-experience which is only experienced in full in a real NDE. With unnecessary irony he goes on: *'Not only those who cheat death in the very last instance experience such extreme situations. The same happens to those who experience a moment of horror with their bodies unscathed. A shaman also oscillates backwards and forwards in trance – his way to and from work, so to speak.'*
All this does not really refute the possibility that some cases might have been real NDEs, because if NDEs are indeed a biological program for preparing people for their physical death and the unimpeded escape of the spirit from the body, then, of course, the *psychological* proximity of death could be playing just as an important role in causing an NDE as the *real* proximity itself. If the brain, as I claim, is an *interface* between body and spirit, such a 'farewell program' must also show the notorious two sides of the same coin.
And all the 'worldly' stimulants or even techniques suitable for causing certain NDE-elements to occur, are themselves a part or at least analogues on the physical side of the coin. In other words: since they belong to the 'physical side' they are primarily responsible for the 'brain-

induced' execution of the biologically embodied and reflex-like starting program.
The more the NDE-affected person approaches to the border of his actual biological death, the more complete, detailed and emotionally loaded (spiritual side of the coin!) all these universal patterns become; they become embodied in his NDE due to the increasing involvement of the other side, the spiritual side.

Are NDEs induced by a shortage of oxygen, or delirium?

"Okay," Alexander changes the direction of our conversation, "let's talk about some of the other causes which are also discussed. Most scientists claim that NDEs are just a result of an oxygen deficiency in the blood..."
"... so-called *hypoxia,* yes," I jump in, "and others think too much carbon monoxide (CO_2), so-called *hypercarbia*, causes NDEs. While both of these conditions can indeed cause one or the other component of NDEs, possibly even several at the same time, neither of them can explain NDEs generally and completely."
"Why not?" Martin shows tense interest, "oxygen deficiency could be a sensible explanation, couldn't it? A person is near to death and slowly his 'life spirit' passes away. Finally his respiration and his heart beat stops. Now, less blood passes through his brain and, due to that, less oxygen."
"Yes," Alexander takes the same line, "the brain then produces hallucinations which are very similar to those experienced by others when they are nearing death – after all, a similar biochemical scenario must be taking place in their brain."
"You know," I start to answer, "another typical characteristic is that NDE-affected persons are always completely free of pain..." But I cannot complete my sentence.
"That's easy to explain: after all, in dangerous situations, the brain produces pain-killing substances known as endorphins. You can read this in any newspaper. They are responsible for taking away the pain."
"In principle that is right," I pick up my thread again, "but why is it that endorphins are *always* produced only during 'real' NDEs and are thus part of the biological program of death preparation while when

experimentally invoked this is not always the case. We are confronted with another correlation here, which only seems to happen *automatically completely and perfectly* during 'real' NDEs. Both, oxygen deficiency (O_2) and excess carbon monoxide (CO_2), certainly induce *single elements* of NDEs.

Hallucinations, especially, may occur which are indeed similar to NDEs, but, as I already explained, they can in no way explain NDE-visions really comprehensively.

During the fifties of the last century when the inhalation of CO_2 was used in psychotherapeutic sessions, it was observed that NDE-like hallucinations occurred. An increased concentration of CO_2 in the blood is the direct result of an oxygen deficiency.

This in turn causes delirium. In fact, in a delirium the affected person can also experience the tunnel impression and the feeling of being surrounded by light. Never, however, are there contacts with beings of light or the experience of a consistent life review covering the positive as well as the negative aspects which is always described in vivid detail. The feeling of loving and of being loved never sets in during a delirium, nor are there any later changes in personality.

Furthermore, people in delirium usually feel disorientated and their faculty of perception of their environment is gravely impaired.

In contrast to this, an NDE-affected person is always very well orientated and can usually recall in detail everything that happened around him.

The memory of a delirium-affected person, on the other hand, is rather fragmentary later on, whereas that of NDE-affected persons stays almost euphorically exact even for decades and only these people report of spiritual encounters. Furthermore, NDE-affected persons always participate *actively* in the process, whereas delirium-affected persons hallucinate in a kind of nightmare and everything they 'experience' happens in a *passive* way, without them really taking part – as if they were not involved.

This again supports the claim that *hypoxia* and *hypercarbia* cannot convincingly explain NDEs. They usually do play a role in the real proximity of death but not in the mere presentiment of death.

In such a situation they cannot explain NDEs at all.

Above all, NDEs occur – notwithstanding all reductionistic views of doubters – even in cases in which the blood of those affected shows an

increased concentration of oxygen although they are standing on the very threshold of death.
The American researchers for NDEs, *Kenneth Ring* and *Raymond Moody*, for example, make this point as well."
"Can you give us some examples?" Martin is still highly concentrated.
"The heart surgeon *Michael Sabom* from Atlanta/Ga. thoroughly documented some such cases. *Sabom* used to be a sceptic – just as I was a long time ago – and he rejected NDEs as being possibly pre-programmed, spiritual-religious death preparations. On the strength of his own experiences, however, he adopted a different view later.
It started when *Sabom* by chance measured the O_2-concentration of a patient's blood exactly at the moment when the patient was going through a profound near-death experience. To his amazement the concentration of oxygen was significantly higher than expected. Even if NDEs or elements thereof may often occur under oxygen deficiency it does not mean that they are in any way dependent on this condition.
In fact, there is *no* causal connection between NDEs and O_2-deficiency. We may merely remark that correlations, i.e. interactions, are possible.
The Swiss author *Evelyn Elsaesser-Valarino* once interviewed the writer *Monsignore Jean Vernette* about this subject. He is adviser to the Vatican and the delegate for problems concerning sects and new religious phenomena for the French episcopate. She asked him whether he considered oxygen deficiency, carbon monoxide surplus and hallucinations in general as being useful arguments against the real existence of NDEs, and whether for him these conditions possibly even provide a rational explanation for NDEs. *Vernette* denied this and explained further: *'Hallucinations are a means for projecting inner visions, a means of reassurance and a reflection of inner needs. NDEs do not have the character of optical illusions expressing the hopes and fears of the dying. They purport to be 'proper' reports which have a specific consistency and a certain objective density.' Vernette* added that *NDEs* very rarely possess religious aspects."[125]

---

[125] E. Elsaesser-Valarino, "On the Other Side of Life – Exploring the Phenomenon of the Near-Death experience" Perseus Books (1999), see List of References

Why is it that not all people experience NDEs?

"Why is it that only approximately one third of all people have NDEs when they come close to dying?" Alexander ponders.
"I believe everybody has these experiences when they die. However, I cannot really tell you why not everybody, who was clinically dead and was brought back to life, talks about it," I reply, "but I would like to offer some speculations.
"Probably they are just dreams?" Martin will not let go.
"No. You know, of course, that practically everyone dreams at night several times," I start, "but only a few of us can remember more than one of these dreams. Of course, everyone will experience an NDE when he is on the threshold of death.
No-one can tell us when exactly such an NDE occurs during the process of dying and at what point in time in actual proximity to death. I assume that most people experience it when the moment of return into this life has already passed.
Those who experience an NDE so early on that they can talk about it after they have returned to this life are probably simply a minority. It is possible that their NDEs heralding the definite separation of body and spirit, start too early – similar to contractions which sometimes set in far too early before the actual birth process commences, thus causing the period of labour to take an awful long time.
Others might actually experience NDEs, but are unable to remember them later, as with most dreams which cannot be recalled."
"Then you are contradicting yourself," Martin takes me to task, "after all, you are of the opinion that NDEs are real and not like dreams which are but shadows. Then people should remember their experience, shouldn't they?"
"Not necessarily," I contradict him on this point. "There are sufficient examples for real events which we nevertheless do not remember later. Just think of sleep-walking. Of course, that is something absolutely real – people walk around in the middle of the night and may even seriously endanger themselves or others – but they do not realize it. When they are told of their expeditions later, after they have woken up, they know nothing about it and they cannot believe it either.
Another example: doctors in hospitals are often expected to be on duty for long periods of day and night shifts, although by law it is not allowed.

It sometimes happens then that a nurse calls them during the night. The nurse might ask, for example, whether a certain patient is allowed to take a specific medicine – let's say against high blood pressure, or what she should give a patient who wants to pass water but is unable to do so. The doctor is probably torn from his deepest dreams and makes an absolutely plausible and right decision on the telephone; the next day, however, he cannot recall the incident at all.

This is by no means an unusual occurrence and the person concerned was most certainly absolutely in control when he gave his orders over the telephone. In this case nobody will deny that this nocturnal telephone conversation actually took place.

Not being able to remember a real incident that happened while we were asleep is no argument for claiming that it never happened. After all, many NDEs have the nature of dreams, even if they are not 'real' dreams, as I have already explained. This and the realization nowadays that the so-called temporal lobes of the brain are involved and assist forgetfulness *(Schröter-Kunhardt)*, should give further plausible support to the theory that if only one third of NDEs is remembered there is no reason to assume that they are not a reality."

Can out-of-body experiences provide proof of NDEs?

"One of the most important arguments for believers in NDEs are out-of-body experiences. They are also known as excursions or OBEs for short," Alexander raises another and very important aspect concerning all NDEs.

"You are right, and they are the best 'proof' if we really want to use this expression," I agree.

"That is exactly what I do not believe," he keeps playing the devil's advocate. On the one hand you talk of a special form of hallucinations, the 'hauto-something-hallucinations', which could occur, for example, after somebody has taken drugs. On the other hand it seems that OBEs can even be provoked in experiments by means of electrical stimulation of the brain without the use of drugs."

"All that is correct," I agree, "it all depends on the small but decisive differences:

To experience an OBE you do not have to be near death. I myself once had an OBE which had nothing to do with proximity of death and this surely happens more often than we think."
A friend of our family believes neither in God nor in a life after death – he simply does not believe in anything at all that cannot be seen, heard or touched. We have often discussed this together. When we visited him and his family in their house once – Martin, you came with us – he suddenly stopped the discussion for a moment and told us about an experience he had had as a child. Until this discussion he had completely forgotten all about it and he had never told anyone, not even his wife to whom he had been married for many years – because, according to his own words, it *'admittedly did not fit into his materialistic view of the world'*.
Well, he must have been about eleven years old, when he was sitting in the bathtub at home one day. Suddenly, he looked down on his own body in the bathtub from a height of about one metre. It seemed very clear to him that he was no longer in his body but was hovering above it. For him it was absolutely real that he was floating above the bathtub as a completely intact person and personality. For him it was only his body that was still sitting in the bath, practically lifeless, and that this had nothing to do with him anymore. He could see and describe every detail of his body. He still experiences this today as he did more than 40 years ago as being a completely real incident.
To answer the first part of your question: the fact that OBEs occur without the proximity of death does not speak against OBEs as being an integral component of real NDEs, nor does it speak against OBEs as being a real separation of spirit and body.
If there is a life after death in the sense that I assume, namely that the body just 'dies away' one day and that the spirit is left behind, then obviously there must be biological mechanisms which spring into action at the right moment.
The corresponding program is probably rather complex since in the actual case of death it covers all areas of a personality and severs them from the other side of the coin, the brain."

A grand concert with an amazing orchestra

"As you know, there are no really relevant biochemical traces in the brain of our emotions, experiences or of the contents of our consciousness or memory. Of course, many things which we register with our brain in the course of our life is (also) processed and stored in the brain. I wrote about this in my book "Life".
All this seems to happen in a purely physical mode – and everything that is really important is thoroughly wiped out when body and spirit are finally severed. The spirit must get it out and take it away. All the 'stops are pulled out' so that the most diverse patterns of the brain become visible and audible to the person concerned. This might explain, for example, why it is that in some experiments some elements similar to those of 'real' NDEs can be observed. However, it is always only parts of these elements that are provoked in laboratories and they are usually of a different quality, e.g. incomplete in their details."
"You mean to say that 'real NDEs' are like a fantastic concert," Martin comes up with a beautiful metaphor. "A large group of musicians with many different instruments plays a whole symphony perfectly..."
"...and intentional experimental provocations with whatever kind of instrument may mean that only a few musicians play on only one kind of instrument. And in addition the symphony is now full of gaps or it is not as melodic and harmonic as if the whole orchestra were playing..." Alexander adds. I think they both just had a real 'eureka-experience'.
"Fantastic," I am overjoyed and absolutely over the moon.
I hasten to add: "And the whole orchestra only plays really sweetly if there is a suitable conductor. If 'at the wrong time' only single musicians are forced to play then there is no conductor..."

The brain, the interface to the spirit

We must now consider dreams and hallucinations from a different point of view. They are independent, 'real' products of the *interface* 'brain': as the mediator between body and spirit the brain is as much responsible for the processing and storing of experiences as it is for storing 'informative copies' (backups) of everything and for channelling fundamentally important items correctly and permitting them to pass in the right direction (e.g. towards the spirit). In connection with NDEs some centres seem to play an important role especially as they participate greatly in everything emotional.

This applies, for example, to the 'limbic system', which, among other things, interconnects various areas of the brain which are on completely different hierarchical levels. The so-called temporal lobes also fit in here and especially the frontal lobe which could possibly be the all-important *portal* for a number of deliberate conscious influences the spirit exerts on *its* brain.

We humans have a comprehension problem here. In our modern, computer-controlled times, we know what the expression *'interface'* means, but many of us can only handle *one* interface as this is usually sufficient to communicate with the internet via a modem, for example.

The spirit and *its* brain, however, are continuously connected with one another via innumerable *interfaces*, a wideband data communication so to speak. These interfaces are spread all over the cortex and they are responsible day-in day-out for a wide variety of tasks. Dreams, which are probably due to maintenance work being undertaken at some of these countless and complicated *interfaces,* could but must not necessarily establish a connection with the 'spiritual internet', at the same time. First and foremost dreams will usually reflect pictures from the 'brain's own' memory store.

These scenes are then probably replenished with those of its own 'spiritual intranet' which is directly connected with the memory store.

„So you think the contents of our dreams are usually produced *in* our own brain," Martin tries to sum up what I had just said in a simple, concise and even more understandable way, and Alexander adds immediately:

"And sometimes they take a look at the 'next door's garden', i.e. the spirit?"

"Exactly – I am thrilled by your cooperation," I continue, "and it is probably similar with hallucinations. They also have to be considered from both sides: on the one hand we rightly define them as tricks of the senses generally due to some kind of mental disease. Usually they are illusions caused by certain illnesses – and that means diseases of the brain not of the spirit. Often they are due to data transmission failures at the synapses, i.e. at the innumerable transmission points between single nerves. Therefore, we can provoke them by taking certain substances, such as specific hormones, narcotics and many others. Here the same applies: we cannot really judge the significance and the 'spiritual-emotional depth' from outside. Most hallucinations will produce pictures and combinations of pictures which are drawn from our own brain and its stores.

Some of these pictures might even go a step further and base themselves additionally on contents of our own personal but already purely 'spiritual intranet'. They are then already from another, namely spiritual, world but, as Martin expressed it, they are still products of our own brain since they are solely projected from our own personal intranet. Other pictures again possess elements which go beyond our own brain because they reflect pictures and scenes from a world extending beyond our own personal spiritual area. They arise from a purely spiritual connection and are taken, as Alexander expressed it so nicely, from our 'next-door's garden'.

Thus the term 'hallucination' must encompass much more and is not necessarily just mean something caused by mental diseases.

Maybe we should distinguish between 'real hallucinations' and *'hallucinoid realities'*." [126]

"This would mean that there are different kinds of OBEs – real ones and half-real ones?" Martin sums it up.

"Yes, that's right and then there are independent OBEs and others which are part of a complex program," I agree.

"And as part of such a complex 'combined brain-spirit program' they belong to NDEs which prepare for the spirit to be severed from the body?" Alexander adds.

"Exactly, that is an apt explanation," I comment his question. "Spirit and body are severed – and the closer death approaches the clearer it becomes and the better this is realized by everyone concerned.

After the terminal, physical death, the spirit remains once and for all severed since only the spirit will go on existing for ever. The body just dies and the spirit stays behind."

---

[126] I coined the term 'hallucinoid reality' myself. It stands for a hallucination with the character of a real experience, i.e. something hallucination-like. This term only makes sense if there is an out-of-body world of experiences which is of a purely spiritual nature and of whose existence I am convinced.

OBEs: Real excursions or visual hallucinations of one's own double?

"What about the 'hauto-something-hallucinations'?" Alexander repeats one of his earlier questions.
"You mean (he-)autoscopic hallucinations," I correct him.[127] "This is also known as the visual hallucinations of one's body image. This is a phenomenon of a certain mental disorder and has nothing at all to do with 'real' excursions or OBEs. The affected persons see the image of their own bodies projected into their own visions. They 'see' themselves in the same way as they would see another person, i.e. in a mirror image. In a 'real' OBE, one acts from the new position outside the 'former' body. At first, the affected persons usually find themselves at a kind of vantage point outside their own physical body. They look at it from a bird's eye perspective. The physical body stays behind, it remains solid and does not become transparent.
Our friend, who suddenly saw himself from above while he was sitting in the bathtub, has most certainly experienced a 'real' OBE.
The 'spiritual body' is always the attentive part during a 'real' OBE. At that moment, the physical body is nothing but an empty – or rather – *inactive* shell; still solid but without life.
In a hallucinated out-of-body experience, however, the physical body continues to be the attentive part. During a 'real' OBE the 'real' body stays behind and remains immovable, whereas the merely hallucinated mirror image of a (second) body even imitates the movements of the 'real' body. Such phenomena could but must not necessarily also occur during migraine attacks, epileptic seizures caused by the temporal lobes and strokes."
"'Real' OBEs as well, then?" Martin wants to be sure.
"Yes, both kinds," I agree. "They can even be induced artificially if certain areas of the brain, the temporal lobes of the cortex, are stimulated.
Some brain researchers do this because they believe that this could be the crucial 'proof' for NDEs being nothing more than 'nice farewell presents' of our brain – as, they assume, are the religious experiences which can also be provoked.

---

[127] Greek: autoscopic = self viewing

In the Canadian town of *Sudbury* the neuro-psychologist *Michael Persinger* has a fully equipped laboratory specially built for brain research. As other researchers also, using dozens of brain electrodes he stimulates the brains of volunteers, thereby creating NDE-similar pictures and even OBEs."
"Isn't he right then with his materialistic view?" Alexander is back to his former scepticism.
"No," I am not willing to compromise, "his conclusions are simply incorrect: first of all, not all epileptics and volunteers whose temporal lobes had been stimulated, had OBEs or religious, NDE-similar experiences. On the contrary, the temporal lobe epileptics especially experience fear far more often.
There are also common features, of course. This is understandable and must be so if my *interface theory* is correct; certain areas of the brain naturally play a role in NDEs and must do so. However, this cooperation can neither comprehensively explain 'real' NDEs as a whole nor their most important part, namely 'real' OBEs.
Apart from the temporal lobes in the cortex another very important structure is also made responsible for NDEs: I am talking of the *limbic system* which connects various brain areas of different hierarchical positions with one another.
However, not only do the feelings of fear, which occur far more often during an external stimulation, refute this theory. Stimulated or pathological, i.e. epileptic-induced OBEs are *always* accompanied by movement disorders, so-called motorial automatisms, and the body sensation of those affected is often severely *disturbed*.
Patients with 'real' OBEs never feel pain, others do so very much. 'Real' OBE-patients never suffer spasms, they do not feel dizzy and do not erupt in sudden outbursts of emotions *(Schröter-Kunhardt)*.
Especially important, however, is the fact that 'real' OBE-patients are in no way restricted in their spiritual performance: on the contrary, they are always in spiritual top form and they are full of awareness and attention.
The spirit and the brain of an NDE-affected person show supreme performance!
In cases of 'real' OBEs, some incidents must evidently really have happened unless we want to explain them with the much more complicated ESP-theories[128] of parapsychologists. Persons affected by

---

[128] ESP = extrasensory perception

'real' OBEs have obviously been to other places. They have sometimes been able to describe events and situations which happened nowhere near their hospital room or their place of accident. The author *Urs Willmann*, who wrote an article in the German weekly newspaper '*Die Zeit*', unjustifiably full of cutting mockery, says: '*The* (American) *television program 'X-Files' usually embellishes such episodes with a memory sequence including a red shoe on the hospital roof, sheets blowing about in the wind on the lower balcony or persons in the adjoining room: this is supposed to 'prove' that the out-of-body experience must actually have happened'.*[129]

The author does the cause no justice simply because he is not prepared to do so. Such anecdotes and events might occasionally be effectively embellished for the media – which does not mean they are invariably wrong. Many can indeed clearly be proven. The heart surgeon *Michael Sabom,* for example, has studied 32 excursion experiences, i.e. OBEs, of patients who had been resuscitated. He then compared their descriptions of the resuscitation process with, as he called it, the '*well-founded assumptions*' about reanimation processes compiled by a control group of 25 medically well-versed patients. *Sabom* was able to prove that 23 out of 25 of the members of the control group had made serious mistakes when giving their exact description of the reanimation measures. All of the 'OBE-returnees', however, without exception, described all resuscitation measures correctly and completely. A controlled study is presently in progress at the *Southampton General Hospital* in the South of England on NDEs with respect to cardiologic events. Sceptics, such as the Scotsman, *Chris Freeman,* from the *Royal Hospital Edinburgh,* believe that the NDEs described by those that experienced them could be explained by the fact that nobody can prove they really happened during the phase of 'deepest mental derangement' but that they might have happened during the subsequent phase of physical recovery. This assumption, however, is contradicted by the fact that NDEs also occur during isoelectric EEGs and during the period of resuscitation when patients are able to describe the resuscitation process authentically in every detail.

In other cases of 'real' OBEs due to NDEs, even *blind people* could evidently describe their surroundings in detail, they could even recall colours correctly.

They could never have done that at any other time."

---

[129] "Die Zeit" (29/1999), "Once to Hell and Back"

"I read somewhere that the light and tunnel phenomena are induced by the visual cortex in the brain," Alexander chips in.
"Yes," I reply, "my counterarguments would still remain the same if that were indeed the case. Only, this observation has a flaw: if the temporal lobes are removed, people no longer experience experimentally induced light and tunnel phenomena – nor do they if the visual cortex is stimulated or if drugs are administered, e.g. LSD[130]. In this case that which otherwise would always show a result does not happen."
"But aren't light and tunnel phenomena products of the brain which we can erase from the 'spiritual' NDE-pattern?" Martin throws in.
"Why that?" I want to know. "You cannot merely provoke them in a laboratory after the temporal lobes have been removed. That does not mean, however, that they are *produced* by the temporal lobes. These areas only have something to do with them. I think that they *participate* greatly in the process of channelling these experiences correctly."

Are NDEs induced by psychogenic drugs?

"Papa, you have already given us the cue," Alexander is again changing the direction of our conversation. "LSD, a drug, is also able to provoke many of these experiences. Other substances can do the same, obviously. Couldn't that be the key for a brain-induced NDE?"
"No," is my short reply; I am no longer on the defensive. "I think that all these drugs are in general the same – no matter whether they are specific remedies, such as transmitters at the synapses, hallucinogens[131] or substances inducing a feeling of utter happiness or even sleeping pills or narcotics. They are all, without doubt, able to induce NDE-similar experiences or only parts of them. Those patients, however, who had a real NDE in their proximity to death, were never under the influence of such substances.
NDEs and drugs could influence each other but they not necessarily depend on each other.

---

[130] LSD = lysergic acid diethylamide; a half-synthetic hallucinogen which induces temporal disruptions in the brain accompanied by hallucinations.
[131] Especially hashish (Cannabis = Indian hemp); it is made from the resin of the Indian hemp. The Mexican hemp-variety is known as Marihuana.

Now we could argue that this does not apply to endogenously produced substances, i.e. substances produced by our own body, such as certain hormones which induce the feeling of blissful happiness in us. They are always produced in the proximity of death and could therefore be responsible for NDEs. Many people try to find here a plausible and comprehensive explanation for NDEs.

However, the same applies to these substances: all hallucinogens, endogenous ones too, *could* in principle cause NDE-similar effects, but *in fact* this happens only rarely. In 'real' NDEs, on the other hand, the well-known NDE-typical experiences occur.

Under the influence of hallucinogens, however, the psychotic, pathological effects dominate *(Schröter-Kunhardt)*. Furthermore, the affected person always recognizes that his excursions are only trips into a world of illusions. He is always aware that his experiences are *not* real. Therefore it would be better to speak of 'pseudo-hallucinations'.

One single exception is the so-called 'real' depersonalisation[132], better known as the 'horror trip'. At first glance they are easily mistaken for OBEs. However, the expression 'horror trip' says everything: such an experience is always an emotionally negative incident and, in contrast to 'real' OBEs, is accompanied by disorders in body integrity and body sensation. A person experiencing a 'real' OBE sees his own 'self' outside his 'real' body and still completely intact. Such drug-induced alienations could possibly explain some negative NDEs but they certainly do not offer a comprehensive explanation for the phenomena of NDEs and OBEs.

Furthermore, depersonalisations never occur in children, although, as you know, children do indeed experience NDEs. After such a drug-induced trip everything seems to blow away unless the person lapses into a deep, possibly even long-lasting depressive hole.

The 'real' NDE-affected person, on the other hand, will all his life look back – the longer his NDE lasted and the nearer to death he actually was the more intensive his feeling will remain with him – on a deeply satisfying, fulfilling and, from his point of view, absolutely *real* experience, which he usually never forgets and which changes his personality for ever."

---

[132] "depersonalisation" or "estrangement"

Attempts at psychological explanations

"There are many sceptics especially among psychologists," Martin turns to another aspect, "why is that?"
"If I wanted to be a bit sarcastic," I digress a little, "I would say that psychologists like to build on old materialistic foundations – and they love to do that especially where there are no real foundations.
It's the old veterans like *Sigmund Freud* who are responsible for that.
In this way whole model 'cities' are built quickly– when in fact they are merely houses of cards."
"Now you are being rather nasty," Alexander attacks me, "there must be something behind their perceptions, mustn't there?"
"All right, maybe I am going a bit too far, but I just want to put some of their core theories into perspective," I try to pacify him again. "In fact, I just cannot understand some of their doctrines. In my opinion some of their theories are still 'only theses'. That means, they are assumed to contain much more truth than they really do. Later this shaky foundation collapses completely. Often such theories are then presented as evidence whereby many problems are made even bigger then they already are.
Therefore, I like to compare them to cities with houses of cards. With regard to NDEs, from a psychological point of view, they are sometimes considered as being 'desired ideals', sometimes as 'archetypes of the collective unconscious' and at other times as 'memories of our earliest childhood'. These psychologists even invent a 'psychodynamic explanation' for all this and parapsychologists philosophise about ESP-waves possibly *produced* in the human brain by an ESP-organ which (of course) has not yet been found but which they assume to be *in* the right hemisphere of the brain. [133]
As you can see, they are at least rather busy."
"Do I hear a slight cynicism there?" Alexander smiles.
"Maybe a teeny weeny bit," I answer visibly exposed.
"You already mentioned 'wishful thinking' at the beginning of our discussion," Martin joins in again, "or would you like to add something to that?"
"Yes indeed I would, for example with regard to encounters with the dead," I commence, "some psychologists consider this to be the

---

[133] ESP = extrasensory perception

'granting of an infantile wishful dream'. That even non-religious people have NDEs, even though they do not believe in a life after death, they try to explain with the theory that, in spite of their pronounced aversions, everyone possesses religious tendencies deep down which are only suppressed.

If NDEs were mere pictures induced by wishful dreams, then negative NDEs would most certainly not exist. The life review, which many NDE-affected persons experience very realistically, shows both the positive and negative moments in our lives. Evil deeds and thoughts are even intensively relived and their consequences are now dearly felt. It is, I think, utter nonsense to believe that pure wishful thinking would allow such negative situations.

Furthermore, such dreamed up pictures would only make sense if somebody were, for example, very sick and were to experience in full consciousness that death was drawing closer all the time. Yet many NDEs are reported by people who experienced a sudden almost fatal onslaught, e.g. an accident. In these cases the affected persons would not have had enough time to utter their wishes.

Another significant damper is put on this theory by *Elisabeth Kübler-Ross*, *Raymond Moody*, *Kenneth Ring* and others who have collected and evaluated an enormous number of NDEs. If small children are asked, be they healthy or sick, who they would wish to be near them, in 99% of all cases their reply is that they would like best to be with their mothers and/or fathers. Although this survey was carried out in the USA – the result would hardly be different in any other country on Earth. If the NDEs of very sick children were mere dream pictures then we would have to expect a similar result. But reality is completely different.

Elisabeth Kübler-Ross writes in this connection: '...*not one of all these children (...) said anything about having seen their mother or father during their near-death experience since they were still alive.*'

For other aspects of NDEs psychologists have such questionable explanations as: 'encounter with demons as a confrontation with their carnal it-components', or 'compensation for unfulfilled wishes'. This, by the way, is supposed to explain the almost inevitable changes in the personality of an affected person, usually accompanied by very deep emotions, which last for the rest of his life.[134]

---

[134] Quoted according to Michael Schröter-Kunhardt von Ehrenwald, 1981, Gabbard und Twemlow, 1984. In Knoblauch, H. et al, "Todesnähe: Wissenschaftliche Zugänge zu

"You cannot really believe all that, can you?" Martin sees the blatant doubt in my face.

"Exactly," I answer him, a bit at a loss, "I think, here again, the slogan applies that something can't be true because it is not allowed to be true according to the opinion of many people."

"How do you mean that?" Alexander asks.

"Well, there are many people who, by hook or by crook, try to discuss metaphysics away," I reply, "and they don't even notice that they are time and again not only up against ancient human experience passed down to us since the beginnings of mankind, but they are also up against intuition, against all religions – yes, even against all human beings really and ultimately also against their own inner self.

In the end, they are probably the ones who are most frustrated, because they fall prey to pessimism. Do you remember the famous Frenchman *Blaise Pascal* and his bet, which I discussed in detail in Chapter 18 of Part 1? If the pessimist, the one who does not believe in life after death, were right – and I am firmly convinced that he is not – he would never even find out about it. To bet on it is, therefore, completely futile! This tiny bit of logic alone would keep me away from the camp of pessimists all my life."

"But that is no argument, of course, you will have to explain such psychological theories in more detail," Alexander admonishes me.

"Okay, here we go," I pull myself together again. "Now then, according to the so-called 'psychodynamic explanation' a person should abstain from all thoughts concerning his future, if he notices that his death is imminent and he sees no possibility anymore of fighting against it.

He should then automatically turn to his past. Only in remaining passive will he become able to accept his own fate in the end. He will shift himself thereby into a state of happiness thus making his circumstances endurable for himself."

"Isn't that nice, maybe I will have the same feeling at school one of these days, when I have to write a test and I don't know what to write," Martin is amused.

"I wish you all the best," is my fleeting remark. "When addressed with regard to this theory the renowned psychologist and researcher of near-

---

einem außer- gewöhnlichen Phänomen", (not translated *Proximity of Death. A Scientifc Approach to an Extraordinary Phenomenon",*" (1999), see List of References.

death experiences, the American *Kenneth Ring*, gave a short, blunt comment: *'Rubbish'*.[135]
Kenneth Ring added that all psychodynamic explanations are 'inconclusive' and not even useful as partial explanations. Furthermore, they would very much *'distort'* everything. As I explained earlier in connection with other interpretations of NDEs, all psychodynamic explanations also exclude all those parts of NDEs which do not fit into the picture. This applies especially to the life review which, as I already told you, by no means replays only the pleasant parts of one's own life.

It should be added here that in this life review scenes sometimes appear which might indicate certain *possible* developments and situations of our future. For the person so pointedly affected, it is, of course, already certain that 'his time to die has not yet come' and that he has to go back to his life 'on this side of the great divide'. In such a 'preview' perspectives might be shown which may emotionally motivate him to return to his life although previously he had strictly refused to do so – this may include, for example, pictures of what *might* be in store for his family without him.

The very fact that many people vehemently resist having to return to their own body contradicts, of course, the theory that they hallucinate an NDE because they are trying to escape death and that they should then turn their attention to the review of their own life simply wouldn't make sense.

Schröter-Kunhardt disagrees with psychoanalysts when they describe the *'wish for'* or even the *'striving toward immortality'* which may go back to an NDE as the *'denial of death'*. To illustrate the point he says that if this be so, then we must also say that the *'yearning for love is the denial of unkindness.* He is right, of course, when he goes on that it would be *'much more sensible and more apt for humans to call unkindness the suppression of love or of the capacity for love."*

"And what about the archetypes?" Martin reminds me that there are some more psychological perceptions to discuss.

"The expression *archetypes* means original patterns or pictures..." I start my answer, "... which, according to the perceptions of the Swiss depth-psychologist *Carl Gustav Jung,* are like the pieces of a gigantic mosaic. If they are put together in the right way they produce the big picture of the *'collective unconscious'.*

---

[135] In an interview with Evelyn Elsaesser-Valarino, see List of References.

The mosaic pieces themselves are equivalent to the innumerable single bits of information and creative experiences which mankind in its entirety has collected in the course of history and which are still being collected. They are all stored in an unknown but *real* immaterial storeroom which in general is open to access by everyone..."
"That is similar to what you say," Alexander interrupts me, "a kind of spiritual world."
"On this point Jung and I certainly agree," I admit, "and he is in line with *Karl Popper*, the Austrian philosopher, whom I have already mentioned several times in previous books. Like Popper, Jung also avoids the – as I see it – all important step towards a spiritual world which contains all the information of being while leaving enough space for subjective experiences as well.
For them the human spirit itself does not exist eternally, but all of its experiences and ideas remain as something completely anonymous. Therefore, they did not believe in a life after death which fitted in perfectly with the spirit of their time. Maybe *Jung's* information store is comparable with the *Akasha-Chronicle* taken over from Indian philosophy. Everything that cannot be directly connected with our own experiences, e.g. a dream about strange rituals or religions, could be an archetype according to *Jung*. The disciples of the Swiss psychiatrist now consider NDEs as an access to the collective unconscious in which archetypes are reflected.
Jung himself changed his mind later after he had a near-death experience in 1944.
This is shown, for example, in the letter from which I took the quotations written on the first page of this discourse. I would like to quote some more from Jung's letter: '*...Sooner or later all the dead become what we are as well. However, in this reality we know little or nothing of that state of being and what will we still know of the earth after we are dead? The disintegration of our temporary form in eternity is not a loss of sense. It is rather that the finger learns to recognize that it belongs to the hand.*'
One of the pioneers of NDE-research, the American *Moody*, points out that Jung's theory about the projection of a 'collective unconscious' cannot explain NDEs because it cannot explain OBEs. OBEs, however, are important components of all NDEs. And any theory which does not take that into account is simply '*worthless*' for *Moody*.

Parapsychological explanations?

"What is there still to discuss?" Martin asks.
"I know," Alexander has an idea, "we haven't done the perceptions of parapsychology yet."
"Good," I agree, "I will explain them briefly. But first some repetitive remarks:
Parapsychologists investigate so-called PSI-phenomena, i.e. incidents which are actually verifiable but scientifically still inexplicable. In former times the majority of parapsychologists were *spiritualists* who explained paranormal phenomena as being the influence of spiritual existences, e.g. the souls of deceased persons. The majority of *animists* today are of a different opinion. They accept all known natural scientific theories as proven knowledge. Of course, they now assume that they must still be expandable in future so that at some time or other, plausible, 'new-physical' explanations of paranormal incidents can be admitted.
They assume that an as yet unproven ability of the spirit, which for them is tied to the brain, is responsible for all PSI-phenomena. Somewhere in every brain there must be an area where so-called *ESP*-waves are produced. ESP is an acronym for **e**xtra-**s**ensory **p**erception. They call the responsible area in the brain, which has not yet been found, the ESP-organ.
The majority of parapsychologists with an animistic orientation distinguish between three major forms of ESP:
1) Telepathy, whereby subjective information is received or transmitted over great distances from person to person. Telepathy is also known as mind reading.
2) Psychokinesis or telekinesis, meaning the direct influence on the environment or various physical processes exerted solely by (brain-tied) mind-power whereby objects can be moved.
3) Clairvoyance, by which is meant the ability to gather objective information about physical things even if they are in non-transparent containers.
According to animistic-orientated parapsychologists, ESP-waves transmitted from the ESP-organ of the brain pick up information about their environment with the aid of one of the three available abilities mentioned above. From the information obtained, the brain-locked spirit then assembles the corresponding PSI-experience.

An example: a person reports that during an NDE he experienced an OBE. He claims he could describe what a nurse looked like who hurried to him and what she was wearing or what the doctor said while he was trying to reanimate him. Furthermore, he reports that he saw all this from a bird's eye view. As a spiritual being he went through the walls into the adjoining room and on the television set of another patient he watched how the goal keeper in a football match saved a penalty. He goes on to say that the other patient was so overjoyed that he jumped around on his bed so much that finally he fell off and had to be treated for a broken bone.
A spiritualist would say now: okay, the affected person has had a 'real' OBE, i.e. his spirit separated from his body and it actually experienced everything he described.
An animist, however, would argue in a completely different way: he would maintain that the 'nearly dead man' established a telepathic contact with the doctor – maybe even in spite of a baseline on the EEG and lying semiconscious on the stretcher – and 'tapped' his thoughts and words.
By means of clairvoyance he 'saw' what the nurse looked like and the details of her clothing. With the aid of ESP-waves he was able to observe himself from a bird's eye view. In this way he was also able to take a look into the other room and, enabled by clairvoyance, to watch the football match on the TV-set.
Finally from his impressions he formed his perception that he really did make such an excursion. In fact, however, his senses fell prey to an illusion. The 'seventh' sense, responsible for all this, is conveyed by the (still undiscovered) ESP-organ.
For this perception, however, no proof is available as yet."
"Not for yours either," Martin looks at me somehow strangely fascinated.

A comparative discussion of my perceptions

„That is true, only I believe that my perceptions are more plausible and more rational. This I shall try to back up by always putting them into an alternative general context while looking for common features. If we analyse all the sciences involved here, which I also discussed in depth in the three volumes of my last series, and if we put their results into an inter-disciplinary context, then it seems to me that my convictions are much more probable and make more sense.

I would like to distance myself clearly from spiritualists. For them spirit and body are two completely different, practically autonomous forms of life. The spirit can settle in a body and leave it again – at the very latest when the body dies.

"Death transfers us into the state of rest in which we found ourselves before we were born. Should anyone sympathize with the dead he should also sympathize with the unborn." The Roman philosopher *Lucius Seneca* wrote these words long ago.

For me, however, the spirit is to a certain degree *also* a product of any physical development. A spirit is induced by the creation of a body. This, in my opinion, is due to the general ability of *living* bodies to communicate or better, to interact with a world-encompassing and all-penetrating spiritual field.

It is due solely to these constant interactions between a living physical existence and the spiritual field that a personal spirit is developed gradually and is differentiated.

Thus each single spirit becomes a separate part, differentiated in itself, of a world-encompassing and all-penetrating spiritual internet. Each single spirit is an independent part of the whole.

The differentiated single spirit is comparable with today's well-known intranet. Since the spiritual field as an increasingly self-differentiating world of information is infinitely large, everything stored there is significantly more complex and in completely three-dimensional perfection on the highest possible level. Everything can be experienced subjectively.

Every human spirit in this 'world beyond' possesses not only all the attributes of his former personality in his life in 'this world' but also all the information of his earlier corporeality – quasi through all the layers and fibres.

This is what I call the fully differentiated part of the whole.

In my opinion, here lies the key to intuitively religious knowledge, that everything belongs together and is in itself a rational part of a greater whole on a higher level, etc..

Although – from an objective point of view – the spirit possesses not even the slightest trace of physical matter, this is hardly less – when viewed just as objectively – than matter itself.
I pointed this out regularly in my earlier books:
All matter is composed of single atoms. Every atom in itself appears to be only a tiny 'particle' which we pretentiously call 'mass'. In reality, however, we could compare it to a large field including kilometres and kilometres of nothing but empty space. For example, the nucleus of a hydrogen atom, the father (or mother) of all atoms, consists of only one proton and its shell has only one electron. And even these two items are ultimately only 'frozen energy' (according to *Albert Einstein*), something fundamentally volatile.
If we now imagine the proton as being the size of a cherry stone, then the diameter of the electron measures only a fraction of a millimetre while the electron orbits the nucleus at a distance of approximately one kilometre. And between these two almost nothings there is really only nothing!
Matter is in reality 99,99% absolutely empty space. Nevertheless we consider it as being a solid substance and difficult to penetrate (and we experience it as such daily).
For us, who are composed of the same material, it must appear so. But in fact any kind of mass is only an illusion!"
"Would you say then that matter is not more real than the OBE which an NDE-affected person experiences?" Alexander muses.
"I would say it in a different way," I reply and at the same time I am planning to end this discussion soon, "matter is *as* real as the OBE which an NDE-affected person experiences and *as* real as his NDE.
As a 'real' experience they prepare us for our survival after death in the case of our death being close and they are, depending on the actual temporal proximity of our final death, already the first step towards our survival in a spiritual world."
"That is a really good closing remark," says Martin, and Alexander and I nod in agreement.

Part 3:
No Death is Final - Epilogue

"To fear death, citizens, is no different from considering oneself to be wise and not being so; since this would mean imagining to possess knowledge, which we do not have."
Socrates (469-399 BC) in: Plato, Defence Speech of Socrates

"Just thinking about death and instability also induces us not to occupy our mind solely with superficial things which only deal with this life.
Death will certainly come.
Tenzin Gyatso, the XIVth Dalai Lama (*1935)

"The individual human spirit lives forever according to our definition of existence. Its existence is just one endless schooling.
Among other subjects we have to learn about love, kindness and how to understand it all. ... The physical death is like leaving primary school. It is the spirit's decision to change to a grammar school."
My own words: Excerpt from the memorial address on the occasion of my fathers funeral (1996)

In press reports concerning my work it has already been reported that I can prove a survival after physical death.
Of course, I cannot do that. Nobody can, but no one is in a position to prove that death is the end of everything either!
It is, however, a symptom of our times that the burden of proof is imposed only on someone, who has decided to believe in a survival of his own physical death, be it by intuition, by experience, or be it religiously motivated or after having gone thoroughly through all the arguments; he is expected to produce the proof.

The central theme of my last five books has been death.
For a long time now I have been convinced that the human spirit survives what we call death in full consciousness, perfectly and unimpaired and with all imaginable attributes and information about its body, its personality and its immense world of thoughts and emotions, and that it will go on living for ever according to our earthly definition.
Of course, my theory stands in stark contrast to the doctrines of modern natural science.
Therefore, I considered it necessary to take a very broad view and scrutinize critically the currently accepted natural scientific perceptions of "God and the world".
It has long been clear to me that many present doctrines are not based on real knowledge at all, but that, often due to interpretations of actual observations and measurements, they have a strong subjective slant.
Interpretations, however, are also opinions. For each theory a plausible counter-theory is possible.
This makes all prevalent doctrines and world models mere products of the state of knowledge and the beliefs of the scientists involved and the spirit of the times in which the research was done.
All new natural scientific theories must of course concur with current observations. However, they should also be inter-disciplinarily matched; our world most certainly forms one integrated whole.
All phenomena and natural laws in this world must, therefore, follow and obey the same principles.
From this perspective, it seems to me that our world cannot be as it is described by many of those who jump to conclusions and seek a definite and final judgement all too hastily, for my feeling.

Even in the most important, even fundamental points our world probably differs significantly from the picture presented to the majority of people today and which is so effectively disseminated by our modern media.

It seems to be mathematics with its simple geometry and its infinite sequence of ordinal numbers and their reciprocal values which initially shows us the right way. Even later on, in all further reflections, it remains a visible, valuable aid to orientation.

Mathematics is obviously a decisive key to recognising the truth. Mathematics provides us with the certain realization that *nothing* in this world could have come from NOTHING but that everything that "IS" must have been created from something utterly indescribable, which here we call "GOD".

Mathematics also leads us inexorably to the conclusion that there must be an all-enveloping spiritual world which controls our universe and, also, any form of evolution discreetly from the background while clearly adhering to strict rules and narrow limits. And not only that: mathematics itself must be an essential controlling device.

From this all-embracing spiritual world, and together with it, our physical universe is engendered, the world of all physical matter, which includes us humans.

Everything that has ever been created in this physical cosmos in the course of its existence over almost immeasurable periods of time, serves the sole purpose of creating ever more spiritual variety and, what is more, ever higher levels of spiritual differentiation. Growing quantitatively and qualitatively the previously "childlike" spirit will and must finally "come of age" and return to itself. The day it set out on its journey it was still "naked", comparable to a seed. Its aim was to perfect itself by striving for the maximum variety and for the highest possible perfection. It seems as if a "new God" were created with all the life in this world.

Only a few basic rules determine further development and paramount of these is the *"law of symmetry and polarity"*.

This manifests itself in the creation of matter from spirit. The world is thereby divided into two real, symmetrical and simultaneously opposing levels of existence, which are mutually dependent. All matter is created by the spirit and will one day return to the spirit. The most beautiful and apt representation depicting this mutually dependent symmetry and

polarity is, in my opinion, the "yin and yang symbols" of Chinese philosophy.
Wherever matter is produced this law applies. All physical matter in this world has a second, a spiritual side, which corresponds with the simple information of "BEING", and each atom, be it ever so small, possesses this information and spreads it. It follows that for such complex matter there must be a pattern, similarly complex, giving information about its existence.
Although every "body" is theoretically infinitely divisible towards its purely physical side facing inward, the space is limited. This corresponds with the infinite sequence of the reciprocal values of all ordinal numbers between 1 and zero in mathematics.
Towards its spiritual side facing outward, every physical "body" "radiates" its own specific information pattern:
It stretches infinitely and without limit into eternity. This fact corresponds with the infinite and unlimited sequence of all ordinal numbers.
The outer shell of any three-dimensional, finite body in this world thus becomes an *interface* between the physical interior and the spiritual exterior of its existence.
I called this universal trinity the *"Universal Law of the Tripartite Unity"*.[136]
The following extremely important conclusion arises from the above:
The physical universe as we experience it is full of *interfaces* which are situated between the relevant physical and spiritual side of every existence. They all possess, therefore, aspects of both sides and act increasingly as mediators between those two sides.
The smallest geometrical figure is a circle. It is of no consequence how small we might imagine a point to be, it is always a circle as long as it is finite.
In past centuries mathematicians nearly despaired at the fact that every circle is clearly finite from a geometrical point of view, but not if we want to express it arithmetically, i.e. in numbers: then an infinite mystery is revealed, and that is the number π. /[137]
Not even if we worked for ever and ever, using all the computers in the world, would we be able to decipher the mystery of this infinite number:

---

[136] For the first time mentioned in: "Arguments for a Life after Death and a Different View of the World" (1999), which is up until now only available in German, see List of References.
[137] It is pronounced [pie] and it denotes the ratio of the circumference of a circle to its diameter which is approximately 3,1415929....! It is an infinite number in spite of what disbelievers say.

it shows no regularity whatsoever. Several billion places after the decimal point have already been calculated. Yet, it remains a futile venture of people who refuse to recognize the character of our world – or who enjoy the frustration.

The circle is the *geometrical interface* between the two worlds "spirit and matter". By mirror-imaging the planes of this circle the sphere as the smallest finite body is created.[138]

Another *interface* is found in arithmetic, in the world of numbers, which is symmetrical and polar again to geometry: it is the number "1".

On the one hand it is pure information: "1" tells us that there "IS" something. It is the information of all "BEING". Its cosmic counterpart is the "quantum" or "photon", the smallest physical, yet mass-less reality in our universe.

The "1" stands at the beginning of the infinite sequence of all ordinal numbers (1, 2, 3, ... ∞) and at the end of the finite sequence of their reciprocal values (1/1, 1/2, 1/3, ... 1/∞ etc.).

It is thus positioned between the infinity of the limited space between "1" and "0" on the one hand and the unlimited infinity towards the outside (1 to ∞) on the other.

The physical counterpart of the number „1" is, therefore, the "quantum" or "photon" as the smallest energy particle. Light consists of photons.

That makes light another *interface*: a photon possesses no mass and is thus pure information of "BEING".

Therefore, it is primarily the expression of the spiritual world. On the other hand, however, as an "energy dot", it is also the "smallest unit" of matter.

The spiritual world is just as real as our physical world and there are many among us who erroneously assume today that this is the only that exists.

The spiritual world and the physical cosmos are only two parts of one common whole and yet they are quite different.

They are symmetrical and simultaneously polar to one another, i.e. not just the mirror image but also the opposite.

A new higher *interface* is "life" itself.

It is not the organic substances that already constitute life, they are only the physical side of it. Life is generated by the ability of complex three-dimensional bodies, i.e. organic molecules and their compounds, to

---

[138] See Appendix: "Straight to the Point"

remain in constant contact with the spiritual world, the infinite world of information, and to communicate with it. Today, we would say living beings are alive because they are constantly "online". In addition to magnetic elements, which can work as aerials and thus receive the information, it is their three-dimensional structure more than anything else which makes organic molecules and various organic structures first-class resonance bodies and storages for (light) information.

However, just to produce "naked" life was not enough for evolution which received its marching orders from the spirit.

The spirit itself wants to learn and must constantly do so; it must develop ever further, it must grow and thrive.

Its programmed aims are: achieving the widest possible variety and the highest possible differentiation and perfection.

Of course, this demands ever better equipment. Soon it will not be sufficient just to be constantly "online". After a while this equipment should enable its users to become actively involved in the process of evolution. For a long time this remains an unconscious participation.

The best possible success is only granted when the users at some time or other recognize the ways and the aims of evolution: consciousness and self-awareness will facilitate this later. Without them evolution would be doomed to fail in the end.

On the physical side – here on earth – an ever more complex and strictly hierarchically structured nervous system is created. Its highest form to date is the human brain: it is of a degree of perfection never before unachieved.

This gives a human being the opportunity to act as a partner of evolution and to assist evolution actively and consciously to fulfil its tasks faster and better and to achieve the expected success far into the future.

However, as we unfortunately experience again and again, it is seemingly a long and stony path before humans will be mature enough to recognize this.

This path will now become even more difficult since humans no longer mature jointly as a collective species but rather as individuals and each single individual becoming responsible. This results in singular evolutionary differences developing within the humans species. And this development poses an immense risk for evolution as a whole.

Yet there is no alternative to evolution. The perfection, towards which it consistently strives, leaves no alternative. Only all things together without exception must eventually reach the goal, without leaving anyone behind. But even this highest risk can only be a calculated risk, otherwise it is not feasible.

This alone in my opinion justifies our looking into the future with great optimism, in spite of all the problems.

The human brain is thus the presently youngest *interface* between spirit and matter. With the brain the course is set for spiritual diversity and spiritual growth to the highest possible perfection.

However, there is another, ancient *interface* between matter and spirit: it is "death"!

On the one hand it suddenly terminates the development of the spirit which is in theory infinite but has narrow temporal limits – but only on its physical side.

On the other hand, as an *interface* it opens the door directly and immediately for the spirit to its true world. Death leads us all to the side of the pure spirit, where infinite diversity and infinite growth become possible in eternity.

Although death is an end, it is not the end of the human being himself but only of his body. As one of many *interfaces* it limits solely the physical matter and nothing else.

Everything that identifies us humans as being a gigantic complex of the most diverse information remains completely intact after death.

This applies to all kinds of information about our body at any time of its existence as well as to the information about our self-aware spirit, our great emotions, our thoughts and all deeds – yes, our entire personality. Nothing of that will ever be lost, since

Those who die are not dead!
So, death is not the end – really nobody ever dies!

Or as William Penn says:

Death cannot kill what never dies!
(William Penn „Some Fruits of Solitude" (1693)

Appendix

1) from: Chapter 8, Monologue, "Summing it up" in "A Better History of our World, Vol. 1: The Universe"

1.1) The start:

We start with the smallest real, finite point – a *circle* (K1). It is clearly defined by three (also real, but spiritual information-) points. The circle is the smallest imaginable two-dimensional form whose internal dimensions can *theoretically* (or purely *numerically*) be structured (divided) infinitely. Its centre is M1. Its radius is a (randomly chosen) unit, e.g. simply 1 (standard circle).

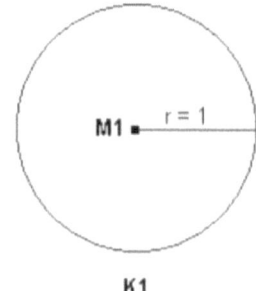

1.2) The first expansion:

The central point (M11) of a new second circle (K11) is a randomly chosen point on the circumference of the circle K1. The second circle, however, is only an auxiliary circle in the duplication process of the first circle and is not independent and only supports the derivation of circles.

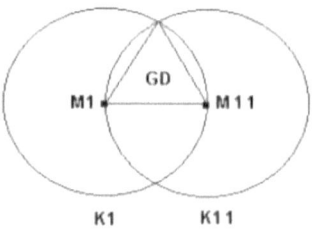

The distance between M1 and M11 is equal to the radius of the first circle with the unit "1" and thus the circle K11 is generated around the point M11.
When the centre of the circles and the points of intersection of circle K1 and K11 are connected, *equilateral triangles (GD)* are automatically generated. They are also perfect geometrical forms and they give *internal* structure to the circles. Equilateral triangles are inevitably produced and they divide the enclosed space internally. This division can *theoretically (spiritually)* be continued into infinity thereby creating an infinite number of ever decreasing triangles in dimensions of between zero and 1. This is, of course, purely hypothetical since there cannot be an infinite number of finite things. On the other hand, the division of the number sequence on which this is based can be continued into infinity since numbers are always immaterial and spiritual.

1.3) The first duplication:

With the second independent circle (K2) in one line, generated by a symmetrical duplication, i.e. by a still "one-dimensional" (or better: single-axis) form, the creation of another completely new, *symmetrical* and *polar* existence starts.

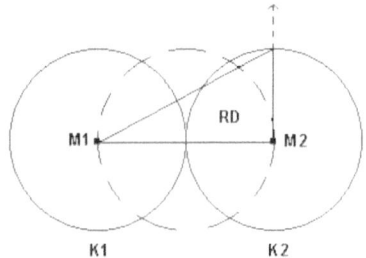

For this new circle (point) prolongs the line "r" since it stands practically in opposition to the first circle, i.e. it is its mirror image. After the appearance of this first new, i.e. independent, existence, we can now start to develop a new, symmetrical and polar dimension. This stands *optimally* at right angles to the centre M2. This line intersects the new circle K2 and facilitates the generation of a new closed form between the centre of the first circle (M1), the centre of this second independent circle (M2) and the intersection point of the vertical on M2. A *rectangular triangle* is generated, the very first of its kind.

1.4) The Golden Section:

The intersection point of the (longer) part of the hypotenuse starting at M1 with the circle K2 establishes a new radius for the larger circle (GK1).

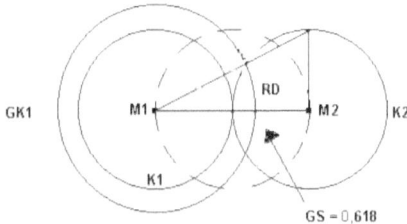

Only after this "reproduction" can a controlled "*growth*" start within the clearly defined predetermined dimensions, of course. This larger circle (GK1) intersects the straight line between the two centres M1 and M2 in the ratio of the *Golden Section (GS)*. After only a few stages of development from singularity to multiplicity the most important number sequence **6-1-8** is *automatically* generated. A further reproduction of the larger circles is achieved in the same manner and according to the same controlling laws.

1.5) The second dimension, the equilateral triangle, circle 3:

In opening up into the second dimension in multiplicity (the plane) after the creation of another auxiliary circle (K21) and a third (independent) circle (K3) vertical to the starting line, the centres of the independent circles, when connected, i.e. M1, M2 and M3, form an *isosceles triangle (GSD)*. All perfect forms of triangles have now been generated.

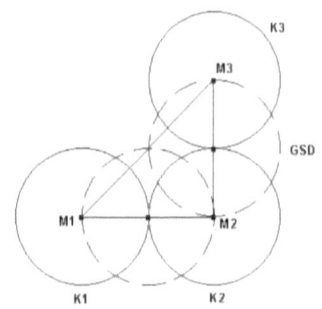

1.6) The perfect, "expanded" multiplicity: the square:

In the second dimension of multiplicity (the plane) the first real perfection is achieved by the isosceles triangle being mirrored over its hypotenuse. Thus a square is generated by developing circle K4.
It is the first and next largest, perfect singularity in the multiplicity and corresponds with the circle.

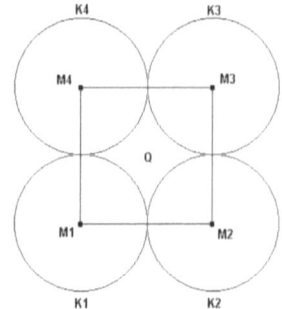

It has been clearly defined by the four circles and is thus the result of the reproduction from a standard circle to the square form.
Geometrically incorrect, but understandable in a purely analogical sense, I used to describe the standard circle as "mono-angle".

1.7. Between multiplicity and singularity: 2-7-3:

The square is the first perfect form of multiplicity which simult-aneously encloses and contains the original circle, i.e. the singularity. The ration of the area of the square to that of the original circle is the same as 1,**273** to 1. *Stelzner* rightly describes the number **273** as a *"measure of the imprisonment in the square"*.

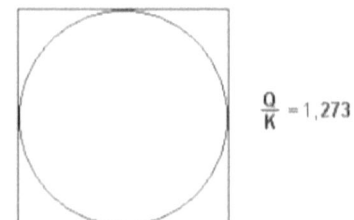

$\frac{Q}{K} = 1{,}273$

8) The order of 24 for every perfect flat plane of multiplicity:

The square now being the most perfect form in this newly developed outward two-dimensionality in multiplicity is defined by four circles. Each circle, when internally structured, automatically creates **6** equilateral triangles by constructing the radius of the circle six times. With the new multiplicity **24** such triangles are thereby produced.

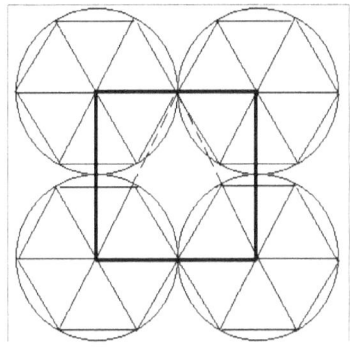

This seems to me to be the geometrically verifiable reason for the cyclical **24**-rhythm which is characteristic for any *outwardly* expanding order. This also seems to be the reason for our time unit which was invented by the *Babylonians* and is still valid and very useful today.

2) from Chapter 5, Monologue, "The Three Musketeers", in "A Better History of our World, Vol. 1: "The Universe"

Chapter 1) of this Appendix shows that: after only a few steps and with the help of the ordinal numbers 1 to 4 we arrive at the number sequence **6-1-8** as the measurement of the "Golden Section" and thus for "optimal fulfilment", and also the number sequence **2-7-3** as the measure of the maximum expansion of our universe.
The numbers **10, 24** and **81**, which I introduced as the "Three Musketeers", can also be directly calculated from the first four ordinal numbers.
As is: $\qquad\qquad\qquad\qquad\qquad\qquad\qquad\qquad$ $1 + 2 + 3 + 4 = 10.$
So is also: $\qquad\qquad\qquad\qquad\qquad\qquad\qquad\quad$ $1 \cdot 2 \cdot 3 \cdot 4 = 24.$
The first four ordinal numbers lead us to the first two "Musketeers", one by addition and the other by multiplication.
But what about the number **81** and what is its special significance in this world?

Here is the mathematical answer:
It is: $\qquad\qquad\qquad\qquad\qquad\qquad\qquad\qquad\qquad\quad$ $1^2 \cdot 3^4 = 81.$
Here also the first **four** ordinal numbers are combined by introduction of the next higher type of arithmetical operation just as we did when we introduced the **24**.
If we work with powers alone then we arrive at the starting number **1** again, because
it is: $\qquad\qquad\qquad\qquad\qquad\qquad\qquad\qquad\qquad\;$ $1^{2 \cdot 3 \cdot 4} = 1.$

The numbers **10** and **24**, in exactly this order, describe the purely spiritual and immaterial basis of our universe: The number **10** defines the numerical system to which all things relate. All numerical systems are in principle equal in worth but one is favoured. It is the first and lowest step for all decisions, it is the basis on which the numbers are to work and control. Mathematically the smallest musketeer can also be derived from the simplest arithmetical operation, the addition.

When it has been clarified just *how* mathematics is to work in our world, then it must be decided on the next level *how* the world is to expand. This involves the question of the space *in which* our physical universe will later exist.

A decision must be made at this point as to *how* everything should be arranged in number and form and how it should all expand.

The most obvious form is the "circle" which is defined and controlled by the number **24** (see next Chapter). It results from the next higher arithmetical operation, the multiplication of the first four integers. This arithmetical operation is also still "homogenous" since the result is still something immaterial: the purely spiritual information for order and expansion of all processes and events.

But the third number, the **81**, is the first having anything to do with matter. It defines the maximum quantitative expansion, i.e. the number and distribution of the most important goods *within* the *already expanded* space. Now, at this point, something of utmost importance happens: although **81** can also be derived from the first four numbers, now, for the first time, it is reached by two different arithmetical operations. The number 3^4, which itself results in **81**, stands for the maximum expansion of all purely physical matter. But, in consequence, the factor 1^2 is now a sign that all matter is in actual fact a combination of two completely different parts, one of which can be and is easily overlooked since it possesses nothing physical. The 1^2 proves in a purely mathematical way that every kind of matter simultaneously possesses something that "adheres" to it, which seems to be "invisible" but nevertheless belongs to it imperatively: it is the pure information *"to be"* – or, in other words, the information of *its own existence*. Every kind of matter informs us of its existence by way of the *"being"* which is inseparably connected with it. This idea is unambiguously induced by *mathematics*. This information of *being* is something purely spiritual and immaterial.

Mathematics provides the *proof* that there is a universal very subtle dualism between the spiritual information of all existence and its physical part. And since the omission of the arithmetical operation 1^2 is perfectly possible from the mathematical point of view when calculating the number 81, it proves that the connection between spirit and matter is not bound to obey the *thermo-dynamic conservation laws*! All kinds of matter in this world actually possess a non-physical *and* a physical existence simultaneously. This explains why any expansion, any formation and any construction of physical existence inevitably possesses a spiritual quality at the same time. Therefore, all matter has an eternal nature since it is not of physical quality alone but also of spiritual quality.

3) from Chapter 6, Monologue, "Prime Numbers", in "A Better History of our World, Vol. 1: "The Universe"

Drawing by Martin: In a circle defined by the number 24 all prime numbers can be seen along the 8 rays in this drawing. Optically, they form a Maltese or St. John's cross. The question certainly arises as to whether this form of cross, which is frequently used, or even any form of cross in general has not been based on an intuitive knowledge of the mathematical basics of this world.

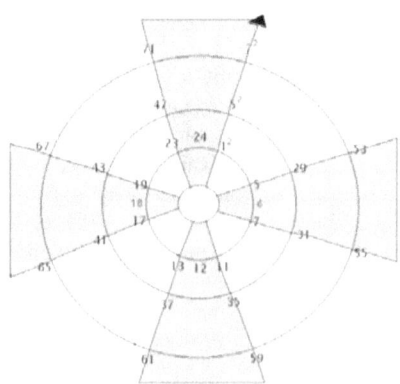

Drawing by Martin: Due to the concentric arrangement of the shells over the number 24 we see at 1 o'clock a ray pointing outward on which mainly the squares or products of all imaginable prime numbers can be found, starting with 1^2, 5^2, 7^2 etc., all obeying the formula "6n±1". Between the shells of two adjacent prime number twins we find some shells with single prime numbers, whose growing number gives us the sequence of all *even* numbers.

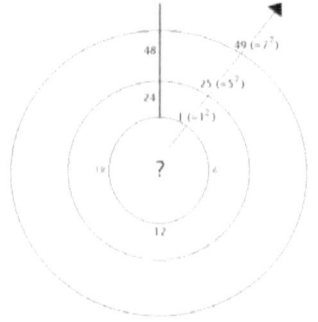

But also between two shells with the squares or products of prime number twins – e.g. between 5^2 and 7^2 or 23^2 and 25^2 - there is a growing number (since the number of prime number twins decreases!) of other shells with single prime numbers. They give the sequence of all ordinal numbers, starting with two times zero.
Plichta coined the term "prime ray" for it. Now it makes sense to
write the 1 on the inner shell of this ray as 1^2. I put a question mark in the centre of the circle since the origin of all things has been discussed somewhere else.

243

4) from Chapter 5, Monologue, "The Number 81 and the Genetic Code", in "A Better History of our World, Vol. 2: "Life"

Illustration "Code-Sun" by Alexander: By means of four organic bases, which are always arranged in groups of three, known as nucleotide-triplets, the genetic code of all 20 amino acids (AA) which are combined to proteins in biological bodies can be encoded. In so doing several triplets may determine one and the same AA. For example, 9 AAs are linked by 2 triplets each.

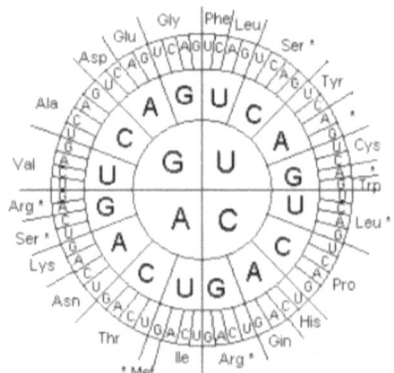

In total **84** code positions can be created. Three of them, however, encode so-called nonsense-triplets, i.e. there is no AA available for them and they always terminate a synthesizing process. Thus exactly **81** $(= 3^4)$ real possible code positions remain. One triplet always operates as the start-codon (AUG). Since the start-codon AUG takes a special place the genotype is also based on the number **81** in the form of **"80+1"** (analogue to the 80 stable and naturally existing elements plus one special starting element, hydrogen). In the same way as 20 so-called *pure* forms of elements exist among these 80 chemical elements, exactly 20 *alpha*-amino acids are encoded by 80 possible combinations.
If we assume now that the genetic code is based on exactly 81 position data then it becomes clear that single mutations cannot have a devastating effect on the reading process by means of which the production of proteins is induced (protein biosynthesis). Incorrectly positioned bases would immediately become apparent during the protein synthesis and the repairing forces of the body would be able to eliminate them. This would confirm the common observation that mutations, which can cause severe damage (e.g. cancer), happen constantly, but that the organism is usually able to conquer them. It recognizes them, I presume, because they carry the "wrong number"! The ability to recognize defects and to repair them decreases in all organisms with advancing age and this is why cancer occurs more often in old age.
But for evolution also my theory shows tremendous consequences: mutations as the drive behind evolution are slowly degraded (they are, however, not eliminated). While at the beginning mutations may (also) have played a decisive role in the evolution of all life, later on evolution employs other means. Evolutionary mechanisms are further developed and support evolution in the construction of increasingly purposeful and deliberate tools which influence the entire evolution.

5) from Chapter 3, Monologue, "Extraordinary Constants in Nature", in "A Better History of our World", Vol. 2: "Life"

The first **three** ordinal numbers are naturally of special importance in our world for **three**-dimensional, i.e. finite closed spaces and bodies. The spatial **four**-dimensionality of the infinite cosmos adds the number **4**. The sum of the first **four** numbers is the number **10**. It seems to be no mere coincidence that in this world we favour the **decimal** system for calculations. If the first **four** ordinal numbers are multiplied by one another we arrive at the number **24**, and by combining multiplication and exponentiation of these four numbers in a *rational* way, we arrive at the number **81**.
Both are important key numbers in our universe, as I have already mentioned. They will also play an important role in the following chapters.
These two numbers and the number sequences **273** and **618** are important key numbers in our universe as I explained in detail with the help of many examples in all my previous books.
If the most important so-called natural constants are considered from this point of view, amazing things become apparent:
Natural constants are unchangeable physical quantities which have been established by experiment and which describe those special standard values found in science for the existence of all matter in the physical universe as we know it. One of the declared aims of dedicated scientists is, of course, to connect these numbers in a rational way, i.e. to develop a common universal theory. However, they have not yet succeeded in doing so, and indeed my proposals in this direction also seem to be rather far fetched, at first glance at least. I admit, they seem quite speculative. Nonetheless, I believe this is a legitimate attempt at lending support to my combining hypothesis which is consistently based on number-theoretical considerations.
Each of these natural constants fluctuates only very slightly around the measured value – at the very most by a few percentage points. Were they not as stable as they obviously are – and that is undisputed among all scientists involved – then our universe could not exist – nor could atoms or solid matter, nor could galaxies, planetary systems or planets – and, of course, there could be no life whatsoever.

One of the most important natural constants is the phenomenal **velocity of light c**.
Its measured value is $2.99792458 \cdot 10^8$ m/s, i.e. nearly 300,000 kilometres per hour. I believe that in all probability the ordinal number **3** actually stands behind this measured value and is thus the actual decisive, orientating "spiritual" value[139].
In the decimal system the upper limit of the actual measured value mentioned above is reached by multiplying the number **3** with a multiple of the number **10** (i.e.

---

[139] This was firstly established by *Plichta* and I took it up gratefully in my previous books and explained it in detail.

10^n, where n is any whole integer) according to the decimal unit of measurement chosen (i.e. m/s or km/h).
We recognize that the actual measured values in our physical world always fluctuate slightly around their "spiritual", i.e. "number based orientations" and they are never really absolutely exact. At this point I spontaneously recall that so beautiful and fitting dialogue in Peter Höeg's thriller *"Miss Smilla's Feeling for Snow"* in which is suggested that there must be an ideal in our world which exists unrecognised in the background and which serves as an orientation but is never quite realized in its physical manifestation.[140]
The speed of light is a constant which also attains not quite precisely the "ideal" on which it is obviously based, the decimal multiple of the ordinal number **3**. (The divergence of the actually measured value from the number 3 is a mere **0.069%**). The speed of light is expressed by the product $3 \cdot 10^n$ since light is not caused by the interaction of two bodies but is related to the expansion of space.

The effects of interdependent bodies, on the other hand, are expressed by the reciprocal value.
Instead of $3 \cdot 10^n$ these are expressed by the factor $1 : (3 \cdot 10^n)$ or $1/3 \cdot 10^{-n}$.
Gravitation is always in force between at least **two** three-dimensional bodies. Using my number theory, we can form a product by multiplying the number **2** by the reciprocal value mentioned above, i.e.: $2 \cdot (1/3 \cdot 10^{-n})$ or $2/3 \cdot 10^{-n}$ which equals **6,6666...** $\cdot 10^{-n}$.
This would mean that gravitation has the same velocity orientated on the number 3. The most important constant in our universe after the velocity of light is the **gravitation constant**.
It has the value $G = 6.67259 \cdot 10^{-19}$ (Nm^2/kg^2) which shows a deviation of only **0.088%** from its calculated value mentioned above.

Planck's elementary quantum of action, also known as Planck's constant (h) is similar. It expresses the constant measure of the smallest effect between **two** bodies in our universe and is represented by $h = 6.626075 \cdot 10^{-34}$ (J/s).[141] The deviation here is only **0.61%** from $2/3 \cdot 10^{-n}$, the reciprocal value mentioned above. The **two** most important nuclear particles, the "proton" and the "electron" may be considered as being polar to each other. The hydrogen atom, which is by far the most important and most common atom in the entire universe, contains only these two. And they are in fact two extreme opposites, not only with regard to their opposing charges but also especially with regard to the difference in their sizes

---

[140] The exact dialogue is quoted in Volume 1, "The Universe", Monologue, Chapter 14.
[141] J = Joule is also a decimal unit for energy. It is 1J = 1Nm (Newton metre) = 10 kgm^2/s^2

which is also expressed in the proportions of their masses to one another. This so-called **mass quotient** is also a natural constant and amounts to: **1,836.152701**.
Is it not astonishing that the factor **2/3 · 10ⁿ** (here: n=1) which I mentioned above, multiplied by the parameter for maximum expansion, i.e. **273**, again gives very nearly the same result?
It is: **2/3 · 10¹ · 273 = 1,820.9**. Rounded up, the deviation is only **0.84%**.

The **elementary charge** is also an important natural constant.
It was certainly meant to be an *optimal* value. To demonstrate this, the mathematical construction plan for our world, as I have defined it, provides us with the "Golden Section", that is with the number **618** after the decimal point, i.e. the ratio **1.618** : 1. The actually measured value for the elementary charge is:
1.60217733 · 10⁻¹⁹ (C) /¹⁴². The deviation amounts to a mere **0.99%**.
And finally we arrive at the so-called *__fine structure constant__* α, which determines the limit for distances between each **two** smallest physical particles in the atom.
If its value were not **1 : 137.0359895** (± a bit!) then atoms could not combine to molecules as they do. Instead of water, metal, stone and sand, for example, we would have nothing but a hotchpotch of atoms. Thus, it also seems to have something to do with the number sequence for the limits of expansion, that is the number **273**.
This boils down to the ratio **2 : 273** which after simple reduction becomes **1 : 136.5** and which shows a mere **0.39%** deviation from the actual measured value.

To summarize:
The first three ordinal numbers, **1, 2** and **3** and also the next number, **4**, the decimal factor, **10**, which is the sum of these numbers and finally the standard values for maximum and optimum, i.e. the number sequences **273** and **618**, they all seem to be key players in the essential natural constants which I have mentioned. Not one of the deviations between calculated values and the known measured values of the natural constants amounts to more than 1% - they are usually much less.

---

¹⁴² C = Coulomb = As = Ampère second, which is a decimal measure of the quantity of electricity.

6) Some examples for the Occurrence of the Number Sequences 273 and 618 (Golden Section) in the Decimal System (Basis 10 = 1 + 2 + 3 + 4):

- absolute zero in centigrade:	-273
- Gay-Lussac (volume reduction per centigrade by):	1/273
- ratio of the moon's radius to that of the earth	0.273
- Moon acceleration on the orbit of the earth in cm/s^2	0.273
- sidereal month: orbit of the moon around the earth in days	27.3
- reciprocal value of days per year	
(The year is the orbit of the earth around the sun)	273
- synodical sun rotation in days	27.3
- gravitational acceleration on the sun in m/s^2	273
- average duration of pregnancy for humans in days	273
- temperature of background radiation in the universe	
in Kelvin	2.73
- ratio of oxygen to nitrogen in the air	0.273

- structure of petals and pine cones results in	1.618
- the distances between the spirals of a snail-shell	1.618
- the distances between the spiral arms of a galaxy	1.618
- distances between the sun and the nine planets	
(Titius-Bode-Law)	1.618
- ratio of revolution periods of planets	
in our planetary system	1.618
- ratio of length of arms to width of shoulders in humans	1.618
- ratio between finger phalanxes	1.618
- ratio between a perfect musical fifth to a fourth	
(Johannes Kepler)	1.618

Glossary

Adenauer, Konrad (*05.01.1876 - +19.04.1967); first Chancellor of the Federal Republic of Germany 1949-1963. Mayor of Cologne 1917-1933 and 1948.
Akasha-Chronicle, Sanskrit: akasha = space, ether; describes a kind of world memory in which everything that ever existed is supposed to be recorded.
Albertus Magnus (Albert the Great), originally Graf Albrecht von Bollstädt (approx. *1193 - †15.11.1280 in Cologne). Dominican, bishop, theologist, philosopher and naturalist. The University of Cologne, where he taught, was named after him. He was canonized by the Catholic Church.
Alexander the Great (*356 - †13.06.323 BC), King of Macedonia (336-323 BC), world conqueror by his own grace, "King of Asia" after the death of the Persian king Dareios (331 BC)
altruism, Latin.: alter = the other; uncalculated sacrifice of oneself for the good of others.
animism, Latin anima = the soul: the belief that material objects and the physical environment are imbued with some kind of soul or spirit. The belief is based on Aristotle's conviction that the soul is mortal and that only a part of it is a separately existing, but not especially individual, spirit which survives the death of humans. Animism in parapsychology maintains that PSI-phenomena are induced by the soul or the unconscious. Although this term is no longer used in modern parapsychology I will still use it in non-spiritualistic contexts for clear distinction.
apocrypha, hidden or secret things, applied especially to certain books in the Old Testament
archetype, Greek: arche = beginning, origin, and typos = pattern, form, good example.
Aristarchus of Samos (*c. 320 BC - †c. 250 BC) Greek astronomer. He was the first to propose a heliocentric picture of the world.
Aristotle (*384 - †322 BC). His father was the personal physician of King Amyntas of Macedonia.
arithmetic, the science of numbers, the part of mathematics dealing with the laws of calculation.
astronomy = the science concerning celestial bodies and the cosmos.
atom Greek: atomos = indivisible, uncut. It denotes the smallest physical particles of →elements which still demonstrate the properties of the element concerned. They cannot be divided chemically.
Augustinus, Aurelius (*13.11.354 - †28.08.430 AD), was a Latin church father and scholar.
Autism a pathological, extreme inability to take up contact with reality.
Babylonian astronomy: goes back to the 3rd millennium BC. Reached its peak about 500-600 BC, ended during the last century before Christ. The astronomical data were so exact that variations to the data established by most modern devices

today are usually extremely small and are probably due to conditions actually having varied in the meantime!
background radiation (BGR): This is a thermal cosmic radiation of micro-waves emanating almost uniformly from all directions. Variations detected by the satellite → COBE are extremely small at only about a thirty-millionth degree.
Bar do thos grol, translated: Liberation by hearing in an interim state. Tibetan name for the Tibetan Book of the Dead.
Barnard, Christiaan (*08.11.1922 - †02.09.2001); carried out the first successful heart transplant with a human heart on 03rd December 1967 in the "Groote-Schuur-Hospital" in Cape Town / South Africa.
Baryons, subatomic particles, consisting of three so-called valence quarks. In this context it is sufficient to acknowledge that a standardized particle size was chosen for a better comparison. It has been proved in experiments that the number of baryons in a closed system remains the same under all presently known interactions, it does not alter! In order to maintain the theory of the Big Bang it became necessary to introduce the claim that immediately after the Big Bang the number of baryons was not conserved since for every baryon (matter) there is an anti-baryon (anti-matter)! In fact, matter and anti-matter should have annihilated each another completely. However, for unknown reasons, more matter-baryons are supposed to have existed as anti-matter baryons so that the universe could be generated!
Bender, Hans (*05.02.1907 - †07.05.1991); German psychologist. First holder of the Chair for →parapsychology in Germany at the University Freiburg/Breisgau.
Berkeley, George (*12.03.1684 - †23.01.1753), Engl. philosopher and bishop.
Billroth, Theodor (*26.04.1829 - †06.02.1894); German surgeon
Bohr, Niels (*07.10.1885 - †18.11.1962); Danish physicist; known for his atom model which applied quantum theoretical principles to → *Rutherford's* shell model. Developed his complementary principle in 1927 which states that light and all other EMR consists simultaneously of particles and waves.
de Broglie, Louis-Victor, Duc (*15.08.1892 - †19.03.1987); French physicist; Nobel prize winner 1929.
Bruno, Giordano (*1548 - †17.02.1600), Italian astronomer and philosopher. Arrested by the Catholic Inquisition in 1592 and burnt at the stake.
Buddha, (*543 BC - †483 BC); originally Siddharta Gautama, Sanskrit: = the enlightened. Founder of *Buddhism*.
causal, Latin: causa = the reason, the cause.
Caesar, Gajus Julius, (*13.07.100 BC - †15.03.44 BC); Roman statesman and army commander, elected dictator for life in 45 BC. Introduced the Julian Calendar. He was murdered by Brutus and Cassius.
Cavendish, Henry (*10.10.1731 - †24.02.1810). English naturalist. He discovered the chemical element hydrogen in 1776. He called hydrogen "burnable air".
Celsius, Anders (*27.11.1701 - †25.04.1744), Swedish astronomer.

chromosome, Greek: chroma = colour, and soma =body; rod-like or bow-like structure within the cell nucleus of plants, animals and humans carrying the genes. Consists of DNA or RNA.
Cicero, Marcus Tulius, (*03.01.106 BC - †07.12.43 BC), Roman orator and statesman. Murdered by order of the Roman Emperor Marcus Aurelius one year after Caesar's assassination. 58 of his speeches and philosophical scripts have survived.
COBE-satellite: = Cosmic Background Explorer, orbiting the earth since 1989. In 1992 it was able to measure the cosmic background radiation of slightly over 2.73 K which is the most exact measurement to date. It was also possible to measure extremely small temperature fluctuations (ripples) of about a thirty millionth fraction of one degree which are curiously *interpreted* as being a proof for the big bang theory.
Cocteau, Jean (*05.07.1889 - †11.10.1963); French author and film director.
coherence = Latin: cohaerere = coherent. Coherence means a systematically ordered state caused by the property of two or more waves of a beam of light having the same frequency and the same phase or a constant phase difference.
coincidence, Latin: cum = with and incidere = to fall into something, to happen. It means the simultaneous occurrence or existence of things or events.
computed tomography (CT), a computer-controlled X-ray examination in layers.
Confucius (*551 BC - †479 BC); also Kongfuzi or K'ung Fu-tse, Chinese philosopher and spiritual founder of the Chinese obsequiousness towards state authority.
contemplation: Latin contemplatio = contemplation, observation; the act of recognizing viewing.
contingent: Latin: contingere = to touch; it means the accidental occurrence, incidental but not essential.
convergence, Latin: convergere = to tend to the same point; means the development of similar characters in animals or plants of different groups.
Copernicus, Nicolaus (*19.02.1473 - †24.05.1543); German physician, lawyer and astronomer; adopted the heliocentric view of the world from →*Aristarchus of Samos*, according to which the planets orbit the eccentric Sun.
cookie, small files by means of which the central computer, the server, can establish whether a user has visited the home page more than once. *Cookies* facilitate the identification of internet-surfers and prevent repeated registration.
correlation, Latin: cor (cum) = with, together with and relatus (referre) = to refer to. It means: two things are in mutual relation, they correspond to each other.
Correns, Carl (*19.09.1864 - †14.02.1933); German botanist.
cosmos: Greek: kosmos = world order, the ordered and harmonious universe; it denotes our universe, the "smallest", the micro-cosmos, the world below the threshold of visibility as well as the "largest", the macro-cosmos, the universe with its planets, stars and galaxies. *Cosmology* is the science that deals with the character of the universe as a cosmos, it is part of the sciences of physics and astronomy.
Crick, Francis Harry Compton (*08.06.1916); English genetics researcher.
Cusanus, Nikolaus: originally →Nikolaus Krebs, known as Nikolaus of Kues.

Dacqué, Edgar (*08.07.1878 - †14.09.1945); German palaeontologist, naturalist and nature philosopher.
Dalai Lama, born 1935 as Tenzin Gyatso. 14th head of the Buddhist "Yellow Church" in Tibet, the Lamaism (since the 8th century.). 1989 Winner of Nobel Peace Prize.
Dante, Alighieri (*Mai 1265 - †14.09.1321); Italian poet; famous mainly for his poem "La Divina Commedia" (1307-1321), one of the great poems of the world.
Darwin, Charles Robert (*12.02.1809 - †19.04.1882); Engl. naturalist. Founder of the evolution theory, according to which all living beings have developed from preliminary levels by natural selection.
Democritus (*460 - †371 BC), Greek philosopher and naturalist.
deoxyribonucleic acid- and ribonucleic acid (DNA and RNA); basic components of the genome. They always possess 3 components: one molecule of phosophoric acid, one molecule of deoxyribose, a pentose (five-carbon) sugar and one organic base. There are 4 bases: adenine, cytosine, guanine and thymine. In RNA thymine is replaced by uracil. The bases are important components for the encoding of DNA and RNA.
They are spatially structured giant molecules. Carriers of the genes necessary for the generation of living organisms. Special forms are m-RNA = messenger RNA and t-RNA = transport RNA.
Descartes, René (*31.03.1596 - †11.02.1650); French philosopher, mathematician and naturalist.
descriptive: Latin: describere = to describe, to characterize, to write down; means: to describe verbally
determinism: Latin determinare = to determine, to limit. Theory that everything in the world is unambiguously and inevitably determined in advance. There are several variants: it starts with the "radical →"indeterminism", according to which an unlimited and totally free will exists; there is the "moderate indeterminism", which stands for a relatively free will but recognizes that it is more or less influenced by various factors which sometimes cannot be influenced at all and which therefore force the events, and lastly there is the "radical determinism" according to which no free will exists at all, everything is completely determined without any possibility of influencing events.
discontinuous, opposite of continuous. Marked by breaks or gaps.
dissipative structures: theory developed by →Ilya *Prigogine*, according to which an input of energy causes large numbers of organic molecules to change suddenly from a chaotic state into an ordered one in which they behave cooperatively as a unit. If the energy supply is interrupted, however, they disintegrate again and fall back into their chaotic state.
dogmatism: Greek: dogma = principle; unyielding belief in authoritative doctrines; uncritical acceptance of rigid beliefs and principles.
Doppler, Christian (*29.11.1803 - †17.03.1853); Austrian mathematician and physicist.
Eckermann, Johann Peter (*21.09.1792 - †03.12.1854); German writer; published "Conversations with Goethe" between 1837 and 1848.

Eckhart, Meister (=Master) Eckhart, *approx. 1200 - †30.04.1328); Dominican, most important of the German speculative mystics. He published the first philosophical scripts in German.
Eccles, John C.(*27.01.1903 - †02.05.1997), Australian philosopher and physician; brain researcher; was awarded the Nobel prize in 1963 for his work on the transmission of nervous impulses across synapses in the brain.
Eddington, Sir Arthur Stanley (*28.12.1882 - †22.11.1944); English mathematician and astrophysicist.
Edison, Thomas Alva (*11.02.1847 - †18.10.1931); American engineer and inventor, e.g. gramophone, electric bulb, electric generator, electric accumulator, concrete casting process; held more than 1000 patents.
Einstein, Albert (*14.03.1879 - †18.04.1955); German physicist, Nobel prize winner; discovered the relativity between time and space. With his equation Einstein proved that any mass if moved with the speed of light would expand into infinity. At the same time the Lorentz contraction (1899) states that a moving body contracts in the direction of its motion into infinity.
electrons: their existence as elementary particles with an extremely small mass of $0,9109389 \cdot 10^{-27}$ g was proved by the English physicist →Joseph J. Thomson (*18.12.1856 - †30.08.1940) in 1897.
electro-encephalography (EEG) = the tracing of brain waves.
elements are pure matter which cannot be decomposed further into simpler substances by chemical processes.
emanation, Latin: emanare = to flow, to spring from a source.
emergence: Latin: emergere = to emerge; to bring forth or to generate from a lower level through evolution a new, usually higher, level of existence
empiricism: Latin: empirice, = school of medical practice founded on experience without the aid of science or theory; generally: the practice of emphasizing experience in science.
empirism: Greek: empeiria = Experience, knowledge, practice; based on experience.
Engels, Friedrich (*28.11.1820 - †05.08.1895); German Marxist and supporter of →Karl Marx
entity, Latin: ens, entis = the thing, the being; existing being.
enzyme: Greek en = in, and zymos = leaven; proteins, very complex multi-chained macro-molecules essential to life by acting as catalysts inducing, promoting or accelerating chemical reactions and metabolic processes.
epilepsy = a group of nervous disorders that feature repeated episodes of sudden convulsive seizures, sensory disorders and blackouts.
epiphenomenon = an additional or secondary symptom
epistemology = the study of the method and grounds of knowledge, especially with reference to its limits and validity.
esoterics: Greek: esoteros = within, inner; a kind of mysterious and secret doctrine or science taught to the initiated only. Today it is rather used as a collective term for all non-scientifically approved theories, including supernatural phenomena.
ethics = a branch of philosophy concerned with the morally good and bad.

Euclid (about 300 BC), Greek mathematician. Wrote a textbook including the entire known mathematics of his time. The classical geometry of the three-dimensional space is named after him Euclidean geometry.
Feuerbach, Ludwig Andreas (*28.07.1804 - †13.09.1872); German philosopher and theologist.
Freud, Sigmund (*06.05.1856 - †23.09.1939); Austrian neurologist and psychiatrist; founder of psychoanalysis.
Gabriel: one of the highest in God's hierarchy of angels according to Christian belief.
Galilei, Galileo (*15.02.1564 - †08.01.1642); Italian astronomer, mathematician and physicist.
Galton, Sir Francis (*16.02.1822 - †17.01.1911); English naturalist and anthropologist; detective.
Gellert, Christian Fürchtegott (*04.07.1715 - †13.12.1769); German poet and novelist.
gene denotes the smallest unit determining and transmitting hereditary characteristics. One gene may consist of several →nucleotides which are thus responsible for the generation of one or more proteins which in turn determine one characteristic.
geometry = part of mathematics which deals with two-dimensional planes and three-dimensional bodies.
gluon, hypothetical quantum which is supposed to act as a glue inducing the powerful interaction between nucleonic particles keeping them together.
gnostic, late Hellenistic, then Christian groupings, which maintain that the salvation of the individual depends on the cognition of God and on the revelation of the divine mystery. Later, Gnosticism reappeared in Christian sects, which took on other religious elements and mystical speculations on the differences between God and matter and was therefore suppressed by the Christian church as a heresy.
Goethe, Johann Wolfgang (*28.08.1749 - †22.03.1832); German writer, philosopher and naturalist; was knighted in 1782 and was thereafter known as "von Goethe".
graviton, hypothetical quantum which is supposed to induce gravitation.
Gregory the Great, (* before 540 - †12.03.604); Father of the Church; first monk to become Pope.
Gurwitsch, Alexander Gawrilowitsch (*1874 - †1954); Russian physician and biologist; tried to explain the biological process of morphogenesis. Discovered "mitogenetic" radiation.
Haeckel, Ernst (*16.02.1834 - †19.08.1919); German zoologist; monist, materialist and Darwinist.
Hawking, Stephen (*08.01.1942); British physicist and cosmologist. Holder of the famous Lucasian Professorship of Mathematics at Cambridge since 1997, the same professorship that →*Isaac Newton* once held. Became world famous with his book: *"A Brief History of Time"*. Supporter of a materialistic view of the world.
heart ventricular fibrillation: a very fast, very uneven heartbeat arising from a ventricle. The condition is marked by a complete lack of regular heartbeat, i.e. an

insufficient amount of blood is pumped into the circulation. Ventricular fibrillation leads to a so-called "haemodynamic cardiac arrest". Without immediate initiation of adequate resuscitation measures the patient is practically (clinically) dead!
Heraclitus (ca. *544 - †483 BC); Greek philosopher.
Hertz, Heinrich (*22.02.1857 - †01.01.1894); German physicist. The unit of frequency known as hertz Hz is named after him. He confirmed Maxwell's prediction on the existence of electromagnetic waves, both in the form of light and radio waves.
Hildegard von Bingen (*1098 - †17.09.1179); Benedictine abbess; important mystic, visions of the "living light ".
Hippocrates (*460 - †377 BC); Greek physician. The physicians' oath, the Hippocratic oath, is named after him.
Hölderlin, Johann Christian Friedrich (*20.03.1770 - †07.06.1843); German theologist and poet.
Homer, (about 8th century BC); the most famous Greek poet, although it is not sure whether he really lived or whether the works attributed to him were not really written by several authors who adopted a "collective nom de plume" known as Homer.
Hoyle, Sir Fred (*24.06.1915), British astrophysicist and cosmologist, also author of science-fiction novels.
Hubble, Edwin Powell (*20.11.1889 - †28.09.1953). The space telescope launched by the USA in April 1990 to explore space while orbiting the earth is named after him. Hubble discovered that distant nebulae in space are really galaxies. The so-called redshift gave him the idea that the universe was expanding and that the expansion followed the formula v=H d, in which v is the velocity of recession, H is the Hubble constant multiplied by d, the distance. The greater the distance between the galaxies the faster they are supposed to move apart.
Hume, David (*07.05.1711 - †25.08.1776); Scottish philosopher and historian.
Huygens, Christiaan (*14.04.1629 - †08.06.1695); Dutch mathematician and physicist.
hypercapnia = increased level of carbon-dioxide in the blood.
hypoxia = oxygen deficiency in the blood and organs.
IANDS = International Association for Near Death Studies. Founded 1981 at the University of Connecticut by Kenneth Ring, Bruce Greyson and John Audette. Some years later national branches of this research centre were also established in Australia and some European countries.
ideology, Greek: idea = appearance, form; logos = word, discourse; legein = to say, to talk, to explain. It means the manner or the content of the thinking characteristic of an individual, a group or a culture, medical, legal, political or other.
imaginary number "i": Negative numbers area mere mirror images of positive numbers. This means that it should also be possible to extract the square root of negative numbers. However, there is no number which, multiplied by itself, results in a negative number again. Therefore, it is denoted by "i". It follows $\sqrt{(-4)}=2i$.
instinct: Latin: instinctus = drive, impulse, inspiration. In biology instinct means an "innate" tendency to behave in a particular way.

intelligence quotient: The mean value is determined with 100 for the average population. 60 is considered to be mentally deficient.
interpretation, Latin: interpretari = to mediate, explain, to elucidate.
Internet, virtual, world-wide data net.
Intranet, part of the internet, which can only be used by authorized persons who gain access by means of a pass word.
intuition, Latin: intueri = to look at, to inspect, to contemplate (especially in the spiritual sense); it means the act or process of coming to direct knowledge of the truth or relationships by a revelation of innate feeling without reasoning but by inspiration.
irrational number: a number that can be expressed to any degree of desired accuracy but not as an exact fraction, the fraction is infinite yet not periodical. An irrational number is calculated from a →*rational number*, e.g. $\sqrt{2}$.
Islam means "surrender to God". Islam and muslim are in fact synonyms.
isotropy = Greek: isos = equal and tropos = direction: equally distributed in all directions without preference.
James, William (*11.01.1842 - †26.08.1910); American philosopher, anatomist and psychologist; main developer of →Pragmatism which emphasizes the value of a creative personality and the pluralistic variety of reality.
Jesus, in Christian faith the Son of God. According to latest research he was born either in 4 BC or in 7 BC.
Judgement Day, synonym: "Doomsday"; according to Christian and Islamic belief the day when the world as we know it will come to a dramatic end.
Jung, Carl Gustav (*26.07.1875 - †06.06.1961); Swiss psychiatrist, psycho-therapist. Pupil of →*Freud*.
Jürgenson, Friedrich (*08.02.1903 - †15.12.1987); Ukrainian-German musician, painter and writer.
Kant, Immanuel (*22.04.1724 - †12.02.1804); German mathematician and philosopher. He spent his entire life in and around Koenigsberg, formerly East Prussia, Germany, now Russia. He was Professor of Logic and Metaphysics at the University of Koenigsberg.
Kelvin: Decimal (!) temperature unit, Abbr.: "K"; named after the British physicist Sir William → Thomson, Baron Kelvin of Largs.
Kepler, Johannes (*27.12.1571 - †15.11.1630); German theologian, mathematician and astronomer. He established the three laws of planetary motion, known as Kepler's laws.
von Klinger, Friedrich Maximilian (*17.02.1752 - †09.03.1831); German poet; in later life he became a Russian officer. He was a friend of Goethe when they were young.
Koran or Qur-an; Arabic = reading; revelation of Mohammed, divided into 114 suras (chapters), arranged according to length.
Kostolany, André (*09.02.1906 - †14.09.1999); Hungarian businessman, writer and famous expert at the stock exchange.

Kronecker, Leopold (*07.12.1823 - †29.12.1891); Polish-German mathematician. Basic works in the fields of algebra and number theory.
Kübler-Ross, Elisabeth (*08.07.1926); Swiss physician and psychiatrist; research on near death experiences.
Lamarck, Jean-Baptiste de Monet, Chevalier de, (*01.08.1744 - †18.12.1829); French naturalist. Founder of the theory of evolution, the Lamarckism.
Lao Tzu (*604 BC according to Chinese tradition; it is certain that he lived at the end of the 7th century BC). Chinese philosopher. He held official rank as archivist at the imperial court in Loyang (today known as Honan Province). He wrote a book about "sense" (probably better translated as "invisible spiritual laws of the world) and "life" which contains 5,000 Chinese characters (→ Tao Te Ching).
Laplace, Pierre Simon de L. (*28.03.1749 - †05.03.1827); French mathematician and astronomer.
LASER = "light amplification by stimulated emission of radiation". The technical laser emits a very strong and intensive light which is highly focused. It is coherent and has a defined frequency.
Leibniz, Gottfried Wilhelm (*01.07.1646 - †14.11.1716); German philosopher and naturalist.
Leucippus of Milet (middle of the 5th century BC); Greek philosopher and co-founder of *Atomism*.
Locke, John (*29.08.1632 - †28.10.1704); English philosopher, politician and teacher.
logic, a science that deals with correct reasoning and the correct use of terms.
light, or better, so-called white light, can be dispersed into colours by a prism. Spectral colour means light of a defined wave length. A light source containing only a limited number of wavelengths, gives a spectrum of a number of lines of different colours.
limbic system, denoting the paired brain structures at or near the edge of the medial wall of the cerebral hemispheres connecting the cortex to lower parts of the brain. These structures are supposed to function as a kind of guard responsible for sorting emotional and memory contents.
Lorentz, Hendrik (*18.07.1853 - †04.02.1928); Dutch physicist. He established the theory that objects travelling at high speed are contracting (at the velocity of light they contract to infinity).
LSD = lysergic acid diethylamide; LSD is a synthetically produced hallucinogen which can cause psychotic symptoms and hallucinations.
Lucrecius, Titus Lucretius Carus (* about 97 BC - †55 BC); Roman poet. He wrote e.g. the epic poem "On the nature of things" (De rerum natura). It is an exposition on the origin of the world in which he attempts to liberate mankind from the anguish and misery caused by superstitious terror of death and various divinities.
macro-structure = the anatomy or structures revealed by visual examination with little or no magnification;. the opposite is micro-structure.
magnetic resonance imaging (MRI), also known as "computed nuclear spin resonance tomography" or "nuclear magnetic resonance imaging". The protons of

hydrogen have a certain spin which makes them behave as tiny nuclear magnets. After having been aligned by a strong magnetic field the nuclei are subjected to pulses of radio-frequency radiation which "tips" them away from the strong field alignment. The nuclear magnets begin to "wobble". The speed at which the nuclei return to the steady state is the relaxation time which is measured. This method is used to detect both anatomical and functional defects in brain tissue

Maimonides Moses (Rabbi Mose ben Maimon, *30.03.1135 - †13.12.1204); Jewish physician, philosopher and Theologist. He systemized the Talmud.

Marx, Karl Heinrich (*05.05.1818 - †14.03.1883); founder of "Scientific Marxism".

Mendel, Gregor (*22.07.1822 - †06.01.1884); German naturalist, botanist, monk and prior of the Augustinian hermits.

Messiah: Latin: mittere = to send; the one sent by God. Synonym for →Jesus Christ.

metaphysics: Greek: "after physics"; by →*Aristotle* originally meant in a temporal sense because he was referring to one of his works which followed his writings about physics! Metaphysics today means primarily that part of theoretical physics which deals with central questions such as structure, sense and reason of reality and existence.

Michelson, Albert Abraham (*19.12.1852 - †09.05.1931); American naval officer and physicist.

mimicry, Greek: mimikos = imitating; the resemblance of one animal to another which has usually evolved as a means of protection.

Mohammed (ca. *570 AD - †08.06.632 AD.). Prophet and founder of Islam.

molecule, the smallest unit of a chemical component which still possesses its chemical characteristics.

monad: Greek: monados = unit; monos = sole, lone, single. According to →*Leibniz* the smallest spiritual, indivisible entity of the universe inherent in everything.

Monod, Jacques (*09.02.1910 - †31.05.1976); French physiologist. Was awarded the Nobel Prize for medicine in 1965.

Morley, Edward Williams (*1838 - †1923); chemist, became world famous as physicist.

morphologic, Greek: morphos = form; it means relating to form, also Latin: anatomic.

Moses , (about 13th century BC); Hebrew Moscheh, Latin Moses; important figure in the Old Testament; mediator between God and mankind.

mutation: Latin: mutare = to change; a sudden random change in the genetic material of a cell.

mysteriousness: Greek: myein, to initiate. It means a "secret", a mystery, a basic form of a direct intercourse with God or another transcendental existence in an elevated religious feeling.

nature-philosophy = speculative theorizing about the phenomena of nature and experiences in nature science.

Newton, Isaac (*4.01.1643 - †31.03.1727). English physicist; professor at Cambridge university, holder of the Lucasian Chair, President of the Royal Society (1704-1727). Was raised to the peerage in 1705 and hence called "Sir". He lies buried in Westminster Abbey in London. The unit "1 newton" is named after him. This is the unit of force, being the force required to give a mass of one kilogram an acceleration of 1 m/s.
Nikolaus Krebs (*1401 - †11.08.1464), son of a fisherman in Kues on the Mosel, Germany, later Bishop of Brixen; known as Nikolaus →*Cusanus*. Theologist, philosopher and naturalist.
null, Latin: nulla figura = having no character or the value of zero.
OBE = Out of Body Experience;
panta rhei, Greek: everything flows. This quotation goes back to the Greek philosopher Heraclitus (about 544-483 BC)
pantheism = doctrine that God is *everywhere* in nature.
Paracelsus (*10.12.1493 - †24.09.1541); original name: Theophrastus Bombastus of Hohenheim; German physician and natural philosopher. He treated people as a unit of body and soul.
paranoia = mental disorder characterized by the presence of systematized delusions, often of a persecutory character.
parapsychology is a part of psychology (Greek: para = beside, next to); a science concerned with the supernatural (occult) phenomena. The first professorial chair for parapsychology was established in Freiburg, Black Forest, Germany. The first professor to hold this chair was Prof. Dr. Hans Bender; German psychologist.
particle zoo: modern expression for the innumerable often instable or even only hypothetical smallest particles which scientists believe are part of the atomic nucleus or which they believe exert a certain force or effect.
Pascal, Blaise (*19.06.1623 - †19.08.1662); French philosopher and mathematician. In his "Logic of Reason", reason is portrayed as being inadequate. The final questions can only be solved in a personally satisfying manner by faithfully experienced religious revelations ("Logic of the Heart").
Penzias, Arno A. (*26.04.1933) ; German-American astrophysicist; discovered, together with his co-worker, the American physicist →Robert W. Wilson, the cosmic microwave background radiation. The discovery was made accidentally while they were searching for the reason for interferences in satellite radio communications. They were awarded the Nobel prize for physics in 1978.
philosophy, Greek: philos = friend, sophia = wisdom.
philosophy of **religion** = investigation of religions and the drawing of comparisons to other philosophical disciplines.
physics, the study of the laws concerned with lifeless matter.
Pi: symbol π. It denotes the ratio of the circumference of a circle to its diameter. It is a transcendental number.
Planck, Max Karl Ernst Ludwig (*23.04.1858 - †4.10.1947); German physicist. He established the theory that energy is not emitted continuously but in "smallest portions", so-called quanta.

Plato, (ca. *427 - †347 BC); pupil of Socrates, Greek philosopher and thinker.
Plotin(os) (205-270 AD); Greek philosopher. Founder of the School of Philosophy in Rome.
pluripotent, Latin: plures = more, having or being more than one; potere or posse = to be able, powerful, mighty, strongly influential: to be effective in more than one way.
Popp, Fritz Albert, German physicist. Established certain proof for biological matter, e.g. cells, e.g. DNA, being light encoded.
Popper, Sir Karl Raimund (*28.07.1902 - †17.091994); Austrian philosopher and psychologist.
positron emission tomography (PET): electro-magnetic scanning method which detects local changes in the blood supply of the brain, so that brain reactions can be identified exactly.
pragmatism, Greek: pragmateia = study of one matter, eager striving. Pragmatism is a doctrine that estimates any actions solely by its practical value.
Prigogine, Ilya (*25.01.1917); Belgian physicist and chemist, born in Russia. Developed the theory of →*dissipative structures*. Was awarded the Nobel prize for chemistry in 1997.
Ptolemaeus, Claudius (about *100 - †170 AD) lived in Alexandria; Greek geographer, mathematician and astronomer. His theory was based on the assumption that the earth was the centre of the universe in which the sun, the moon and the planets moved around the earth in so-called epicycles.
pulsar, the remains of a star which periodically emit radio waves; they were discovered in 1967.
Pythagoras, (*about 580 - †ca.496 BC), Greek philosopher and mathematician. The Pythagoreans recognized that $\sqrt{2}$ in the diagonal calculation of a square does not result in a number in the usual sense. Pythagoras's theorem: In a right-angled triangle the area of the square on the hypotenuse (the longest side) is equal to the sum of the areas of the squares drawn on the other two sides. Integers fulfilling this condition are known as Pythagorean numbers. 3 ,4 and 5, and their squares 9 + 16 = 25, therefore, are the first Pythagorean numbers.
rational numbers, Latin: ratio = the reason. In mathematics these are any positive integers (= natural numbers, parts of rational numbers) and negative integers, zero and any number that can be expressed as the ratio of two integers resulting in a finite or an infinite but periodical decimal fraction.
religion, Latin: religio = considerate, conscientious observance; Latin: religens = god-fearing, possibly going back to Latin: religere = to obey considerately. The Latin syllable "re" means "again" and the word ligere means to obey, to note, to respect.
resonance, Latin: resonare = to resound, to echo.
quantum, originally the "action quantum" introduced by →*Max Planck*. Today it usually denotes the minimum amount by which a smallest or quantized physical quantity of energy or angular momentum, for example, can change. The difference in energy between two conditions is often determined by one particle which is

added or taken away. It is then called a quantum. The smallest quantum of light or of electromagnetic radiation is a photon.
Quasars: so-called quasi-stellar objects (QSO) or quasi-stellar radio sources (QSS), they are star-like objects; possibly collapsed galaxies.
Ranke, Leopold von (*21.12.1795 - †23.05.1886); German historian; professor at the Berlin University, advisor to several kings and emperors.
reanimation, Latin re = back; anima = soul; it means resuscitation.
reductionism: a variant of →*monism* in which the differences in the essence of elements is generally dismissed and everything is traced back to only one form of being.
regressive, Latin: regressus = move backwards; it means to relapse.
regression therapists try to take people back to their early childhood by hypnosis techniques. Some believe that people can even be taken back to "earlier lives".
recessive, opposite of →*dominant.*
Rilke, Rainer Maria (*04.12.1875 - †29.12.1926); Czech-German writer.
Sacks, Oliver (*1933); British physician, neurologist and neuro-psychologist, professor of clinical neurology at the Albert Einstein College of Medicine in New York.
schizophrenia, derived from the Greek, it means split mind. It is a mental disorder marked by the disconnection between thoughts feelings and actions.
scholastic, Latin: schola = school, or scholasticus = pupil. A term for the theology and philosophy schools of the church in the middle ages.
Seneca, Lucius Anneus (*about 4 BC - †65 AD); Roman philosopher.
Sheldrake, Rupert (*1946), Engl. biologist.
signs of death: in contrast to "clinical" death the "terminal" death is diagnosed only when "sure" signs of death are visible. Among others these are:
rigor mortis, post-mortem lividity, and signs of commencing decomposition. An essential *uncertain* sign for the diagnosis "clinically dead" is the so-called baseline in the →EEG.
singularity: physically an infinite point where the usually valid laws of physics do not apply.
Socrates (*469 - †399 BC) Greek philosopher, who was put on trial on a charge of impiety and corruption of the youth and was sentenced to death by drinking a cup of hemlock (a poisonous fungus).
Spinoza, Baruch de (24.11.1632 - †21.02.1677), Dutch mathematician and philosopher.
Steiner, Rudolf (*27.02.1861 - †30.03.1925); Croatian-German writer. Founder of anthroposophy (1912), the theory of scientific research in the spiritual world.
stoics = people with an unshakeable composure. It is a philosophical system founded about 300 BC in Greece and is based on the so-called "stoa (poikile)", which means "Painted Porch", where the teaching took place. Everything real and physical is filled with divinity, the elemental force.
Strindberg, Johann August (*22.01.1849 - †14.12.1912); Swedish poet.

stringent, Latin: stringere = to draw together, to bind tightly. It means something with a convincing force of reasoning or argument.

strings, postulated by cosmologists, are sub-microscopic (below 10^{-27}m), massless, one-dimensional "rubber-band like" objects equipped with tremendous energy criss-crossing the universe like threads after the assumed Big Bang and serving as a kind of primeval nucleus for the generation of galaxies. This is supposed to explain the chain-like arrangement of galaxies within huge spaces free of matter.

Suttapitaka (Sanskrit: "Basket of Teachings"), one of three collections of the "Tripitaka" ("Triple Basket"), Buddhist script.

symbiosis, Greek: sym = together, and bios = life;. It means organisms living together for their mutual benefit.

synchronicity: a term coined by →*Carl Gustav Jung* in cooperation with the physicist →*Wolfgang Pauli*. It denotes the sensible coincidence of an objective physical process with an internal psychological event. It remains open whether this coincidence could also be of causal nature, i.e. that one event, e.g. an objective incident, could even have induced the other event, the psychic incident. This would, however, go beyond the term *synchronicity* and scientists dismiss this possibility. Critics, however, explain the accidental coincident of synchronic events with selective perception. Age-old traditions and, of course, people's own experiences, however, contradict this theory convincingly. In any case, those experiencing a synchronistic event are usually extraordinarily moved.

Talmud, Hebrew: to learn, the instruction, the authoritative body of Jewish law and tradition developed during the 3rd and 6th century AD.

tantrism a religious movement originating in India. It is named after the Tantras, the religious scripts of the Shakta sect who are worshippers of Shakti, the female creative energy.

Tao Te Ching, is the book (=Ching) of the "sense" (=Tao, or better translated as "the invisible spiritual rules of the world") and "life" (=Te). It was written by → Lao Tzu.

Teilhard de Chardin, Pierre (*01.05.1881 - †0.04.1955); French anthropologist and philosopher, geologist, palaeontologist.

teleology, the philosophical study of evidences of the expedients and purposeful design in nature. Was introduced by the German philosopher Christian Wolff (*1679 - †1754) in 1728.

Theognis, (6th century BC); Greek poet, possibly from Megara.

Thomas of Aquinus (*1225 - †07.03.1274); German Dominican, theologian and church scholar, was canonized by the Catholic Church.

Thomson, Sir Joseph John (*18.12.1856 - +30.08.1940); proved among other things the existence of →electrons as mass particles.

Thomson, Sir William (*26.06.1824 - †17.12.1907); raised to the British peerage as Baron →*Kelvin* of Largs in 1892. He helped to carry out fundamental research into thermodynamics.

trance: Latin: transire = to pass away, to change: sleep-like condition of profound abstraction.

transcendent, Latin: transcendere = going beyond, exceeding the usual limits: supernatural; to go beyond the limits of the normal sensory perception and lying outside these limits. Contrasted with immanent (within the world). Transcendental numbers cannot be expressed by an algebraic equation with a rational coefficient, e.g. Euler's number or π.
Upanishad, Sanskrit "act of sitting down near something" (near a teacher). Denotes a group of religious revelation scripts of Hinduism with philosophical-mystic contents.
Vedic religion, the Veda (=Sanskrit: "knowledge"), is one of the oldest scripts of Indian literature which consists of four collections (Rigveda, Samaveda, Yajurveda and Atharveda). It contains the mythic-religious perceptions of Indo-Arian immigrants who invaded the Indian sub-continent during the 2nd century BC. The Vedic religion and influences already existing in India merged into a new religion known as →Hinduism.
Virgil, originally Publius Vergilius Marco (*15.10.70 - †21.09.19 BC); Roman poet. He wrote, for example, Aeneid; "Father of the Occident".
Vries, Jan, de (*11.02.1890 - +23.07.1964); Dutch botanist.
Wagner, Richard (*22.05.1813 - †13.02.1883); German composer
water, (chemical formula H_2O) consists to 99,85% of the pure molecule H_2O with only 1 proton. A "water mixture", however, contains in addition 0,15% of other isotopes deuterium (1 proton + 1 neutron) and tritium (1 proton + 2 neutrons).
Watson, James Dewey (*26.04.1928); American biologist, biochemist.
Weismann, August (*17.01.1834 - †05.11.1914); German zoologist, neo-Darwinist.
Wiles, Andrew (* 1953 in Cambridge); Engl. mathematician
Wilson, Robert W. (*08.06.1936); American physicist; discovered microwave background radiation by accident together with the German-American physicist →Arno A. Penzias in 1965 while they were searching for the reasons of interference effects in satellite radio communications. They were awarded the Nobel prize for physics in 1978.
Zenon of Elea (about 460 BC); Greek philosopher, quoted by Aristotle.
Zoroastra (about *600 - about +533 BC); ancient Iranian founder of a religion

References

Altea, R., „The Eagle and the Rose", Warner, New York (1995)
D'Aquili, E.G., A.B. Newberg, "The Mystical Mind: Probing the Biology of Religious Experience", Augsburg Fortress Publishers (1999)
Araoz, D.L., "Selbsthypnose – Kreative Imagination in Beruf und Alltag", Econ (1992)
Ash, D., P. Hewitt, „Science of the gods", Gateway books, UK (1990)
Asimov, I., J. Asimov, "Frontiers II", Truman Tally Books, N.Y. (1993)
Bache, Ch. M., „Lifecycles: Reincarnation and the Web of Life", Paragon House (1990)
Bagemihl, B., "Biological exuberance: animal homsex. and natural diversity", St. Martin's Press (1999)
Barbour, J., "The End of Time", Oxford Univ. Press (2000)
Barrow, J.D., "Theories for Everything. The Quest for Ultim. Explan.", Oxf Press (1990)
Barrow, J.D., "Pi in the Sky", Oxford Univ. Press (1992)
Barrow, J.D., J. Silk, "The left Hand of Creation", Basic Books, N.Y. (1983)
Bauby, J.D., "The diving-bell and the butterfly", Wheeler Pub. (1997)
Bell, J.S., „Speakable and Unspeakable in Quantum Mechan.", Cambr. Univ. Press (1987)
Berger, K., „Ist mit dem Tod alles aus ?", Quell (1997)
Bischof, M., „Biophotonen - Das Licht in unseren Zellen", Zweitausendeins (1995)
Breuer, R., „Immer Ärger mit dem Urknall", rororo (1996)
Briggs, J., F.D. Peat, „Turbulent Mirror. An Illustrated Guide to Chaos Theory and the Science of Wholeness", Harper & Ross, NY (1989)
Brocher, T., „Stufen des Lebens", Kreuz, Stuttgart
Capra, F., „The Turning Point", USA (1987)
Capra, F., „Uncommon Wisdom. Coversations with Remarkable People", USA (1987)
Cerminaria, G., „Many Mansions", W. Sloane Ass., New York (1950)
Combs, A., M. Holland, "Synchronicity – Science, Myth and the Trickster" Paragon (1992)
Conze, E., "Buddhist Scriptures", Harmondsworth/Great Britain (1959)
Coward, H., „Life after Death in the Worlds Religions", Orbis Books, N.Y. (1997)
Cox-Chapman, M., „The Case for Heaven", G.P. Putnam's Sons, NY (1995)
Cumont, F., "After Life in Roman Paganism", New Haven (1922)
Dacqué, E.: „Vermächtnis der Urzeit. Grundprobleme der Erdgeschichte". Aus dem Nachlaß hrsg. von M. Schröter (1948)
Dalei Lama, "A human approach to world peace", Wisdom Pub. (1984)

Dam, W.C. van, „Tote sterben nicht - Erfahrungsber. zw. Leben u. Tod", Weltbild (1995)
Damman, E., „Erkenntnisse jenseits von Zeit und Raum --- Die Wende im naturwissenschaftlichen Denken", Knaur (1990)
Davidson, J., „Natural Creation & the Formative Mind", Element Books Ltd., UK (1991)
Davies, P., „God and the New Physics", J.M. Dent & Sons, London (1986)
Davies, P., „About Time. Einstein's Unfinished Revolution", Simon&Schuster, NY (1995)
Diamond, J., "Why Is Sex Fun?" BasicBooks, N.Y.(1997)
Diederichs, E., „Laotse - Tao te king - Das Buch vom Sinn und Leben", Diederichs (1972)
Ditfurth, H. von, „Wir sind nicht nur von dieser Welt", dtv (1985)
Different auth., "Forschung im 21. Jahrhundert", Spektrum d. Wissensch. Spez. (2000)
Different auth., "Gravitation – Urkraft des Kosmos", Sterne-Weltraum, Spez. 6 (2001)
Different auth., "Schöpf. ohne Ende - Die Geburt d. Kosm.", Sterne-Weltr Spez. 2 (2002)
Different auth., "Die Evolution des Menschen", Spektrum d Wissenschaft, Dossier (2002)
Doucet, F.W., „Die Toten leben unter uns --- Forschungsobjekt Jenseits", Ariston (1987)
Dürr, H.-P., "Physik und Transzendenz", Scherz (1989)
Dürr, H.-P., W. Ch. Zimmerli, „Geist und Natur --- Über den Widerspruch zwischen naturwissenschaftlicher Erkenntnis und philosophischer Welterfahrung", Scherz (1991)
Durant, W., "The Story of Civilization", Simon & Schuster
Eady, B., „Embraced by the Light", Gold Leaf Press, CA/USA (1994)
Eccles, J.C., D.N. Robinson, "The Wonder of Being Human. Our Brain and Our Mind", The Free Press, New York (1984)
Eccles, J. C., „Creation of the Self", Routledge, London, New York (1989)
Eccles, J.C., „Gehirn und Seele. Erkenntnisse der Neurophysiologie", Piper (1991)
Eccles, J. C., „How the Self controls its Brain", Springer (1994)
Eddington, A., „Wissenschaft und Mystizismus", aus: „Das Weltbild der Physik und ein Versuch seiner philosophischen Deutung", F. Vieweg & Sohn (1935)
Einstein, A., L. Infeld, „Die Evolution der Physik", Weltbild (1991)
Elsaesser-Valarino, E., "On the Other Side of Life – Exploring the phenomenon of the near-death experience", Perseus books (1999)
Erben, H.K., „Die Entwicklung der Lebewesen", Piper (1988)
Ernst, H., „Die Weisheit des Körpers - Kräfte der Selbstheilung", Piper (1993)
Ewald, G., „Die Physik und das Jenseits --- Spurensuche zwischen Philosophie und Naturwissenschaft", Pattloch (1998)
Ferris, T., „The Mind's Sky, Bantam Books, New York (1992)
Findlay, A., „Beweise für ein Leben nach dem Tod", Bauer (1983)

Fischback Powers, M., "Footprints: the story behind the poem that inspired millions", Harper Collins Publ., Toronto, Canada (1993)
Ford, A., „Unknown but Known. My Adventure into the Meditative Dimension", Harper & Row, New York (1968)
Ford, A., "The Life beyond Death", G.P. Putnam's Sons, N.Y. (1971)
Fox, M., R. Sheldrake, "The Physics of Angels. A Realm where Spirit a .Sci. meet", (1996)
Genz, H., „Die Entdeckung des Nichts - Leere und Fülle im Universum", Hanser (1994)
Ghyka, M., "The Geometry of Art and Life", Dover/New York (1977)
Goldberg, Ph., „Die Kraft der Intuition", Scherz (1988)
Gribbin, J., „In the Beginning. After COBE and before the Big Bang", Little, Brown and Company, Boston (1993)
Gribbin, J., M. Rees, „Cosmic Coincidences. Dark Matter, Mankind, and Anthropic Cosmology", Bantam Books, New York (1989)
Gribbin, J., "Schrödinger's Kitten and the Search for Reality", Weidenfeld & Nicholson, London (1995)
Guggenheim, B., J. Guggenheim, „Hello from Heaven", ADC Project, Longwood, FL/USA (1995)
Gurwitsch, A.G., „Über den Begriff des embryonlaen Feldes". Wilhelm Roux' Archiv für Entwicklungsmechanik der Organismen. Bd. 51 (1922)
Hallmann, W., W. Ley, "Handbuch Raumfahrttechnik", Hanser (1999)
Haug, M., E.W. West, "The book of Arda Viraf", Bombay/London (1872)
Hawking, St.W., "A Brief History of Time: From the Big Bang to Black Holes", Bantam Books, New York (1988)
Hawking, St.W., "Is the End in Sight for Theoretical Physics? – An Inaugural Lecture", Press Syndicate of the Univ. of Cambridge, UK (1980)
Hayward, J.W., „Shifting Worlds, Changing Minds", Shambhala Publ., Bost., MA, (1987)
Hengge, P., „Es steht in der Bibel", Verlag Wissenschaft und Politik (1994)
Herbig, J., „Im Anfang war das Wort", Hanser (1985)
Herneck, F., „Einstein und sein Weltbild", Buchverlag Der Morgen (1976)
Högl, St., "Near-Death Experiences, Religions and the World Beyond. A Glance at the Other Side of Life and its Influence on Mankinds Religions", Magisterial-Treatise, University of Regensburg (1996)
Hoffmann, B., „Relativity and Its Roots", Scient. Amer. Books, NY (1983)
Holy Bible: Die Heilige Schrift des Alten und Neuen Bundes, Herder (1965)
Holy Bible: die vierundzwanzig Bücher der Heiligen Schrift, übersetzt von L. Zunz, Goldschmidt (1995)
Hooper, J., D. Teresi, „The three pound universe", Macmillan Pub. Comp., N.Y. (1986)
Horneck, G., C. Baumstark-Khan, "Astrobiol, The Quest for the Condit. of Life", (2001)
Hornung, E., „Geist der Pharaonenzeit", Artemis (1989)

Hornung, E., „Die Nachtfahrt d Sonne - Eine altägypt. Beschr. d. Jens.", Artemis (1991)
Huber, G., „Das Fortleben nach dem Tode", Origo (1996)
Ikeda, D., „LIFE – An Enigma, a Precious Jewel", Kodansha Int. Ltd. (1982)
Jürgenson, F., „Sprechfunk m. Verstorb.-Prakt. Kontaktherst. m. d. Jens.", Goldm. (1981)
Jung, C.G., „Briefe, Erster Band 1906-1945", Walter (1972)
Jung, C.G., A. Jaffé, „Erinnerungen, Träume, Gedanken von C.G. Jung", Walter (1976)
Kahan, G., „Einsteins Relativitätstheor. – z. leicht. Verständn. f. jederm.", Dumont (1987)
Kaku, M., „Hyperspace. A Scientific Odyssey Through Parallel Universes, Time Warps, And The Tenth Dimension", Oxford Univ. Press, N.Y. (1995)
Kaplan, R.W., „Der Urspr. d. Lebens. Biogen. ein Forsch.Geb. heut. Naturwiss.", (1978)
Klimkeit, H.J., "Der iranische Auferstehungsglaube. Tod und Jenseits im Glauben der Völker", Harrassowitz (1978)
Klivington, K.A., "The Science of Mind", MIT Press, Cambridge/USA (1989)
Knoblauch, H., "Berichte aus dem Jenseits. Mythos und Realität der Nahtod-Erfahrung", Herder/Spektrum (1999)
Knoblauch, H., H.G. Soeffner, I. Schmied und B. Schnettler, "Todesnähe. Interdisz. Zugänge zu einem außergewöhnlichen Phänomen", Universitätsverl. Konstanz 1999
Krisciunas, K., B. Yenne, „Atlas des Universums", Lechner (1992)
Kübler - Ross, E., „Über den Tod und das Leben danach", Silberschnur (1994)
Kübler - Ross, E., „Sterben lernen - Leben lernen - Fragen u. Antw.", Silberschnur (1995)
Kübler - Ross, E., „The Wheel of Life", Scribner, New York (1997)
Küng, H., „Ewiges Leben?", Piper (1982)
Kunsch, K., St. Kunsch, "Der Mensch in Zahlen – Eine Datensammlung in Tabellen mit über 20.000 Einzelwerten", Spektrum (2000)
Laack, W. van, "Plädoyer für ein Leben nach dem Tod und eine etwas andere Sicht der Welt", (1999 & 2000) see p. 272
Laack, W. van, "Der Schlüssel zur Ewigkeit", (1999 & 2000), see p. 272
Laack, W. van, "Key to Eternity", (2000), see p. 272
Laack, W. van, "Eine bessere Geschichte unserer Welt, Bd. 1, Das Universum" (2000), Bd. 2, Das Leben (2001), Bd. 3, Der Tod (2002), see p. 272
Laack, W. van, "A Better History of Our World, Vol. 1, The Universe" (2001), Vol. 2, Life (2002), Vol. 3, Death (2003), see p. 272
Laack, W. van, "Wer stirbt, ist nicht tot!", ISBN 3-936624-00-3 (SC) BoD-Libri, Hamburg (2003) und ISBN 3-936624-06-2 (HC, 2. Aufl.), BoD-Hamburg (2005)
Laack, W. van, "Mit Logik die Welt begreifen", ISBN 3-936624-04-6 (SC), BoD-Libri, Hamburg (2005)

Laack, W. van, "Nah-Todeserfahrungen – Vorhof zum Himmel oder bloß Hirngespinste?", die Drei, Z. f. Anthroposophie in Wissenschaft, Kunst und sozialem Leben, 12 (2004)
Laack, W. van, "Ohne Geist läuft wenig! – Teil 1, Kann aus Neuronen Bewusstsein entstehen?", die Drei, Z. f. Anthroposophie in Wissenschaft, Kunst und sozialem Leben, 2 (2005)
Laack, W. van, "Ohne Geist läuft wenig! - Teil 2, Zur Unfreiheit verdammt?", die Drei, Z. f. Anthroposophie in Wissenschaft, Kunst und sozialem Leben, 3(2005)
Lashley, K.S., „Brain Mechanism and Intelligence", Chicago Univ. Press (1929)
Lashley, K.S., „In Search of the Engram", Sympos. Soc. Exp. Biol. 4 (1950)
Laudert-Ruhm, G., „Jesus von Nazareth, Das gesicherte Basiswissen", Kreuz (1996)
LeCron, L.M., "The complete guide to hypnosis", USA (1973)
Lederman, L., D. Teresi, "The God Particle", Houghton Mifflin, NY (1993)
Löw, R., „Die neuen Gottesbeweise", Pattloch (1994)
Lomborg, B., "The Sceptical Enviromentalist", Cambridge Press (2001)
Lüth, P., "Der Mensch ist kein Zufall", Deutsche Verlags-Anstalt (1983)
Mann, A.T., „The Elements of Reincarnation", Element Books, UK (1995)
Mann, A.T., ";Millenium Porphecies", Element Books, London (1992)
Margenau, H., „The Miracle of Existence", Ox Bow, Woodbridge (1984)
Matthiesen, E., „Das persönliche Überleben des Todes", de Gruyter (1987)
Meckelburg, E., „Hyperwelt --- Erfahrungen mit dem Jenseits", Langen-Müller (1995)
Meckelburg, E., "Wir alle sind unsterblich", Langen Müller (2000)
Méric, E., A. Ysabeau, „Seele ohne Grenzen: Übernatürliche Phänomene u. d. menschliche Körper als Indikator der Persönlichkeit", Gondrom (1997)
Mielke, Th.R.P., "Coelln – Stadt, Dom, Fluss", Schneekluth (2000)
Miller, S.L., H.C. Urey, „Org. compound synth. on the primit. earth", In: Sci., 130 (1959)
Miller, S., „After Death. Mapping the Journey", Simon &Schuster, NY (1997)
Moody, R.A., „Life after Life", Mockingbird Books, USA (1975)
Moody, R.A., „Reflections on Life after Life", Bantam Books, NY (1977)
Moody, R.A., „The Light Beyond", Bantam Books, New York (1988)
Moody, R.A., P. Perry, „Reunions. Vision. Encount. with Departed Loved Ones", Vill.ard Books, NY (1993)
Moody, R.A., P. Perry, „Coming Back. A Research Odyssey into the Meaning of Past Lives", Bantam Books, New York (1991)
Morgan, M., "Mutant Message Down Under", Harper Collins, N.Y. (1994)
Morse, M., „Closer to the Light", (1990)
Morse, M., P. Perry, „Verwandelt vom Licht. Über die transformierende Wirkung von Nahtodeserfahrungen", Knaur (1994)
Newberg, A., V. Rause, "Why God won't go away: Brain Science and the Biology of Belief", (2001)
Nuland, Sh. B., „How we die", A. A. Knopf, New York (1993)

Oesterreich, K.T. „Der Okkultismus im modernen Weltbild", Dresden (1921)
Ozols, J.,. "Über die Jenseitsvorstellungen des vorgeschichtlichen Menschen". in: Tod und Jenseits im Glauben der Völker. Hg. Hans-Joachim Klimkeit. Harassowitz (1978)
Paulos, J.A., „Beyond Numeracy", A.A. Knopf, New York (1991)
Patch, H.R., "The Other World"
Penfield, W., „The mystery of the Mind", Princeton Univ. Press (1975)
Penfield, W., L. Roberts, „Speech and brain Mechanism", Princeton Univ. Press (1959)
Penrose, R., „Shadows of the Mind", Oxford Univ. Press, New York (1994)
Platon, Sämtliche Werke, Bd. 3: Phaidon, Politeia. Deutsch von F. Schleiermacher. Rowohlts Klassiker d. Literatur und der Wissenschaft Nr.27
Plichta, P., „Gottes geheime Formel --- Die Entschlüsselung des Welträtsels und der Primzahlcode", Langen-Müller (1995)
Popper, K.R., J.C. Eccles, „The Self and Its Brain – An Argument for Interactionism", Springer (1977)
Popper, K.R., „Objektive Erkenntnis -ein evolut. Entwurf", Hoffmann u. Campe (1993)
Popper, K.R., „Alles Leben ist Problemlösen - Über Erkenntnis Geschichte und Politik", Piper (1994)
Pribram, K., „Languages of the Brain", Englewood Cliffs (1971)
Prigogine, I., Vom Sein zum Werden", Piper (1982)
Prigogine, I., I. Stengers, „Dialog m, d. Natur. Neue Wege nat-wiss. Denk.", Piper (1993)
Prigogine, I., I. Stengers, „Das Paradox der Zeit -Zeit, Chaos und Quanten", Piper (1993)
Radhakrishnan, "The Principal Upanishads", London (1953)
Reichholf, J.H., „Das Rätsel der Menschwerdung --- Die Entstehung des Menschen im Wechselspiel mit der Natur", DVA (1990)
Reitz, M., „Leben jenseits der Lichtjahre --- Die Wissenschaften auf der Suche nach außerirdischen Intelligenzen", Insel (1998)
Ricken, F., „Lexikon der Erkenntnistheorie und Metaphysik", Beck (1984)
Ring, K., „Heading Toward Omega", USA (1984)
Riordan, M., "The Shadows of Creation. Dark Matter and the Structure of the Universe", W.H. Freeman & Co., New York (1991)
Rose, St.P.R., S. Harding, „Training increases ^{3}H fucose incorporation in chick brain only if followed by a memory storage", Neuroscience 12 (1984)
Rose, St.P.R., A. Csillag, „Passive avoidance training results in lasting changes in deoxyglucose metabloism in left hemisphere regions of chick brain", Behavioural and Neural Biology 44 (1985)
Ross, D., „The work of Aristotle; Select fragments. ", Clarendon Press, Oxford (1952)
Rüber, G., "Kleine gesammelte Geschichten aus Köln", Engelhorn-Verlag.
Ruppert, H.J., „Okkultismus --- Geisterwelt oder neuer Weltgeist ?", Edit. Coprint (1990)

Ryzl, M., „Das große Handbuch der Parapsychologie", Ariston (1978)
Ryzl, M., „Der Tod ist nicht d. Ende - Von d. Unsterblichk. geist. Energ.", Ariston (1981)
Sabom, M., "Light and Death", Zondervan Publishing House (1998)
Sachs, R., "Perfect Endings. A Conscious Approach to Dying and Death", Healing Arts Press, Rochester (1998)
Sacks, O., „A leg to stand on", G. Duckworth, London (1984)
Sacks, O., "The Man Who Mistook His Wife For a Hat", Summit Books/ Simon & Schuster, New York (1985)
Sagan, C., A. Druyan, „Shadows of Forgotten Ancestors", Random House, N.Y. (1992)
Sahm, P.R., G.P.J. Thiele, "Der Mensch im Kosmos", Verlag Facultas (1998)
Sahm, P.R., G.P.J. Thiele, "Der Mensch im Kosmos II", Shaker Verlag (2000)
Sandvoss, E.R., "Geschichte der Philosophie – Bd. 1 u. 2", dtv (1989)
Schäfer, H., „Brücke zwischen Diesseits und Jenseits --- Theorie und Praxis der Transkommunikation", Bauer (1989)
Schiebler, W., „Der Tod, die Brücke zu neuem Leben --- Beweise für ein persönliches Fortleben nach dem Tod. Der Bericht eines Physikers." Silberschnur (1991)
Schmid, G.B., "The six fundamental characteristics of chaos and their clinical relevance to psychiatry: A new hypothesis for the origin of psychosis. In: **Orsucci, F.**, "The Complex of Matters of Mind", Vol. 6 (1998)
Schmid, G.B., "Is Distant Mentation in Livin Systems a Quantum teleportation Phenomenon? Kantonale Psychiatrische Klinik Rheinau (1999)
Schmid, G.B., "Tod durch Vorstellungskraft – Das Geheimnis psychogener Todesfälle", Bechtermünz Verlag (2001)
Schmidt-Degenhard, M., Die oneiroide Erlebnisform: Zur Problemgeschichte und Psychopathologie des Erlebens fiktiver Wirklichkeiten" (1992)
Scholem, G.G., "Major Trends in Jewish Mysticism" , Schocken Books (1995)
Schroeder, G.L., „Genesis and the Big Bang", Bantam Books, N.Y. (1990)
Schröter-Kunhardt, M., "Das Jenseits in uns", Psychologie heute, Heft 6 (1993)
Schröter-Kunhardt, M., "Erfahrungen Sterbender während des klinischen Todes", in "Sterben und Tod in der Medizin", Wiss. Verlagsgesellschaft (1996)
Schröter-Kunhardt, M., "Nah-Todeserfahrungen aus psychiatrisch-neurologischer Sicht", In: "Todesnähe - Wissensch. Zugänge zu außergew. Phänom.", Univ.-Verl., Konst. (1999)
Senkowski, R., "Transkommunikation", Zeitschrift für Psychobiophysik und interdimensionale Kommunikationssysteme, Fischer-Verlag, Frankfurt
Sheldrake, R., „The Presence of the Past", UK (1988)
Sheldrake, R., „Wunder und Geheimnis des Übersinnlichen --- Sieben Phänomene, die das Denken revolutionieren", Weltbild (1996), engl. "Seven Experiments That Could Change the World", Park Street Press (1995)
Sheldrake, R., "A New Science of Life", Park Street Press (1995)
Siegel, R.K., "The Psychology of Life after Death", in American Psychologist 35 (1980)

Singh, K., „The Mystery of Death", Delhi (1975)
Sngh, P., "Fermat's Last Theorem...", Fourth Estate, London (1997)
Spirik, H.J., H.R. Loos, „Nachrichten aus dem Jenseits --- Erforschung paranormaler Tonbandstimmen", Ennsthaler (1996)
Spitzer, M., "Lernen – Gehirnforschung und die Schule des Lebens", Spektrum (2002)
Sprenger, W., „Der Tag, an dem mein Tod starb", Nie/Nie/Sagen (1995)
Stevenson, I., „Children who remember previous lives", USA (1989)
Stratenwerth, I., Th. Bock, „Stimmen hören –Botschaft. aus d. inner. Welt", Kabel (1998)
Teilhard de Chardin, P., „Die Entstehung des Menschen", C.H. Beck (1981)
Teilhard de Chardin, P., „Der Mensch im Kosmos", C.H. Beck (1981)
Terhart, F., „Das Geheimnis der Eingeweihten --- Was spirituelle Persönlichkeiten uns erschließen", Ariston (1996)
Time-Life-Bücher, „Fernöstliche Weisheiten", Time-Life (1991)
Tipler, F.J., „The Physics of Immortality", Doubleday, New York (1994)
Toynbee, A., "Mankind and Mother Earth – A Narrative History of the World", Oxford Univ. Press, UK (1976)
Trefil, J., "The Dark Side of the Universe", C. Scribner's Sons, NY (1988)
Ulke, K.D., „Vorbilder im Denken", Gondrom (1998)
Wapnick, K., „A Course in Miracles", Roscoe, N.Y. (1983)
Weinberg, St., „The First Three Minutes. A Modern View of the Origin of the Universe", Basic Books Publ., New York (1977)
White, M., J. Gribbin, „Stephen Hawking – A Life in Science", Viking, London (1992)
Wilber, K., „Das holographische Weltbild", Scherz (1986)
Wilber, K., "The Spectrum of Consciousness", USA (1987)
Wilber, K., "Grace and Grit", Shambala Publ. Boston/USA (19991)
Wilder-Smith, A.E., „Die Naturwissenschaften kennen keine Evolution. Experiment. und theoret. Einwände gegen die Evolutionstheorie" (1978)
Wolf, F.A., „The Body Quantum", Universe Seminars Inc. (1986)
Wolpert, L., The Triumph of the Embryo", Oxford Univ. Press (1991)
Woltersdorf, H.W., „Denn der Geist ist`s, der den Körper baut --- Die Irrlehren des wissenschaftlichen Materialismus", Langen-Müller (1991)
Zaleski, C., "Otherworld Journeys. Accounts of Near-Death Experience in Medieval and Modern Times", Oxford Univ. Press (1987)
Zahrint, H., „Jesus aus Nazareth --- Ein Leben", Piper (1987)
Zahrint, H., „Das Leben Gottes - aus einer unendlichen Geschichte", Piper (1997)
Zimmer, C., "Parasitus Rex", Umschau/Braus (2001)

Prof. Dr. med. Walter van Laack

English Books since 2000:

Nobody Ever Dies!
ISBN 3-936624-03-8, Softcover, 272 p., (2005), 24,80 €

A Better History of Our World
Vol. 1, "The Universe"
ISBN 3-8311-1490-0, Softcover, 188 p. (2001), 15,80 €
Vol. 2, "Life"
ISBN 3-8311-2597-X, Softcover, 236 p. (2002), 17,80 €
Vol. 3, "Death"
ISBN 3-936624-01-1, Softcover, 276 p. (2003), 19,80 €

Key To Eternity
ISBN 3-8311-0344-5, Softcover, 256 p. (2000), 17,80 €

German Books since 1999:

Mit Logik die Welt begreifen
ISBN 3-936624-04-6, Softcover, 380 p., (Sept. 2005) 29,80 €

Wer stirbt, ist nicht tot!
ISBN 3-936624-00-3, Softcover, 312 p., (2003), 24,80 €
ISBN 3-936624-06-2, Hardcover, 312 p., 2. edit. (2005), 35,-- €

Eine bessere Geschichte unserer Welt
Band 1, "Das Universum"
ISBN 3-8311-0345-3, Softcover, 196 p. (2000), 15,80 €
Band 2, "Das Leben"
ISBN 3-8311-2114-1, Softcover, 248 p., (2001), 17,80 €
Band 3, "Der Tod"
ISBN 3-8311-3581-9, Softcover, 276 p., (2002), 19,80 €

Der Schlüssel zur Ewigkeit
ISBN 3-9805239-4-2, Hardcover, 288 p.,1. edit. (1999), 24,80 €
ISBN 3-89811-819-3, Softcover, 288 p., 2. edit. (2000), 17,80 €

Plädoyer für ein Leben nach dem Tod und eine etwas andere Sicht der Welt
ISBN 3-89811-818-5; Softcover, 448 p., 2. edit. (1999/2000), 22,90 €

My Books in the Internet: www.van-Laack.de & www.Leseproben-im-Internet.de
Email: webmaster@van-Laack.de
van Laack Book Publishers, Roermonder Str. 312, D - 52072 Aachen, Fax +49-(0)241-174269

www.ingramcontent.com/pod-product-compliance
Lightning Source LLC
Chambersburg PA
CBHW021138230426
43667CB00005B/171